Children of Handicapped Parents

RESEARCH AND CLINICAL PERSPECTIVES

Children of Handicapped Parents
RESEARCH AND CLINICAL PERSPECTIVES

Edited by

S. Kenneth Thurman

Department of Special Education
College of Education
Temple University
Philadelphia, Pennsylvania

1985

ACADEMIC PRESS, INC.

(Harcourt Brace Jovanovich, Publishers)

Orlando San Diego New York London
Toronto Montreal Sydney Tokyo

ACADEMIC PRESS, INC.
Orlando, Florida 32887

United Kingdom Edition published by
ACADEMIC PRESS INC. (LONDON) LTD.
24–28 Oval Road, London NW1 7DX

Library of Congress Cataloging in Publication Data

Main entry under title:

Children of handicapped parents.

    Includes index.
    1. Children of handicapped parents--Addresses,
essays, lectures. 2. Parent and child--Addresses,
essays, lectures. I. Thurman, S. Kenneth.
HV1568.C48 1985   362.8'2   84-21608
ISBN 0-12-690780-3 (alk. paper)

PRINTED IN THE UNITED STATES OF AMERICA

85 86 87 88   9 8 7 6 5 4 3 2 1

This book is dedicated to Doie,
a special parent,
and to Lanny,
a special friend

Contents

Contributors

Numbers in parentheses indicate the pages on which the authors' contributions begin.

BARBARA J. ANDERSON (97), Center for Human Growth and Development, Michigan Diabetes Research and Training Center, University of Michigan, Ann Arbor, Michigan 48109

DEBORAH L. COATES (155), Youth Research Center, Catholic University, Washington, D.C. 20017

RONALD GALLIMORE[1] (69), Mental Retardation Research Center, Neuro-Psychiatric Institute, University of California-Los Angeles, Los Angeles, California 90024

THOMAS K. GILHOOL (11), Public Interest Law Center of Philadelphia, Philadelphia, Pennsylvania 19107

DOROTHEA D. GLASS (145), Temple University School of Medicine, Moss Rehabilitation Hospital, Philadelphia, Pennsylvania 19141

JUDITH A. GRAN (11), Public Interest Law Center of Philadelphia, Philadelphia, Pennsylvania 19107

DAVID B. GRAY (155), Human Learning and Behavior Branch, Center for Research for Mothers and Children, National Institute of Child Health and Human Development, Bethesda, Maryland 20205

BOBBY G. GREER (131), Special Education and Rehabilitation, Memphis State University, Memphis, Tennessee 38152

ROBERT J. HOFFMEISTER (111), Center for the Study of Communication and Deafness and Programs in Deaf Studies, Boston University, Boston, Massachusetts 02215

[1] Present address: Department of Psychiatry & Biobehavioral Sciences, University of California, Los Angeles.

HELEN KORNBLUM (97), Patient Care Division, St. Louis Children's Hospital, St. Louis, Missouri 63110

J.R. NEWBROUGH (181), John F. Kennedy Center for Research on Education and Human Development, George Peabody College of Vanderbilt University, Nashville, Tennessee 37203

ARNOLD J. SAMEROFF (47), Institute for the Study of Developmental Disabilities, University of Illinois at Chicago, Chicago, Illinois 60608

RONALD SEIFER (47), Institute for the Study of Developmental Disabilities, University of Illinois at Chicago, Chicago, Illinois 60608

S. KENNETH THURMAN (1, 35), Department of Special Education, Temple University, Philadelphia, Pennsylvania 19122

PETER M. VIETZE (155), Mental Retardation Research Centers Program, Mental Retardation and Developmental Disabilities Branch, National Institute of Child Health and Human Development, Bethesda, Maryland 20205

MARSHA A. WEINRAUB (1), Infant Behavior Laboratory, Department of Psychology, Temple University, Philadelphia, Pennsylvania 19122

THOMAS S. WEISNER (69), Departments of Psychiatry and Anthropology, University of California, Los Angeles 90024

ANTOINETTE WHALEY (1), Department of Educational Psychology, Temple University, Philadelphia, Pennsylvania 19122

MELVIN ZAX (47), Department of Psychology, University of Rochester, Rochester, New York 14627

ANDREA G. ZETLIN (69), Mental Retardation Research Center, Neuro-Psychiatric Institute, University of California-Los Angeles, Los Angeles, California 90024

Preface

There is little question that the family is the basic social unit in all societies and, as such, provides a primary source of socialization to the children of any culture. The process and course of socialization is significantly affected by the characteristics of the parents within the family. One parental characteristic that heretofore has received relatively little attention is that of handicap. In recognition of this fact, the central purpose of this book is to discuss and delineate how children are affected by the presence of handicapping conditions in their parents. Thus, as the title suggests, this book is about that distinct group of children whose parents have a handicap. By necessity this book is also about families and their reactions and adjustments to the presence of handicapping conditions in their primary adults (viz., parents).

This book should be of interest to researchers and practitioners who have an interest in parent–child relationships or family interactions. This volume raises and clarifies research and clinical problems as they relate to families with handicapped parents. At the same time, it discusses research models and strategies that can be applied to this population.

Because of the broad nature of the topic being considered, the authors represented in this volume come from a wide variety of disciplinary backgrounds, including law, medicine, special education, social work, rehabilitation, anthropology, and community, developmental, and pediatric psychology. As a result, each chapter approaches the topic of handicapped parents from a different perspective and deals with a particular issue within the topic area. The introductory chapter, by Thurman, Whaley, and Weinraub, underscores the central theme of the book by providing a rationale for studying this population. The second chapter, by Gilhool and Gran, discusses legal and public policy issues as they relate to parenthood in handicapped individuals. The third chapter, by Thurman, discusses how families with handicapped parents might be studied using an ecological model to trace the development of the system across time. Sameroff, Seifer, and Zax, in Chapter 4, review the research on the effects of parental emotional handicap on early child development and suggest "that the offspring of schizophrenic women as a group have many development problems [but] that these problems do not appear to be the simple result of maternal schizophrenia." Chapter 5, by Zetlin, Weisner, and Gallimore, demonstrates how qualitative research approaches can be effectively employed to study mentally retarded parents. The authors suggest that, while mentally retarded individuals can demonstrate some effective parenting practices, they often require support and aid from extended family members. Zetlin et al. conclude that this pattern of functioning, while somewhat atypical for the middle and upper classes of American society, is not unusual when compared either with other socioeconomic and subcultural groups in the United States or with several other cultures in other parts of the world.

In Chapter 6, Kornblum and Anderson examine the family environment of children with diabetic parents. Their analysis stems from their own experience as researchers and clinical practitioners serving families with diabetic parents. They conclude by summarizing a number of issues for further study of these families.

Hoffmeister, in Chapter 7, provides insight into deaf families. He contrasts deaf and hearing parents who have deaf and hearing children. He also elucidates the role of the Deaf Community and how that community helps define the function of deaf parents and offers them support and aid.

Both Chapter 8, by Greer, and Chapter 9, by Glass, deal with physical disability and how it can affect parenting and family functioning. Greer focuses on people with physical disabilities who become parents and develops some hypotheses concerning their children. He also provides a discussion of the types of variables that should be considered when studying families with disabled parents. Glass, by contrast, addresses the later onset of physical disability by discussing a variety of issues that must be considered when a previously nonhandicapped parent suddenly becomes physically disabled. She concludes, as does Greer, that more research is needed on the effects of parental physical handicap on children and on family functioning in general.

In Chapter 10, Coates, Vietze, and Gray discuss and analyze the methodological issues in studying children of disabled parents. Their analysis leads to the development of two paradigms: one that addresses congenital disability in parents and another that addresses adventitious disability in parents. These paradigms are meant to provide a beginning for researchers whose interest is to study parental disability.

The final chapter, by Newbrough, provides an analysis and a synthesis of the other chapters in the book. Newbrough does this from his perspective as a community psychologist.

In selecting all of these individuals to contribute to this effort, I attempted to identify people who have made signficant contributions to their fields. The chapters that they have presented speak to their professional competence. In addition, however, several of these authors are either disabled themselves or are children of disabled parents. Thus, they bring a personal as well as a professional perspective to the topic at hand. This combination of perspectives has given this book a unique point of view, one that is scholarly and yet juxtaposes perspectives with actual personal experience.

Several words of thanks are necessary. First, I would like to express my appreciation to the Society of Research in Child Development Study Group Committee, which saw fit to provide funds during early March 1982, for the study group from which this book derives. Thanks, too, to the Foundation for Child Development, whose funds underwrote the study group. The Foundation for Child Development is a private foundation that makes grants to educational and charitable institutions; its main interests are in research, the study of social economic indicators of children's lives, advocacy and public-information projects, and service experiments that help translate theoretical knowledge about children into policies and practices that affect their daily lives.

Within this context I must offer a special word of thanks to Gray Garwood, who chaired the Study Group Committee and provided much-appreciated advice and guidance in the development and conduct of the study group. His actual attendance at the study group as the committee's liaison was an important factor in its success, and his professional contributions to the discussions are gratefully acknowledged.

Of course I want to thank each of my contributors, without whom neither the study group nor this book would ever have become a reality.

I feel a special word of thanks should go to three colleagues and friends, Diane Gallagher, Toni Whaley, and Peter Vietze, whose professional and personal support led me to realize the necessity for the study group and subsequently for this volume. Each of them contributed to this project in his or her unique way and I am grateful.

My thanks, too, to members of the staff of Academic Press for their support, advice, and confidence in the completion of this book.

Finally, my thanks and gratitude go to Marcia and Shane, whose support and love are always there and who have had to endure yet another of my "projects."

1

Studying Families with Handicapped Parents: A Rationale

S. KENNETH THURMAN, ANTOINETTE WHALEY,
and MARSHA A. WEINRAUB

INTRODUCTION

Since the 1960s, there has been growing interest in the effects of family variables on the development of children. This interest has led to studies concentrating on patterns of interaction between parents and their children as well as factors like paternal absence, sex role identification, birth order, family and marital integration, child-rearing practices, and the like. From this research, models have emerged that suggest that eventual developmental outcomes in children result from the ongoing transactions between children and their parents (Sameroff & Chandler, 1975). Other models, like that more recently suggested by McGillicuddy-DeLisi, Sigel, and Johnson (1979), have related factors like parental belief systems to the child's level of cognitive development. In addition, there has been recent emphasis on the different contributions of fathers and mothers in the development of children (Clark-Stewart, 1978; Parke, 1979; Parke & Sawin, 1980; Pederson, 1980; Weinraub, 1978).

Socioeconomic characteristics of parents also have been found to be related to developmental outcomes. In fact, McCall, Hogarty, and Hurlburt (1972) have suggested that socioeconomic status remains the single best predictor of infants' IQ scores as they get older. Golden and Birns (1976) conclude that it may be "process variables such as, nutrition, patterns of mother–child interaction, language experience, etc., which may be associated with social class that may have a direct effect on children's development" (p. 300). Likewise, Sameroff and Seifer

(1983) argue that social status can be divided into component variables, such as parental beliefs, attitudes, and coping abilities, as well as environmental factors, in order to help eliminate individual differences in development. As the discussion below indicates, these variables may have particular relevance in studying handicapped parents and their children.

The preceding discussion clearly indicates that a wide variety of parental characteristics and family variables can be related to and can predict developmental outcomes in children. Nonetheless, one parental characteristic that has been little studied is parental disability. As a result, we possess only limited knowledge of the effects that parental disability have on the development of children. In response to this dearth of information, researchers from a number of disciplines have begun to show an increased interest in studying this population. Consequently, since the late 1970s, an increasing number of articles dealing with this subject have appeared in the scientific literature (see Budd & Greenspan, 1984; Buck & Hohmann, 1983; Zetlin, Weisner, & Gallimore, Chap. 5, this volume).

Given this increased interest in studying the effects of parental disability on the developing child, several important questions may be raised. What do we presently know about the relationship between parental disability and the developing child? What are the critical research questions still to be answered? The remaining chapters of this book address issues clearly related to these two questions. The present chapter provides a context from which the others emerge.

Specifically, this chapter focuses on the importance of studying handicapped parents and their children and the implications of this study for public policy. In addition, it addresses how studying this population can increase our specific knowledge of this type of family and of developmental processes generally.

THE EMERGING LEGAL CONTEXT

In Chapter 2 Gilhool and Gran make it clear that a number of legal positions have emerged that have implications for parenthood in disabled adults. They conclude that some disabled groups have been more successful in gaining parental rights than others. While more and more legal decisions have favored disabled parents and have treated their disabilities as only one factor to be considered, historically, the opportunities for disabled individuals to experience parenthood have been severely limited. In particular, the rights to bear and raise children have been the most restricted among mentally retarded persons.

Indeed, one of the purposes of their institutionalization has been to eliminate any opportunity for mentally retarded persons to procreate (Budd & Greenspan, 1984; Zetlin, Weisner, & Gallimore, Chap. 5, this volume). Although other disability groups have not been denied this right as blatantly as mentally retarded persons have, they too have had less opportunity to exercise their parental rights. Many adoption agencies, for example, will not consider the application of a disabled person to adopt a child (Sandness, 1981), a discriminatory practice sometimes upheld by the courts (Gilhool & Gran, Chap. 2, this volume). In addition, during a custody hearing, a disabled parent may frequently find that his or her disability is used against him or her (Gilhool & Gran, Chap. 2, this volume; Greer, Chap. 8, this volume).

With the rights of disabled people being expanded and with an increased likelihood that they will become parents, the issue of child outcomes takes on an increased relevance. Generation of further public policy in this area requires a firmer empirical basis emanating from studies that examine the effects of parental handicap on children. This research is needed to support the goal of preventing indiscriminant denial of and/or infringement on disabled persons' parental rights without compromising the right of children to be raised in an environment conducive to their maximal development. Reaching this goal requires the cooperation of legal, medical, rehabilitation, and family service professionals. To be successful they need up-to-date information that will help them decide whether a particular disabled parent in a particular set of circumstances places a given child at developmental risk. Specifically, they need to know (1) which parental disabilities, if any, place a child at developmental risk; (2) whether other factors exacerbate or attenuate the effects of that particular parental disability; (3) what intervention support programs, if deemed necessary, would most likely benefit that disabled parent and his or her children; (4) whether that intervention or support exists or could be provided; and (5) whether the effects of the handicap are temporary or permanent. Unfortunately, this kind of information is, for the most part, nonexistent.

As a result of this lack of information, policy makers are being forced to make important decisions about the lives of both disabled parents and their children that, to a large degree, cannot be supported or denied by empirical data. Some of the decisions unnecessarily restrict parental rights, while other decisions create the real possibility that some children are put at a greater risk than is necessary. Without increased study of these populations, policy makers, albeit well-meaning ones, are likely to continue to make ill-informed decisions. This fact provides one important rationale for studying children of handicapped parents. It, however, is not the only one, as can be seen from the ensuing paragraphs.

WHAT IS TO BE LEARNED?

While it is clear that policy makers may require specific data on specific questions in the generation of public policy relating to families (Nye & McDonald, 1979), there are also important questions regarding developmental and social psychological phenomena that can be answered through the study of disabled parents and their children. Buck and Hohmann (1983) have suggested that there is a "dire need for further research as well as better research [with these families]." They further assert that "research assessing children's adjustment to parental disability through childhood, adolescence, and adulthood and at varying periods after the onset of disability needs to be undertaken" (p. 230). Coates, Vietze, and Gray (Chap. 10, this volume) have presented two models that can be employed to study this population further and have expanded upon the variables identified by Buck and Hohmann. They have delineated some of these variables as independent, others as intervening, and still others as dependent. Of course, how each variable is classified within a given study will depend on the specific research questions being posed and will, in turn, provide different perspectives on the results of each study.

Buck and Hohmann have also made a clear distinction between disability and illness. Kornblum and Anderson (Chap. 6, this volume) have provided additional insight into the variables to consider when studying chronic parental illness. While their example is insulin-dependent diabetes, many of the variables they identify have relevance to populations with other types of chronic debilitating illness.

While the positions of these authors would suggest that further study of handicapped parents and their children is needed, their basic premise seems to be that we need more knowledge of this population. This knowledge, as suggested above, could lead to the development of more enlightened policy. In addition, more knowledge about this population will help to determine to what extent different types of services are required to meet the needs of these individuals. Buck and Hohmann (1983) have raised the following unanswered questions regarding children with disabled parents as typical of those needing further study.

1. How do children's reactions to the disablement of a parent vary as a function of the age of the child when the parent is disabled?
2. How do children's reactions to the parent's disability change as a function of time since onset of parental disability?
3. What patterns of adjustment characterize children with disabled parents during early, middle, and late childhood, adolescence, and adulthood?
4. What effects does it have on children to live through the social, emotional, and financial upheaval often associated with parental disablement versus entering the home after the disabled parent has learned to live with his/her disability? (p. 230)

These questions would seem to stem from the basic belief that parental disability does, in fact, make a difference in the developmental outcome of children. We would submit that data are still needed to identify whether parental disability as a single variable is significant in predicting the development status of children at various life stages. To a large degree we have yet to determine whether parental disability is a significant variable in and of itself or whether it is merely a concomitant variable with other factors that predict developmental outcome. Therefore, it may be more important, as Sameroff, Seifer, and Zax (Chap. 4, this volume) suggest, to study how parental handicap combines with other variables to predict developmental outcomes. Unfortunately, the number of variables involved in studying this population, and the complexity of the interaction among these variables, may limit researchers' ability to draw meaningful generalizations.

Although we recognize the difficulties inherent in studying this population, it is clear from the discussion above the much can be learned about families with handicapped parents. On a broader level, study of this population can provide additional knowledge about child development and family systems. For example, it is generally accepted that the visual system mediates bonding and attachment between mother and child (Klaus & Kennell, 1976; Robson, 1967), because it governs the pace and intensity of mother–infant interactions (Brazelton, Koslowski, & Main, 1974; Stern, 1974, 1977). The validity of this theory appears to be strengthened in the light of Fraiberg's (1974) work with sighted mothers and their blind children. Further study of blind mothers and their sighted infants can either provide additional evidence of the importance of vision in this process or force us to modify the theory somewhat by identifying other processes that do or can mediate the attachment of mothers and their infants.[1]

---

[1]One of the authors, Antoinette Whaley, is presently conducting research on the patterns of interaction between sighted infants and their blind mothers. Her data should help elucidate further the role of visual mediation in the development of mother–infant attachment systems.

As Glass (Chap. 9, this volume) points out, it is clear that the onset of physical disability can significantly alter patterns of family interaction and adjustment. By studying such families, researchers can begin to learn more about how families reestablish homeostatic balance following periods of upheaval and stress. In addition, adventitious disability provides researchers the opportunity to study coping patterns in both individuals and the family system. It further creates a situation for studying how the copeability of one member of a family affects that of other family members and even that of the family as a unit.

Another key area of concern among developmental theorists is parental roles and child-rearing practices. Clearly the existence of a parental handicap can alter child-rearing practices and parental roles. By systematically studying these alterations, researchers may begin to understand more about the relationship between child outcomes and parenting practices. By studying both the abilities and disabilities of disabled parents, more insight into the factors that positively and negatively affect children's development can emerge. While the structure of the responses made by disabled parents may be different from those made by nondisabled parents, some qualitative aspects of these responses may remain the same. We would assert that further comparative research on these similarities and differences can shed significant new perspectives on our understanding of parent–child relationships.

Related to parenting practices and parental roles is the issue of sex role development. Because of disability, a parent might be forced to modify his or her role within the family in such a way that he or she is no longer providing a traditional sex role model. Again, basic questions about the function of parental modeling in sex role development could be further elucidated by studying these families.

Another important question of developmental import is "What is a competent parent?" This question has importance not only in the developmental context but also in the legal–policy arena discussed above and in Chapter 2, by Gilhool and Gran. By studying various groups of disabled parents we may begin to identify the parameters of parental competence. What must disabled parents be able to do (as parents) to assure the most desired developmental outcomes in their children? At a more fundamental level, does a disabled parent need to do something more or something differently than a nondisabled parent in order to facilitate the same outcomes in his or her children?

Certainly, there are other questions and other issues that contribute to the rationale for studying disabled parents and their children. We have raised but a few. In one way or another, each chapter in this book raises questions and perspectives that should further build the rationale for studying disabled parents and their children. Our hope is that you, the reader, will raise other questions and set out to find the answers.

A FINAL PERSPECTIVE

One area of concern for all of us as researchers, clinicians, and scholars is our own attitudes, biases, and perceptions. In order to study this population and to render required services to them, it is important to develop our theories and practices with as few a priori assumptions as possible. For example, we cannot assume a priori that any given person with a disability would or would not be, or is or is not, an effective parent. For if we do, our research and services will surely bear out our assumptions.

Professionals' attitudes may surface in many ways. They surface in the way a researcher interacts with the disabled person. They may surface in the design of the study; that is, in the questions that are asked and the instruments that are used to measure the variables. And they may surface in the way one interprets the research data and develops service plans for these families.

We offer three suggestions to help reduce these attitudinal biases. First, before embarking on a project with a particular disabled group, one should learn as much as possible about the etiology of that particular disability; the history of treatment of that disability group, as Hoffmeister has done in Chapter 7; and the problems and characteristics of adjustment associated with it. It is most important to learn, not only about what behaviors are typical in that population, but also, about the range of those behaviors. This knowledge will increase the probability of asking relevant research questions and developing appropriate measures, research designs, and service plans. Furthermore, this knowledge will assist in the analysis and interpretation of research and clinical data since many behaviors that appear aberrant for nondisabled persons are typical and appropriate within a disabled population. In turn, such knowledge will help to determine whether an observed behavior is a result of the person's disability or some other existing or pre-existing condition in the environment. Knowing that a person is disabled no more explains all of his or her behavior than does knowing his or her social class, family configuration, IQ, or any other single characteristic.

Second, analysis should not stop at simple comparisons of differential parental or child outcome in handicapped or nonhandicapped families but should examine within each group those parenting style variables that are correlated with child outcome. Research can go even further to investigate whether the processes that predict optimal developmental outcome are similar across groups (see Ansul & Weinraub, 1984; Weinraub & Wolf, 1983).

Third, researchers and clinicians should explore and examine their own feelings toward disabilities in general and toward the specific disability of concern in particular. By doing so, they will be better able to determine whether their interpretation of the data or reaction to a particular behavior is due to their professional training and observations or to their attitude toward disabled persons. Following these suggestions will not eliminate attitudinal bias but should make researchers and clinicians more aware of their bias and its effect on their own professional practice.

SUMMARY

This chapter has provided several rationales for studying families with handicapped parents. This first rationale stems from the necessity to provide policy makers with data for informed decision making regarding these families. Another rationale grows from the need to know more about the characteristics and needs of these families so that appropriate and adequate services can be developed and maintained when they are required. Finally, through systematic study of these families, some fundamental questions concerning child development and family systems can be further clarified. These questions relate to such critical processes as sex role development, child-rearing practices, parental competence, role modeling, and family adjustment and coping strategies. It is from the context provided by this chapter that the other chapters in this book emerge.

REFERENCES

Ansul, S., & Weinraub, M. *Children's responses to strangers: Effects of family status, stranger sex, and child sex.* Paper presented at the Fourth Biennial International Conference on Infant Studies, New York, April 1984.

Brazelton, T. B., Koslowski, B., & Main, M. The origins of reciprocity: The early mother–infant interaction. In M. Lewis & A. Rosenblum (Eds.), *The effect of the infant on its caregiver.* New York: John Wiley, 1974.

Buck, F. M., & Hohmann, G. W. Parental disability and children's adjustment. In E. L. Pan, T. E. Backer, & C. L. Vash (Eds.), *Annual review of rehabilitation* (Vol. 3). New York: Springer Publishing Co., 1983.

Budd, K. S., & Greenspan, S. Mentally retarded mothers. In E. A. Bleckman (Ed.), Behavior modification with women. New York: Gilford Press, 1984.

Clarke-Stewart, K. A. And daddy makes three: The father's impact on mother and young child. *Child Development*, 1978, *49*, 466–478.

Fraiberg, S. Blind infants and their mothers: An examination of the sign system. In M. Lewis & A. Rosenblum (Eds.), *The effect of the infant on its caregiver*. New York: John Wiley, 1974.

Golden, M., & Birns, B. Social class and infant intelligence. In M. Lewis (Ed.), *Origins of intelligence*. New York: Plenum Press, 1976.

Klaus, M. H., & Kennell, J. H. *Maternal–infant bonding*. St. Louis: Mosby, 1976.

McCall, R. B., Hogarty, P. S., & Hurlburt, N. Transitions in infant sensorimotor development and the prediction of childhood IQ. *American Psychologist*, 1972, *27*, 728–748.

McGillicuddy-DeLisi, A. V., Sigel, I., & Johnson, J. E. The family as a system of mutual influences: Parental beliefs, distancing behavior, and children's representational thinking. In M. Lewis & L. A. Rosenblum (Eds.), *The child and its family*. New York: Plenum Press, 1979.

Nye, F., & McDonald, G. Family policy research: Emergent models and theoretical issues. *Journal of Marriage and the Family*, 1979, *41*, 473–485.

Parke, R. D. Perspectives on father–infant interactions. In J. Osofsky (Ed.), *Handbook of infant development*. New York: John Wiley, 1979.

Parke, R. D., & Sawin, D. B. The family in early infancy: Social interactional and attitudinal analysis. In F. A. Pederson (Ed.), *The father–infant relationship: Observational studies in the Family Setting*. New York: Praeger, 1980.

Pederson, F. A. (Ed.). The father–infant relationship: Observational studies in the family setting. New York: Praeger, 1980.

Robson, K. S. Role of eye to eye contact in maternal–infant attachment. *Journal of Child Psychology and Psychiatry*, 1967, *8*, 13-25.

Sameroff, A., & Chandler, M. J. Reproductive risk and the continuum of care taking casualty. In F. D. Horowitz, M. Hetherington, S. Scarr-Salapatek, & G. Sigal (Eds.), *Review of child development research* (Vol. 4). Chicago: University of Chicago Press, 1975.

Sameroff, A. J., & Seifer, R. Familial risk and child competence. *Child Development*, 1983, *54*, 1254–1268.

Sandness, G. Adoption by parents with disabilities. *Rehabilitation Gazette*, 1981, *24*, 23–25.

Stern, D. N. Mother and infant at play: The dynamic interaction involving facial, vocal, and gaze behaviors. In M. Lewis & L. A. Rosenblum (Eds.), *The effect of the infant on its caregiver*. New York: John Wiley, 1974.

Stern, D. N. *The first relationship: infant and mother*. Cambridge, Mass.: Harvard University Press, 1977.

Weinraub, M. Fatherhood: The myth of the second-class parent. In J. H. Stevens, Jr. & M. Mathews (Eds.), *Mother/child, father/child relationships*. New York: National Association for the Education of Young Children, 1978.

Weinraub, M., & Wolf, B. Effects of stress and social supports on mother–child interaction in single and two-parent families. *Child Development*, 1983, *54*, 1297–1311.

Legal Rights of Disabled Parents

THOMAS K. GILHOOL and JUDITH A. GRAN

In *Meyer v. Nebraska* (1923), the United States Supreme Court recognized that a person's right "to marry, establish a home and bring up children" (p. 399) is a fundamental right protected by the fifth and fourteenth amendments to the Constitution. Yet the rights of disabled parents still do not enjoy the same protection as those of the nondisabled. In important respects, the statutory and common law of most states treats disabled and nondisabled parents unequally. Faced with a custody dispute between a disabled and a nondisabled parent, all but a handful of progressive courts treat a disabled parent's handicap as evidence favoring an award of custody to the nondisabled parent. And almost universally, mentally retarded parents face powerful judicial and statutory presumptions of inadequacy.

This chapter examines some current approaches of courts and legislatures to the parental rights of persons with disabilities. First, it will discuss legal recognition of the disabled person's right to be a parent, that is, the right to procreation. Next, it will discuss recent developments in the law concerning the rights of physically disabled parents. Finally, the article will examine the complex issues that arise in cases concerning the rights of parents with mental retardation.

THE RIGHT TO BECOME A PARENT: RECOGNITION OF THE DISABLED PERSON'S RIGHT TO PROCREATE

In the early decades of this century, during the heyday of the eugenicist movement, many states passed legislation authorizing compulsory sterilization of persons with mental retardation or mental illness and, in some states, persons with physical disabilities such as epilepsy (Sokappa, 1980). In *Buck v. Bell* (1927), the United States Supreme Court upheld the constitutionality of a statute providing for compulsory sterilization of institutionalized retarded persons. In his opinion for the Court, Justice Holmes accepted the eugenicist rationale for compulsory sterilization laws, likening them to vaccination as public health measures to keep society from being "swamped with incompetence." (p. 207)

Despite the holding in *Buck v. Bell*, by the 1940s the constitutionality of state sterilization statutes had been almost completely undermined by two related developments. The first was the recognition by the Supreme Court, first articulated in *Skinner v. Oklahoma* (1942) that procreation is a basic civil right.[1] *Skinner* concerned a constitutional challenge to a state statute mandating the sterilization of thrice-convicted felons. The Court struck down the statute because it was unsupported by any evidence that the children of larcenists, who were subject to sterilization, were any more dangerous to society than the children of embezzlers, who were not.

The Court's analysis in *Skinner* laid the foundation for attacks by other courts on compulsory sterilization statutes. For, in identifying procreation as a fundamental civil right, the Court also defined the state's burden to justify a statute which deprives some categories of persons of this right but not others. Normally, a state statute is entitled to a strong presumption of constitutionality, even when it appears to treat different categories of individuals differently. However, when a statute affects the exercise of fundamental civil rights, its differential treatment of different categories of citizens must be necessary to protect an important state interest. If the justification offered by the state for protecting the rights of some persons less than others is not extremely convincing, the statute will be found unconstitutional.

The second development was the demise of eugenics. With the recognition that only a small percentage of mental retardation is the result of abnormal genes or chromosomes, the rationale behind sterilization statutes as preventive health measures evaporated, and those statutes could not survive the close scrutiny mandated by *Skinner*. Although the Court has never explicitly overruled *Buck*, most authorities agree that its rationale did not survive *Skinner* and subsequent

---

[1]*Skinner* should be distinguished from *Meyer v. Nebraska*, and *Pierce v. Society of Sisters* (1925) in that *Skinner* recognized procreation as a fundamental freedom in its own right. The earlier cases upheld parents' right to direct the education of their children as a corollary of their First Amendment freedom of expression.

cases affirming the fundamental character of procreative rights (*Griswold v. Connecticut*, 1968; see Isaacs, 1980; *Roe v. Wade*, 1973).

After *Skinner*, many compulsory sterilization statutes were invalidated by the courts as unconstitutional or repealed voluntarily by state legislatures. (Note, *South Dakota Law Review*, 1980). Only a small minority of states retain such statutes, and their constitutionality is dubious.

Thus, it is clear today that a person who has a disability but has not been declared incompetent to make his own decisions, by court order, cannot be sterilized without consent. The great majority of retarded persons, then, since they cannot be declared incompetent, cannot be sterilized.

A severely retarded person who has been declared incompetent may be sterilized only by court order. The retarded person's parent or guardian or any other interested person seeking sterilization must file a petition requesting sterilization with the court before the sterilization sought may be performed. In some states, there are statutory criteria to guide the court in deciding whether the petition should be granted; in others, where there is no authorizing legislation, the court may develop its own guidelines[2] or refuse to grant sterilization petitions altogether.

Courts that have chosen to develop their own guidelines have used one of two approaches. Some try to decide whether sterilization is in the best interest of the retarded person; others employ the doctrine of "substituted consent," that is, the fiction that the court is making the decision the person would have made were she capable of meaningful choice (*In re Grady*, 1981). Some courts have refused to develop their own guidelines in the absence of authorizing legislation and have rejected the doctrine of substituted consent, stating that it is facile to assert that there has been genuine choice when in fact there has been none at all. These courts have also rejected the "best interest" standard, stating that the courts cannot decide what constitutes a retarded person's best interest without guidance from the legislature (*In re Eberhardy*, 1981).

In spite of the variety of approaches taken by the courts, it is clear that the only constitutionally sufficient justification for sterilizing a disabled person who has not genuinely chosen it, is the interest of the

---

[2]In *Stump v. Sparkman* (1978), the U.S. Supreme Court held that a court of general jurisdiction has the inherent judicial power to decide whether to grant a sterilization petition, even if there is no authorizing legislation nor any guidelines established by the legislature.

disabled person herself, not the interest of parents, relatives or society (Note, *South Dakota Law Review*, 1980). Yet the strength of judicial protection of the retarded person's right to become a parent contrasts sharply with the ease with which the courts may terminate a retarded person's right to keep the child once she has become a parent. This ironic result of the disappearance of compulsory sterilization laws will be explored later in this chapter.

EQUALITY, DUE PROCESS, AND THE RIGHTS OF PERSONS WITH DISABILITIES

Beside recognition that procreation is a fundamental right, two additional developments in the law have affected the rights of disabled parents. The first is the judicial and legislative trend, beginning in the 1970s, toward higher standards of procedural due process in matters that affect the fundamental rights of persons with mental disabilities. The second is the enactment of statutory schemes to protect disabled persons' right to equal treatment and provide them with the resources to live normal, independent lives in their own communities.

As a result of constitutional challenges, many state statutes that affect disabled persons' basic rights have been revised during the last decade to require courts to rely on facts rather than presumptions. For example, in most states a person can no longer be confined in an institution or mental hospital merely because of retardation or mental illness; it must be shown by clear and convincing evidence that her behavior is dangerous to herself or others (*Goldy v. Beal*, 1976). Similarly, although it was relatively easy in most states a decade ago to terminate a retarded parent's rights even if there was no evidence that the parent actually had neglected her child, by the mid-1970s most states had revised their termination statutes to require evidence of severe parental incapacity—repeated and continued abuse or neglect that could not or would not be remedied—before a retarded parent's relationship with her child could be judicially severed.

During the 1970s, federal legislation was enacted to ensure equal treatment of disabled persons in federally funded programs and to provide disabled persons with the resources needed to live independently in the community. In 1973, as part of a new Rehabilitation Act, Congress enacted a civil rights statute for disabled persons based on the language of Title VI of the Civil Rights Act of 1964 (42 U.S.C.A. §2000d). Section 504 (29 U.S.C.A. §794), provides that

No otherwise qualified handicapped individual in the United States . . . shall, solely by reason of his handicap, be excluded from participation in, be denied the benefits of, or be subjected to discrimination under any program or activity receiving Federal financial assistance.

The section 504 regulations require that programs receiving Federal assistance provide handicapped and nonhandicapped persons with substantially equal opportunities. Disabled persons must be afforded an opportunity to "obtain the same result, to gain the same benefit, or to reach the same level of achievement" as nondisabled persons (45 C.F.R. §84.4[b] [2]). Thus, the mere formal availability of federally funded services to disabled people may not satisfy section 504 if disabled people cannot benefit from them because they are not accessible or appropriate to their needs.

The Comprehensive Services for Independent Living title added to the Rehabilitation Act in 1978 (29 U.S.C.A. §796) authorizes grants to the states to provide services, which include transportation, attendant care, and services for preschool children such as language and communication training and child development services, to severely handicapped persons to enable them to live independently in their own communities. Both the Independent Living Amendments and the Developmentally Disabled Bill of Rights and Assistance Act (42 U.S.C.A. §6000 *et seq.*) reflect congressional recognition that society as a whole benefits when severely disabled persons' potential for achievement and contribution to society are supported by services that allow them to live as independently as possible in their own communities.

In spite of this body of federal legislation, adequate support services for severely disabled parents, especially retarded parents, are almost nonexistent in most states. Yet support services in housekeeping, nutrition, budgeting, and specialized day care and enrichment programs for the child are vitally important to retarded parents and may determine whether or not the parent is able to keep a child. Many state statutes now specify that parental rights be may terminated by a court only after reasonable efforts have been made by social service agencies to remedy the parent's problems and these efforts have failed. Most local child welfare agencies offer rehabilitative services for problem parents, and a reasonable interpretation of section 504 suggests that services made available to nonhandicapped parents must also be made available, with appropriate modifications, to handicapped parents. Unfortunately, regardless of section 504, the absence of appropriate rehabilitative services for mentally disabled parents is a brute fact in most parts of the country, and few courts have been persuaded to order that such services be provided as an alternative to severance of the retarded parent's relationship with a child. In fact, it is only recently that the influence of section 504 has become apparent in cases concerning the rights of physically disabled parents.

PHYSICALLY HANDICAPPED PARENTS

Most adjudications of the rights of physically handicapped parents have arisen in child custody cases. In a custody dispute, the task of the court is to determine which parent will better serve the best interest of the child. Where custody is hotly contested by two conscientious parents, it is difficult for the court to decide which parent will better serve the child's best interest, and the cases suggest that trial judges do not always resist the temptation to let one parent's handicap tip the balance.

Three views of the relation between physical handicap and the best interest of the child have emerged in child custody cases. The first is the view that the handicap establishes a presumption—generally, a rebuttable one—that a handicapped parent is an inadequate parent.

The second, and perhaps the most common view today, is that while handicap is only one of many factors for the court to consider in determining the best interest of the child, it may be treated as prima facie evidence of parental inability; that is, evidence sufficient, unless rebutted, to establish that, other things being equal, a handicapped parent is less capable than a nonhandicapped parent. The handicapped parent may compensate for her disability by evidence of ability in some other area.

The third and most advanced view is the one adopted by the California Supreme Court in *In re Carney* (1979). This view forbids the court the apply any presumption of parental inadequacy based on handicap or to treat handicap as prima facie evidence that the handicapped parent is less capable than the nonhandicapped parent. It requires that the court begin with the "ethical, emotional and intellectual" content of the parent–child relationship and considers "the handicapped person as an individual and the family as a whole" in its inquiry into the best interest of the child.

The following cases illustrate these three approaches.

Handicap as Presumption of Parental Inadequacy

In *Adoption of Richardson* (1967), the California court of appeals held that a categorical or irrebuttable presumption that a handicapped person is incapable of raising a child violates the parent's right to due process and equal protection of the law. In *Richardson*, a married couple in which both spouses were deaf–mute petitioned to adopt an infant boy. The couple introduced expert testimony during the adoption hearings that they had a good relationship with the child and that their disability would have no adverse impact on the child's development. The trial court denied the petition, asking rhetorically,

> Is this a normal, happy home? There is no question about it, it is a happy home, but is it a normal home? I don't think the Court could make a finding that it is a normal home when these poor unfortunate people, they are handicapped, and what can they do in the way of bringing this child up to be the type of citizen we all want him to be. (p. 228)

On appeal, the California court of appeals held that the judge had abused his discretion and had made clearly erroneous findings of fact. The appellate court roundly chastised the judge for his thoughtless, stereotypic remarks and stated that he should have disqualified himself from the case at the outset. (In addition to his other errors, the judge had made a highly improper ex parte contact with the director of the county bureau of adoptions urging that the adoption be "nipped in the bud before these unfortunate people get too attached to the child," p. 229.) The judge's opinion of the abilities of deaf–mutes obviously affected his capacity to render an impartial decision. The court of appeals also held that the judge's application of an irrebutable presumption of the parents' incapacity to raise a child violated the parents' right to due process and equal protection of the law.

The dissenting judge in *Moye v. Moye* (1981) argued that handicap establishes a presumption, though a rebuttable one, of parental inadequacy. Fortunately, both this view and the irrebuttable presumption applied by the trial court in *Richardson* are distinctly minority views today.

Handicap as Prima Facie Evidence of Inability

Treating handicap as prima facie evidence of lesser adequacy as a parent also reflects stereotype, for it treats disability as evidence, sufficient if not rebutted, of parental inability without considering the actual impact of the disability on the parent–child relationship. For example, in *In re Levin* (1980), the California court of appeals rather mechanically weighed the comparative strengths and weaknesses of a disabled and a nondisabled parent, automatically assuming that the mother's disability was a weakness. The mother, Paula Levin, had suffered a stroke during pregnancy and at the time of the custody hearing was confined to a wheelchair. The daughter had been with her father, Barry, since birth because of her mother's stroke. The evidence showed that the daughter had a warm and close relationship with both parents. The weight of expert testimony presented at the hearing favored an award of custody to Paula because Barry had kept their daughter in a nursery school for six to seven hours a day while she was in his custody, and the psychologist expert witness testified that this was too long for a two-year-old child to be in day-care. Nevertheless, the trial court awarded permanent custody to Barry. The court reasoned that it was in the daughter's best interest to remain with her father, "not because of the mother's handicap, but because of the limitations that the handicap imposes upon what I conceive to be the most normal possible life for a child" (p. 988).

The court of appeals remanded the case to the trial court for re reconsideration in light of the California Supreme Court's decision in *In re Carney*, discussed below. However, in its analysis of the record, the court of appeals indicated that the question for the lower court was essentially a quantitative one: Whether Paula's handicap would have a "substantial" adverse impact on the best interest of the child or only a "minor" one. The court appeared to assume that having a mother in a wheelchair would, in some measure, be adverse to the child's best interest. Thus, although the court of appeals cautioned the trial court to consider the facts surrounding the impact of the mother's handicap on the child, it is not clear that the standard articulated by the court of appeals went beyond the notion that disability should ordinarily be considered a negative factor in the equation of two parents' respective strengths and weaknesses.

In a custody dispute between a mother with epilepsy and a non-handicapped father, the Idaho Supreme Court, in *Moye v. Moye* (1981), reversed an award of custody to the father and remanded the case to the trial court for more complete findings of fact. The mother's epilepsy was partially controlled through medication, and she had post-seizure lack of energy and migraine headaches. The trial court had made 10 findings, 6 of them concerning the mother's physical condition. The supreme court held that the trial court had abused its discretion by overemphasizing the mother's disability and that its other findings of fact were insufficient to support the custody award. A strong dissenting opinion would have held, with the trial court, that the mother's handicap established a presumption of inadequacy.

Despite the difference between the majority and the dissent, there was essential agreement that a parent's disability may be treated as evidence that, other things being equal, the disabled parent is less able than the nondisabled parent. The majority differed with the dissent only in concluding that handicap should not ordinarily be the decisive factor in a custody case.

In a custody dispute between a parent and a nonparent, the natural parent ordinarily is entitled to a strong presumption of fitness. However, in 1979 in *Rains v. Alston*, the Arkansas Supreme Court affirmed an award of custody of the child of a blind and epileptic mother to the child's grandparents. Although the mother supported herself and her child at a full-time job, the trial court held that her disability made her an unfit parent. The supreme court affirmed this in an unpublished opinion and did not take issue with the trial court's findings of fact. Subsequently, in response to public protests, the court issued a new opinion to emphasize that the trial court had found the mother unfit for reasons apart from her handicap.

Indeed, most of the evidence recited by the supreme court from the trial record revealed that Ms. Rains' basic problem was poverty, not blindness. She worked full-time but did not earn enough to employ a housekeeper or an aide. Although with housekeeping services, Ms. Rains could have overcome the problems created by her blindness, the court did not consider whether some arrangement could or should be made to provide these services so that she would not have to relinquish custody of her child.

Rains v. Alston illustrates a painful dilemma of parents who are poor as well as disabled. A disabled parent who turns to public agencies because she knows she cannot provide for her child's needs by herself gives evidence of her acknowledged inadequacies as a parent; and experience demonstrates that the response will not always by sympathetic (many petitions for termination of parental rights are initiated by social service agencies). Even when the parent turns to family and friends for help, her decision may be construed as evidence of her inability to manage. Ms. Rains had asked her parents for help with her young child because she felt she could not take proper care of a baby while working full-time. The court suggested that had she been a fit parent, she could have managed without her parents' help.

Most of the factors cited by the supreme court to justify its decision (dirt, roaches, primitive open heaters in the home) concerned the physical environment of the home rather than the quality of the mother's relationship with her child. The court did not even consider the benefit to the child from maintaining close emotional ties with the mother; nor did it ask whether that benefit was outweighed by the harm to the child from the poor environmental conditions exacerbated by the mother's disability.

Beyond Stereotype: *In re Carney*

In re Carney (1979) is one of the few child custody decisions to show a strong awareness by the court of the public policies underlying federal statutory mandates of equal opportunity for disabled persons. In *Carney*, the California Supreme Court reversed a trial court's transfer of custody of two children from their father to their mother after the father became a quadriplegic in an automobile accident. The parents had separated five years before the accident, and the mother had formally relinquished custody of the boys at the time of the separation. After the accident, the father, William, moved to dissolve the marriage; and his estranged wife, Ellen, moved for an immediate award of custody of the two boys. The trial court granted Ellen's request on the ground that it would be detrimental to the boys to grow up in the custody of a quadriplegic father.

> *It wouldn't be a normal relationship between father and boys. . . .* [William] has to have help bathing and dressing and undressing. *He can't do anything for the boys himself except maybe talk to them, and teach them, be a tutor, which is good, but it's not enough.* I feel that it's in the best interest of the two boys to be with their mother, even though she hasn't had them for five years. (p. 735) (Emphasis in original.)

The supreme court, in a unanimous opinion written by Justice Mosk, reversed. The court condemned the trial court's overemphasis on the father's inability to join his sons on the playing field as "sex-stereotypical thinking," pointing out that a normal father–son relationship may be built upon shared experiences in many other activities besides sports. The court chastised the trial judge for relying on stereotyped preconceptions about William's physical disability and for ignoring the positive effect of his sophisticated wheelchair on his mobility. The court noted the growing body of legislation designed to enhance the participation of handicapped persons in the everyday life of the community, concluding that both technology and social and legal change have contributed to maximize the ability of disabled persons to participate in their children's lives.

Especially significant, from a legal perspective, was Justice Mosk's use of the policies underlying section 504 and other civil rights legislation for the disabled. The court's method of handling the evidence and allocating the burden of proof in child custody disputes, he wrote, must be consistent with the policy goal of encouraging "total integration of handicapped persons into the mainstream of society" (p. 740). In the custody case, therefore, it is impermissible to use evidence of

handicap as "prima facie evidence of the person's unfitness as a parent
or of probable detriment to the child" (p. 736). The court may consider
the parent's handicap only as part of the family's situation as a whole.
This means inquiring into the person's actual *and potential* physical
capabilities, how he or she has adapted to the disability and manages
its problems, how other members of the family have adjusted to the
disability. The inquiry "must take into account the special contributions the person may make to the family despite—*of even because of*—
the handicap" (p. 736) (emphasis added).

In its instructions for handling evidence of a parent's disability, the
supreme court warned lower courts against considering handicap, on
its face, as a negative factor in weighing comparative parental quali-
fications. In fact, Justice Mosk wrote, handicap may be a parental asset
rather than a deficit. "Few can pass through the crucible of a severe
physical disability without learning enduring lessons in patience and
tolerance" (p. 739). Handicap can strengthen family unity; can help
children become more responsible; and can enhance the ethical, emotional and intellectual environment for the child. Justice Mosk's emphasis on the positive role that handicap can play in the moral
environment of the home contrasts sharply with the overemphasis by
other courts on the effect of the parent's disability on the child's physical environment (which in itself may be an indirect way of treating
handicap as prima facie evidence of parental unfitness).

In *Hatz v. Hatz* (1982), a New York court adopted the California
Supreme Court's approach. In *Hatz*, as in *Carney*, the noncustodial
parent sought custody after the custodial parent was disabled in an
auto accident. The *Hatz* court paid special attention to the child's adjustment to the parent's disability. The court noted with approval the
opinion of an expert witness that the child should have an opportunity
to come to grips with her mother's handicap:

> He did not think it fair to take her away from the situation and possibly miss
> the opportunity to adjust to this painful event in her life. This adjustment
> would be more likely to occur were the child to live through the situation
> rather than be taken away from it. (p. 2215)

Ultimately, the approach taken by the courts in *Carney* and *Hatz*
rests on the conviction that to have a disability, even a severe one, is
not to be *less* than a nondisabled person; it is to have one's own way
of being in the world. It follows that the courts must examine the quality of the environment actually created by the disabled parent for his
child rather than assume without question that he would have provided a better environment if he were not disabled. It is hoped that the

California Supreme Court's pioneering decision in *Carney* eventually will be followed by the courts of other states, just as its pioneering decisions have been followed in other areas of law.

PARENTS WITH MENTAL RETARDATION

Cases concerning mentally handicapped parents arise most often in neglect and termination proceedings; that is, proceedings brought by a public agency to sever permanently the parent's relationship with her child. The principal issues that these cases raise include (1) the unfitness required before the parent's rights can be terminated, and (2) the duty of public agencies to provide the handicapped parent with training in parenting as an alternative to termination.

All states have statutory proceedings authorizing the state to intervene to protect abused or neglected children, and all but five have statutory procedures permitting a court to sever permanently a parent's rights in her children. In most states, this process requires two separate hearings: one a fact-finding hearing to establish whether the parent's conduct constitutes neglect, the other a dispositional hearing focusing on the placement that will serve the child's best interest once she has been found neglected (Bell, 1981). Thus, only after a child has been found to be neglected may the court decide whether termination would be best for the child, as measured by the balance of harm and benefit to the child in being removed from his parent's custody. Termination decisively affects fundamental individual rights, and due process therefore requires that the evidence supporting a finding of neglect be "clear and convincing" before parental ties can be severed (*Santosky v. Kramer*, 1982).

Despite substantial changes in state termination statutes during the 1970s to provide increased procedural protections and limit the courts' discretion to terminate parental rights for vague or imprecise reasons such as "moral unfitness," many termination statutes still treat retarded parents differently from nonretarded parents. In the 1970s, it was common for social service agencies to seek judicial severance of a retarded parent's rights soon after the child was born, or even before, on the ground that the parent would "inevitably" neglect her child (Note, *Stanford Law Review*, 1979). And although a person with retardation cannot be sterilized against her will merely because she is retarded, the statutes of 16 states still permit termination of parental rights on the ground of retardation alone. In effect, statutes such as Nebraska's section 43-292(5) allow the court to find parental abuse and neglect prospectively, before it has occured (*In re Holley*, 1981; see also *In re J. L. P.*, 1982).

Courts have upheld this "irrebutable presumption" that a retarded parent is necessarily unfit. In *Watkins v. Department of Human Resources* (1977), a mentally retarded father's parental rights were terminated although he had never had an opportunity to demonstrate whether he was or was not a fit parent. The trial court found that the father, because of his mental age, "did not have the basic intellectual qualities to raise children," and the appellate court affirmed the termination order on the basis of this finding. Courts have issued termination orders on the basis of a parent's low IQ alone, although other evidence indicated that the parent was satisfactory and there was no other evidence of abuse or neglect (*In re Orlando F.*, 1976).

Since the mid-1970s, the termination statutes of most states have been revised to require the party seeking termination to establish with particularity that the children have been or will be harmed by the retarded parent (see *In re Jeanie M. and Emma M.*, 1982). This requirement has also been imposed by the courts. For example, in *In re Green* (1978), a New York court strongly criticized a social welfare agency for deciding before birth that the mother would be inadequate and for refusing to provide or even consider rehabilitative services to help her correct her alleged deficiencies.

However, even where proof of parental neglect is required, retarded and nonretarded parents may not be treated equally. Several states have termination statutes that classify retarded and nonretarded parents separately and establish different grounds and procedures for each. For example, an Arizona statute (*Arizona Revised Statutes Annotated*, § 8–533) authorizes termination of a retarded parent's rights if retardation renders the parent "unable to discharge her parental responsibilities" and the condition is "unlikely to change." For nonretarded parents, much more specific grounds for termination (abuse, neglect, abandonment, commission of a felony) are required.

In New York, a bifurcated proceeding is required for nonretarded parents, but only a single proceeding for retarded parents. (*New York Social Service Law*, § 384[b][4][C]) In cases involving nonretarded parents, the court must first find that the child is neglected or dependent; only then may termination proceedings, including a separate dispositional hearing, be instituted. However, a separate proceeding to establish neglect is not required where it has been established that the parent is retarded. Nonretarded parents can be denied bifurcated termination proceedings only in the case of abandonment or severe and repeated abuse.

As noted above, a statute that treats different categories or persons unequally and that affects a fundamental right violates the Equal Protection Clause of the 14th amendment unless unequal treatment is justified by an important state interest (*Dunn v. Blumstein*, 1972; *Plyler v. Doe*, 1982; *Shapiro v. Thompson*, 1969; *Stanley v. Illinois*, 1972). At least one New York state court has held that the New York statute authorizing unequal treatment of retarded and nonretarded parents in termination proceedings violates the retarded parent's right to equal protection of the law (*In re Gross*, 1980; *Cardinal McCloskey School & Home v. Mendes;* 1980). However, another family court, in *In re Daniel A.D.* (1980), upheld the statute's constitutionality, stating that the classification of mentally retarded parents versus other parents was rational because "the proof surrounding mental retardation or mental illness *may be* closely connected to the proof regarding the best interests of the child" (p. 938) (emphasis added). Although equal protection analysis requires a court to closely scrutinize a statutory classification that affects fundamental rights, in *Daniel A.D.* the court merely assumed that the classification was rational, and declined to examine it to determine whether it was, in fact, rationally based. Similarly, the Arizona statute referred to above, which provides different types of termination proceedings for retarded parents and nonretarded parents, was upheld against an equal protection challenge in *In re Appeal in Maricopa County Juvenile Action No. JS 1308 and JS 1412* (1976).

Many states statutes now require that the party requesting termination show that a meaningful attempt has been made to improve the parent's skills through rehabilitative services, and that the effort has failed, before termination will be granted. Reasonable efforts must be made to remedy the condition that prevents the parent from caring adequately for his child. Thus, in termination cases the outcome may turn on the kind of services the agency is required to provide before the court may decide that the parent's deficiencies cannot be corrected.

The application of this statutory requirement to retarded parents raises a series of questions. How much effort are public agencies required to expend? Who has the burden of proposing and designing an appropriate service plan? Should only curative services—those designed to train the parent to manage on his own—be provided, or should public agencies be required to provide ongoing support services? What happens when appropriate services do not exist? Should the state be required to create them?

In the 1970s, courts placed the burden on the retarded parent to re-habilitate himself, and he would be given no more than a grace period in which to cure his alleged unfitness (see, e.g., *In re McDonald*, 1972). More recently, appellate courts have reversed termination orders be-cause the social agencies requesting termination had made no effort to help the parents improve their skills. For example, in *Chapman v. State ex rel. Juvenile Department of Multomah County* (1981), the court of appeals of Oregon reversed an order terminating the rights of a father with retardation and a mother with schizophrenia because the county Children's Service Division had offered "no services, sugges-tions, encouragement, training or any advice of any kind to the parents to help them to develop skills to care for the child properly," including the counseling services and parenting classes that the parents wanted to attend (p. 835).

But even where the courts agree that there is a duty to provide re-medial services, the problem remains that the necessary services may not exist, the social welfare agency involved may decide that the re-tarded parent cannot benefit from the services it does have, or the ser-vices available may not be appropriate for retarded parents. Courts may treat these facts as adequate justification for failing to provide services because of their own lack of knowledge of the skills retarded persons can learn given adequate training. For example, in *In re McDaniel* (1980), the Children's Service Division had offered the parents no sup-portive services for a long period of time. The same court that decided *Chapman* upheld termination because it was convinced, from its re-view of the record, that no amount of effort could have made it possible to reintegrate the child into the home.

In states where remedial services are required, the parent normally must be given an opportunity to comply with a remedial plan approved by the court. For example, a Colorado statute (*Colorado Revised Stat-utes*, §19–11–101) provides that termination may not be granted unless "an appropriate treatment plan approved by the court has not been reasonably complied with by the parent or parents or has not been suc-cessful." In *People v. C.A.K.* (1981), the Colorado court of appeals held that the court-approved rehabilitation plan must provide a standard by which success in complying with the plan must be measured. In the absence of measurable criteria for determining compliance, a finding that the plan has been unsuccessful cannot serve as a basis for ter-minating the parent–child relationship.

Even where remedial programs are required, however, structural problems, lack of coordination in the service system, and unavailabil-ity of appropriate services interfere with the successful implementation of adequate rehabilitative plans. Most rehabilitation plans are written by child welfare caseworkers and are based on services currently available with which the caseworker is familiar. Many child welfare workers are unfamiliar with the needs and learning patterns of persons with retardation. In addition, specialized services for retarded parents, like the innovative ESPRIT program operated by the Association for Retarded Citizens of Allegheny County, Pennsylvania, are rare and inadequately funded. Even where appropriate services exist, child welfare workers may not be aware of them because of lack of coordination between social service agencies. (A program for retarded parents would probably be sponsored by a local office of mental health–mental retardation, whereas the social service agency that usually intervenes in child neglect cases is the local child and youth services office.) Parents with retardation are unlikely to be receiving appropriate services from the local mental health–mental retardation program unless they were already clients of the program before their children were born or are referred by the children's services office. Specialized daycare programs for children of retarded parents are practically nonexistent, despite their acknowledged importance in helping retarded parents keep their children (see Note, *Stanford Law Review*, 1979).

Moreover, it is not easy for a retarded parent to challenge the appropriateness of a rehabilitation plan during termination proceedings. Most retarded parents are poor and cannot afford private counsel; and although the provision of counsel for indigent parents is required by statute in 30 states (Bell, 1981), the United States Supreme Court held in *Lassiter v. Department of Social Services of Durham County, N.C.* (1981) that parents do not have a constitutional right to appointed counsel in termination proceedings. In states where appointed counsel is not required, many retarded parents cannot effectively challenge a remedial plan proposed by the court even if they disagree with it.

In *In re Brooks* (1980), the Kansas Supreme Court considered the respective burden of parent and party seeking termination to design, implement, and comply with programs to enhance parenting skills. While the court stated that "the drastic remedy of termination of parental rights should not be utilized unless the court is satisfied there is no realistic alternative and so finds" (p. 2046), it also held that the court had no duty to explore specifically every existing program of family support before ordering termination. Instead, the court's duty is simply to "carefully consider any particular alternative remedy proposed by an interested party in the case" (p. 2048) and to state its reasons if it rejects the program. In practice, the interested party proposing a rehabilitative program usually will be the social service agency seeking termination. The duty of the parent to "cooperate with the agency, . . . keep apointments, . . . have a sincere desire to improve their family life and . . . be willing to accept counseling" (p. 2048), conceals the reality that in many cases, the remedial program will be perceived by parents as the imposition of a social service agency's views of proper parenting rather than as a response to their own needs.

The duty of the party seeking termination, and of the court, where no appropriate programs exist for the mentally retarded parent was considered in *In re William, Susan, and Joseph* (1982). In termination proceedings in trial court, a psychiatrist retained by the Rhode Island Department of Children and Families testified that the mother's moderate retardation would not keep her from being a fit parent as long as she had appropriate support services. The doctor admitted, however, that the necessary services were not available from the state. A psychologist retained by the department also recommended that the department attempt gradual reunification of mother and children after providing services including marital counseling. However, the department reported that it had no marital counseling program available for, in the court's words, "limited" persons. The mother contended on appeal from an order terminating her parental rights that the state had not made reasonable efforts to help her learn to care adequately for her children. Nevertheless, the Rhode Island Supreme Court rejected her contention and concluded that the state's efforts were reasonable "in the totality of the circumstances" (pp. 1256–1257). Since the "totality of the circumstances included the absence of services appropriate for parents with the mother's disability, this standard for evaluating the reasonableness of the state's effort allowed the court simply to ratify the agency's decision not to offer services for parents with retardation, but only services designed for nonretarded parents. Although no Section 504 claim was considered by the court in this case, it can certainly be argued that the state's failure to provide counseling services for retarded parents as effective as those it provides for nonretarded parents violated the federal civil rights statute.

The Pennsylvania Superior Court used a radically different approach in *In re C.M.E.* (1982). The lower court that had terminated the mother's parental rights had heard testimony from a psychologist that because of the mother's level of retardation, an intensive educational program of up to two and a half years would be necessary to equip her with the parenting skills necessary to maintain and enhance her child's level of development. The lower court had found that the amount of time and effort required to rehabilitate the mother was prohibitive.

The superior court disagreed, noting that to terminate the mother's parental rights because the services necessary to rehabilitate her were too costly was, in effect, to punish her for the severity of her disability. Unlike the Rhode Island court, the Pennsylvania court measured the state's duty in terms of the mother's needs, not in terms of available services nor the services required to rehabilitate nonretarded parents. The court began by asking "what would be expected of an individual in [the] circumstances [in] which the parent under examination finds herself" (p. 63) and stated that, measured by that standard, the parent had committed no wrong that would justify termination.

> We refuse to punish a parent for her lack of parenting skills which is based, at least in part, on her limited intellectual ability, especially when the evidence leads to the conclusion that she may be able to reach a satisfactory level of parenting skill with the aid of programs available to her. (pp. 63–64)

The court noted that only a single, halfhearted attempt had been made by the county children's services agencies involved and that the parent's own efforts to obtain services had been thwarted by the jurisdictional complexities of the state welfare system. The superior court therefore rejected the trial court's finding that the mother's incapacity could not be remedied as it was unsupported by the evidence.

The Pennsylvania court's approach recognized that a parent's intellectual ability has no necessary relationship to the moral quality of her relationship with a child, that parenting is more than housekeeping, budgeting, feeding or tutoring the child. When a parent's lack of domestic skills is the result of retardation, and not of any moral failing on her part, the state should expend more effort to remedy any deficiencies in her skills than it would if she were not retarded. To do otherwise, the court correctly reasoned, is to punish the mother for her retardation rather than compensate for it by providing appropriate services.

The Pennsylvania court's approach is also more realistic in terms of the state of the art in training and habilitation of persons with retardation. Techniques for training retarded parents in child care and domestic skills must be based on the retarded parent's slower rate of learning. Once weekly visits by service workers may be adequate to teach the nonretarded parent how to budget and plan nutritious meals but totally inadequate for the retarded parent who requires a much more intensive training program. Nevertheless, given adequate training methods, persons with retardation can learn much more than is commonly assumed.

Even with the best training program available, some retarded parents may never acquire the skills to become adequate parents without on-going support. In many cases, long-term support services for retarded parents would benefit both parent and child and are a sensible alternative to termination and long-term foster care for the child. The idea of providing retarded parents with long-term support services would require changes in existing service delivery systems and, in some states, in legislation, since some statutes authorize termination on the ground that the parent's mental deficiency is likely to continue for a prolonged period (Nebraska §43–292 [5]).

The idea that the parent–child relationship may be worth supporting and preserving, even though the parent may never gain adequate intellectual, social, and domestic skills to provide for all the needs of her child, is radical and difficult for courts and service agencies to accept, as the case of Marjorie Lehman (*In re William L.*, 1978) illustrates.

Ms. Lehman, expecting her fourth child, voluntarily placed her three sons with Lycoming County Children's Services in Pennsylvania because she was then living in substandard housing and had difficulty finding daycare services. After her daughter's birth, Children's Services offered her the choice of a small apartment large enough only for Ms. Lehman and her daughter or of waiting until a larger apartment became available. Ms. Lehman chose the smaller apartment with the expectation that she would regain custody of her sons (who had been placed in foster care) as soon as her situation improved. She maintained a regular visiting schedule with her sons and enlisted the help of nutrition aides to help her adequately care for her daughter; the record showed that she maintained a clean, healthy home. However, when the social service agency judged that Ms. Lehman had made "little or no progress" in learning how to cope on her own, the agency requested that she be tested by a psychologist, who concluded that she "lacked the social maturity and intellectual capacity to cope with the continuing responsibilities of raising children" (p. 1239). An action to terminate her parental rights followed.

The petition for termination was granted, and the supreme court of Pennsylvania affirmed the termination order. The court acknowledged that Ms. Lehman was guilty of no parental misconduct. Nevertheless, Justice Roberts' opinion for the majority relied on the findings of the orphan's court that had terminated Ms. Lehman's parental rights that her "very limited social and intellectual development," plus her 5-year separation from her sons, constituted "clear and convincing evidence" that she was incapable of providing minimal care for her children (pp. 1239–1240).

The nutritional and other services Ms. Lehman needed were available from the county, and the agency did not claim that the services did not make her an adequate parent as long as she received them. But the Pennsylvania Supreme Court assumed that the county was under no obligation to provide anything beyond temporary rehabilitative efforts until she improved enough to cope on her own.

The Pennsylvania statute Ms. Lehman challenged requires, before termination may be granted, not only proof of parental incapacity but also proof that the parent's incapacity has *"caused* [italics added] the child to be without essential parental care, control or subsistence"* (23 Pa. C.S.A. §2511[2]). Based on the statute, the Pennsylvania Court had in previous cases reversed termination orders because the trial record did not establish that a parent's retardation had caused her children to be neglected (see *In re Geiger*, 1975). Here, the required causal nexus between retardation and neglect did not exist, because Ms. Lehman had sought voluntarily the assistance of social welfare agencies to ensure that essential care would be provided. As Justice Nix pointed out in his dissenting opinion, Mr. Lehman herself, by acknowledging her limitations and seeking out public services to compensate for them, had ensured that those limitations would not result in neglect.

After termination was upheld by the Pennsylvania Supreme Court, Ms. Lehman filed a petition for habeas corpus in federal court for return of her sons. The denial of her petition eventually was upheld by the United States Supreme Court in a decision that imposes a serious limitation on the power of federal courts, traditionally the guarantors of individual constitutional rights against state authority, to measure state termination procedures against federal constitutional standards. The Court held that Ms. Lehman's children were not "in custody" for habeas purposes, since they were in foster care and not in the direct custody of the state (*Lehman v. Lycoming County Children's Services Agency*, 1982).

CONCLUSION

The law governing the rights of disabled parents is still laden with stereotype. Although physically handicapped parents fare much better in the courts than mentally handicapped parents, only a handful of progressive state courts refuse to treat disability as prima facie evidence of parental unfitness and possible detriment to the child.

In most states, mentally disabled parents are no longer victims of an irrebuttable presumption that they cannot be adequate parents. Most termination statutes now require the party seeking termination of a retarded parent's rights to prove that the child has actually been harmed or neglected. Still, in most states it is easier to terminate a retarded parent's rights than those of a nonretarded parent guilty of the same neglect. Simpler procedures for terminating retarded parents' rights than for terminating a nonretarded parent's rights facilitate the severance of the retarded parent's ties to his child.

But lack of appropriate rehabilitative and support services for retarded parents is more problematic than defects in statutory procedures. Since persons with retardation learn at a slower rate and in a different manner than nonretarded persons, rehabilitative programs that are adequate for nonretarded parents may not be adequate for retarded parents. Thus, even where state law requires that a reasonable effort be made to improve the parent's skills before a request for termination can be granted, there can be no reasonable effort unless appropriate parent training programs exist. As the Pennsylvania superior court noted in *In re C.M.E.*, for a public agency to provide adequate rehabilitation programs for normal persons but not for retarded persons simply punishes the retarded parent for the severity of her handicap. If parental neglect is due to lack of intellectual skills rather than moral unfitness, the burden on the state to remedy the parent's deficiency should be greater, not less. Yet many courts have assumed just the opposite: that the greater time and effort required to teach skills to retarded parents relieves the state of the duty to provide any training at all.

This facile assumption has tragic consequences for parent and child. Severance of the retarded parent's ties to her child does not automatically mean that the child will be provided with an adequate substitute parent. Often, years of temporary foster care are the result. Ironically, the cost to the state and society of refusing to provide support and training for retarded parents may ultimately be much greater than the cost of providing them would have been.

Moreover, when the retarded parent is a decent and moral person, where her relationship with her child is based on parental love and affection, it is easier to support the parent–child relationship with technical services than to replace it. As Judge Berman of the Colorado court of appeals noted in his opinion concurring in the reversal of an order terminating a retarded mother's parental rights (*People v. C.A.K.*, 1981),

> Indisputably, [the child's] welfare would be served, now and in the future by preservation and encouragement of the tender, loving relationship she enjoys with her mother, even though that may not be sufficient to supply the totality of the child's developmental needs. That relationship is, in my view, the sin-

gle most significant factor in determining whether the child will become a
happy, well-adjusted adult. The State can more easily supply mechanisms to
meet the child's other developmental requirements than it can the love of a
parent for its child, and of a child for its parent. (p.143)

The cases discussed in this chapter show how easily a parent's rights
may be severed because of retardation—if no longer merely because of
IQ or mental age, then because of the retarded person's lack of parenting skills. Although it is difficult or impossible to order a retarded
person to be sterilized against her will, it is much easier to terminate
the same person's parental rights once she has borne a child. This contradiction raises troubling policy questions. Would it be kinder to force
retarded persons to be sterilized than to allow them to have children
and then take those children away? If we can determine, after a retarded person has had children, that she can never become a fit parent,
then can't we determine this before she has children and spare her the
pain of severing her ties with them?

Whatever the answer, it is clear that we cannot go back. Having decided that involuntary sterilization of any person, retarded or not, who
has not been declared incompetent violates basic constitutional rights,
we no longer have the option of preventing retarded persons from becoming parents. The only way out of the contradiction is to acknowledge that without the social support that allows retarded parents to
keep their children, their constitutionally protected right to become a
parent is meaningless.

There are many reasons why adequate support systems for retarded
parents do not exist: lack of funding, lack of child welfare workers
trained in retardation, jurisdictional problems, lack of coordination in
the service system, and perhaps above all, the misconception that because retarded persons learn more slowly and need more reinforcement
than nonretarded persons, they cannot learn at all.

These are difficult barriers but not insurmountable ones. As Judge
Berman recognized in *People v. C.A.K.*, it is better to attempt a limited
goal than an impossible one. The state can supplement the parent–
child relationship with housekeeping, nutritional, and child development services. It cannot produce a substitute for something for which
no substitute exists: "the love of a parent for its child, and of a child
for its parent" (p. 143).

REFERENCES

Adoption of Richardson, 251 C.A. 2d 222 (1967).
Arizona Revised Statutes Annotated, §8-533 (Supp. 1983).

Banks v. Department of Human Resources, 233 S.E.2d 449 (Ga. App. 1977).

Bell, D. Termination of Parental Rights: Recent Judicial and Legislative Trends. *Emory Law Journal,* 1981, *30,* 1065.

Buck v. Bell, 274 U.S. 200 (1927).

Cardinal McCloskey School & Home v. Mendes, 6 Family Law Reporter (BNA) 2851 (N.Y. Fam. Ct. 1980); rev'd sub nom. *In re Sylvia M. & Alicia M.,* 7 *Family Law Reporter* (BNA) 2636 (A.D. 1981).

45 C.F.R. §84.4 (1983).

Chapman v. State ex rel. Juvenile Department of Multomah County, 631 P.2d 831 (Or. App. 1981).

Colorado Revised Statutes, §19–11–105(b)(I) (1978).

Dunn v. Blumstein, 405 U.S. 330 (1972).

Goldy v. Beal, 429 F. Supp. 640 (M.D. Pa 1976).

Griswold v. Connecticut, 379 U.S. 926 (1968).

Hatz v. Hatz, 9 *Family Law Reporter* (BNA) 2214 (N.Y. Fam. Ct. 1982).

In re Appeal in Maricopa County Juvenile Action No. J.S. 1308 and J.S. 1412, 555 P. 2d 679 (Ariz. App. 1976).

In re Brooks, 7 *Family Law Reporter* (BNA) 2046 (Kan 1980).

In re C.M.E., 448 A. 2d 59 (Pa. Super. 1982).

In re Carney, 24 Cal. 3d 725 (1979).

In re Daniel A.D., 431 N.Y.S. 936 (N.Y. Fam. Ct. 1980).

In re Eberhardy, 307 N.W. 2d 881 (Wis. 1981).

In re Geiger, 331 A.2d 172 (Pa. 1975).

In re Grady, 426 A. 2d 467 (N.J. 1981).

In re Green, 5 *Family Law Reporter* (BNA) 2173 (N.Y. Fam. Ct. 1978).

In re Gross, 425 N.Y. S. 2d 220 (N.Y. Fam. Ct. 1980).

In re Holley, 308 N.W.2d 341 (Neb. 1981).

In re J.L.P., 8 *Family Law Reporter* (BNA) 2640 (Fla. App. 1982).

In re Jeanie M. and Emma M., 8 *Family Law Reporter* (BNA) 2637 (Ca.App. 1982).

In re Levin, 102 C.A. 3d 981 (1980).

In re McDaniel, 610 P. 2d 321 (Or. App. 1980).

In re McDonald, 201 N.W. 2d 447 (Iowa 1972).

In re Orlando F., 40 N.Y. 2d 103 (1976).

In re Terwilliger, 450 A.2d 1376 (Pa. Super. 1982).

In re William L., 383 A.2d 1228 (Pa. 1978), cert. denied, 439 U.S. 880 (1978).

In re William, Susan and Joseph, 448 A.2d 1250 (R.I. 1982).

Isaacs, S. The Law of Fertility Regulation in the United States: A 1980 Review. *Journal of Family Law,* 1980, *19,* 65.

Katzman, S. Parental Rights of the Mentally Retarded: The Advisability and Constitutionality of the Treatment of Retarded Parents in New York State. *Columbia Journal of Law and Social Problems,* 1981, 16, 521.

Lassiter v. Department of Social Services of Durham County, N.C., 452 U.S. 18 (1981); reh. denied, 453 U.S. 927 (1981).

Lehman v. Lycoming County Children's Services Agency, 458 U.S. 502 (1982).

Meyer v. Nebraska, 262 U.S. 390 (1923).

Moye v. Moye, 627 P. 2d 799 (Id. 1981).

Nebraska, Revised Statutes §43–292(5) (Supp. 1982).

New York Social Service Law §384(b)(4)(c) (McKinney, Supp. 1982).

Note, Involuntary Sterilization of the Mentally Retarded: Blessing or Burden? *South Dakota Law Review,* 1980, *25,* 55.

Note, Retarded Parents in Neglect Proceedings: The Erroneous Assumption of Parental Inadequacy. *Stanford Law Review* 1979, *31,* 785.

23 Pa. C.S.A. §2511 (2)(Supp. 1984).

People v. C.A.K., 638 P. 2d 136 (Colo. App. 1981), rev'd, 652 P.2d 603 (Colo. 1982).

Pierce v. Society of Sisters, 268 U.S. 510 (1925).

Plyler v. Doe, 457 U.S. 202 (1982).

Rains v. Alston, 576 S.W. 2d 505 (Ark. 1979).

Roe v. Wade, 410 U.S. 113 (1973), reh. denied, 410 U.S. 959 (1973).

Santosky v. Kramer, 455 U.S. 745 (1982).

Shapiro v. Thompson, 394 U.S. 618 (1969).

Skinner v. Oklahoma, 316 U.S. 535 (1942).

Sokappa, P. Sterilization petitions: Developing judicial guidelines. *Montana Law Review*, 1980, *44*, 127.

Stanley v. Illinois, 405 U.S. 645 (1972).

Stump v. Sparkman, 435 U.S. 349 (1978); reh. denied, 436 U.S. 951 (1978).

29 U.S.C.A. § 794 (Supp. 1983).

29 U.S.C.A. §796 (Supp. 1983).

42 U.S.C.A. § 2000d (1981).

42 U.S.C.A. §6000 *et seq.* (1983).

Watkins v. Department of Human Resources, 237 S.E. 2d 696 (Ga. App. 1977).

Ecological Congruence in the Study of Families with Handicapped Parents

S. KENNETH THURMAN

BACKGROUND

Human development as an arena of study has always had a focus on behavioral, biological, and psychological changes in human beings over time. Lewis and Starr (1979), for example, have made this point by suggesting that "the study of change demarcates the area of developmental inquiry [and] current theories of development are predominantly descriptions of the child at different points or stages in ontogeny" (p. 653). Developmental research has generally been carried out for two basic purposes. First, developmental researchers have been concerned with describing various developmental sequences and their relationship to each other as exemplified by theories like that of Piaget (1952) or more recently by the research of McCall and his associates (McCall, 1979; McCall, Applebaum, & Hogarty, 1973; McCall, Eichorn, & Hogarty, 1977; and McCall, Hogarty, & Hurlburt, 1972). Second, they have been concerned with identifying factors that account for developmental progress and with how these factors contribute both positively and negatively to the overall process of development. These factors are seen as being either biologically based or environmentally based, and in recent years the point of view that has emerged is that both these sets of factors interact to form the basis for developmental progress in human beings (see Bixler, 1980). Little dispute can be offered to the proposition that developmental change occurs as the result of an organism's interaction with its environment over time. Until the late 1960s and early 1970s, however, developmental researchers tended to overlook the fact that during such interactions, the developing individuals also modify the behavior of the persons with whom they are interacting. Bell (1968) for example, pointed out the reciprocal nature of the mother–child interactive system that later on led to additional concerns about how infants and young children affect their caregivers (see Lewis & Rosenblum, 1974). Thus, we have come to recognize that parents affect their children while in turn being affected by them.

As a result of the basic belief of developmental theorists that the individual develops through interaction with his or her environment, some branches of psychology have been particularly concerned with the effects of various environmental factors on human behavior. These branches most notably include ecological psychology as put forth by Barker (1968) and environmental psychology as described by Proshansky, Ittelson, and Rivlin (1970) and Moos (1976). However, both ecological and environmental psychology tend to de-emphasize the role of the individual as he or she affects the environment. Rather their stress is on how various aspects of human behavior can be accounted for by major factors and conditions in the environment. Bronfenbrenner (1977), however, has recognized that as two interacting individuals mutually affect each other so too there exists a mutual effect between the developing organism and its environment. He suggests therefore that we "must be concerned not only with the developing child but also with the developing ecology" (p. 28). To do this we must begin to establish models that are concerned with the developmental patterns exhibited by interactive human– environment systems. These models will tend to be transactional in nature (Sameroff & Chandler, 1975) and by definition will be concerned with the study of ecologies where the interactional unit (of say child and environment) will become the primary dependent variable. Thus, the focus would become one of studying developmental changes in ecological systems themselves with organism–system niche becoming the basic irreducible unit of analysis (Turvey & Carello, 1982).

It is difficult, however, to begin the application of ecological systems models because of the lack of a theory of behavioral ecological development. Like the early researchers concerned with mother–child relations, we have overlooked the fact that there is a mutuality of effect between the individual and the environment. So called ecological studies have had their focus on explaining how various environmental factors account for human behavior at different points in time. We have, I believe, tended to overlook the effects that individuals have on the environment around them and upon other individuals who simultaneously occupy those environments. What I am suggesting is that it might be fruitful to ask basic questions like: What factors account for any particular ecological system existing as it does? What stages of development did this system pass through to get to its present state? and, How do these stages of development relate to each other? Is, for example, the development of an ecological system continuous or discontinuous? Answering such questions would provide a beginning step in understanding the development of behavioral ecologies.

Ambrose (1977) has suggested that ecology may be defined as "the scientific study of the relationship of living organisms with each other and their environment" (p. 4). Turvey & Carello (1982) have similarly pointed out that ecological realism in the study of cognition "concerns the logical dependence of the organism and the environment" (p. 313). To understand the development of any ecological system in light of these definitions would seem to require us at least to identify (1) what each individual in the system contributes to the development of system both separately and collectively, (2) how the environment contributes to the system, (3) how the environment affects the individual both separately and collectively, (4) how the individuals separately and collectively affect the environment, and (5) how each individual affects each other individual and in turn is affected by them. Put more simply, ecological studies depend on analyzing the nature of environment, the nature of the inhabitants in that environment, and the interaction of both with each other. To study the development of an ecology system requires the additional necessity of examining that system at different points in time.

We must begin to conduct studies that focus on the ecological system and its development in order to enhance our understanding of human–environment relationships. Such studies would shift their emphasis away from delineating developmental patterns within individuals and instead would make their unit of study the ecological system. To begin this type of research, developmental researchers would be required to shift their unit of analysis from individual human beings to specific units of the human ecology, such as the school, home, street corner, or church. The fundamental question would become, Why is this ecological unit functioning the way it is at this particular point in time? or, put another way, What are the necessary and sufficient conditions for explaining the present state of functioning of an ecological unit? Answers to such questions could be sought by using the type of inductive approach suggested by Platt (1964) that depends on successive elimination of alternative hypotheses designed to elucidate the relationship between a given condition and the particular phenomenon under study. In the present case, the phenomenon of interest would be a particular ecological system and various hypotheses that would be identified from answering the five questions raised in the paragraph above.

The ecological congruence model, which I first suggested in Thurman (1977) and which has subsequently been expanded (Thurman & Widerstrom, 1985), may provide a useful framework in which to study the development of ecological systems. In my original paper, I defined the ecological congruence model as having three critical dimensions. These dimensions are illustrated in Figure 3.1 One dimension of the model is the deviancy continuum, a second is the competency continuum, and a third is the tolerance for difference continuum.

Deviancy, according to the ecological congruence model is a function of a label being placed on an individual and/or his or her behavior. Essentially the model regards Simmons' (1969) suggestion that no human behavior is inherently deviant as a valid basis for the conceptualization of deviancy. "The judgment made about a particular behavior or set of characteristics can be made relative only to the social context in which it has occurred. Thus, those conditions accounting for the label placed upon a behavior and subsequently the individual him [her] self, lie within the environmental context in which the behavior occurs" (Thurman, 1977, p. 330).

Competency can, in the simplest terms, be defined as functional

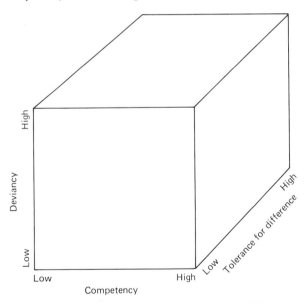

Figure 3.1 The ecological congruence model.

ability. "Just as every social setting defines parameters for deviance, so does it define a certain set of functional behaviors, or behaviors that lead to the completion of a task or job within that setting. Competency/incompetency, unlike deviance, is an attribute of the individuals," since, given a specific task, a person either has or does not have the necessary behavior repertoire or developmental status to perform the task (Thurman, 1977, p. 330). It is important to point out that lack of competence cannot be inferred solely from nonperformance since performance of a task is also a function of other factors, as for example, motivation, and not just one's degree of competence. Simply, lack of performance by an individual does not necessarily mean lack of competence on the part of that individual.

Finally, tolerance for difference is the dimension of the ecological congruence model that determines the goodness of fit between the individual and the environmental–social context. Within every ecological system there is a range of tolerance for difference that is defined by the system itself. When an individual is viewed as different enough either because of an assigned degree of deviancy or a lack of competency in performing tasks within the system, that person is not tolerated by the system. Lack of tolerance by the system establishes an incongruent ecology, one, if you will, that is out of balance. In a recent extension of the concept of tolerance for difference, Thurman and Widerstrom (1985) suggest that incongruence in an ecology may also result from intolerance of the individual for the system. If, in fact, the individual perceives attributes in the system that are intolerable, then a lack of ecological congruence still results. The development of congruent ecologies not only assures the smooth functioning of the ecology itself but also may provide a means to maximize the ontogenetic development of the individual participants within the ecology.

In essence, the ecological congruence model suggests that the rationale for human service interventions ought not be concerned solely with changing the behavior (or developmental progress) of individuals but rather on the premise that interventions should stress the development of harmonious or congruent ecologies. As a result the model stresses the need to change both the individual *and* the environment or setting with which an individual interacts. The model suggests that such interventions focus on making the individual more competent to perform tasks within the environment, that is, making the individual increase his or her developmental status and at the same time exhibit fewer characteristics or behaviors that are viewed by other individuals in the environment as deviant from the norm. Simultaneously, changes are made in the physical environment to accommodate the individual, and the attitudes and affect of all individuals in the environment are made more tolerant of individual and environmental differences. Thus, the model is aimed at designing interventions that develop more congruent, harmonious, and tolerant ecologies.

At a more theoretical level, however, the development of a particular ecology could be characterized by the degree of congruence present in a particular ecology at any point in time. It is likely that the development of any ecology moves forward through the dynamic changes in the levels of congruence within that ecology. Furthermore, it may be possible to predict the degree and qualitative nature of congruence in an ecological system at some future point by knowing those same factors at an earlier point in time and by identifying the necessary and sufficient conditions that account for them.

More specifically, if we accept the premise suggested above that the characteristics of the individuals who participate in a particular ecology are important in defining that ecology and in affecting its development, then we can begin to speculate about ways in which different characteristics of individuals may affect the development of a particular ecology at different points in time. The existence of a handicap in an individual represents the type of characteristic that is apt to affect the congruence of the ecological system of which that individual is part. Within the family ecology, the existence of handicapping conditions can be of special concern since the family for most of us represents our initial point of social involvement and indeed, as Lewis and Feiring (1979) point out, it is the family that provides the basic social network for most infants and young children. Furthermore, early research by Farber (1959) has suggested that at least one severe handicapping condition (viz., mental retardation) can seriously disrupt integration of family units and therefore affect the nature of the family as an ecological system. In addition a number of studies (e.g., Als, Tronick, & Brazelton, 1980; Kogan & Tyler, 1973; Kogan, Wimberger, & Bobbitt, 1969; Vietze, Abernathy, Ashe, & Faulstich, 1978) have presented evidence that parents with handicapped children interact with their children in ways that are different from parents of nonhandicapped children. These studies also clearly suggest that handicap can affect the nature of the family ecology. There is, of course, much research yet to be done before we have a fuller understanding of parent–child interaction when the child possesses a handicap. From an ecological perspective, however, it is also important to consider the effects of handicap as a parental characteristic.

HANDICAPPED PARENTS
AND THE FAMILY ECOLOGY

The presence of handicapping conditions in parents provides a potential threat to the development of congruent ecologies. Perhaps the most basic threat is the degree to which a parent's handicap makes him or her incompetent to perform the tasks necessary for family function. Although I am not suggesting that a disability a priori interferes with a person's competence as a parent or member of a family ecology, I am suggesting that it may. To the extent that it does, the parent may not be tolerated by other members of the family, causing a degree of ecological incongruence. Incompetency, related to disability, may also affect the development of the ecology by putting additional responsibilities onto other individuals in the ecology. This, in turn, may even increase the lack of tolerance toward the handicapped parent.

Another fundamental factor in considering the ecological development of a family is whether one or both parents display a handicap. For example, the ecology of the family where one parent is blind and the other sighted may be quite different than one where both parents are blind. A blind and sighted partner may complement each other in very different ways than two partners who are blind. In addition, blind parenting may require modification of the physical environment to maximize congruence in that items to be used for completion of certain tasks must be arranged so that they are readily accessible.

Similarly, when both parents are deaf it is often necessary to modify the physical environment to accommodate it to their impairments. More important in the case of deaf parents, it may be necessary for their hearing children to leave home during periods of language development. It is obvious that such a necessity for children to leave the family might critically affect the ecological development of the individual family. Simply, the question becomes, How does a family maintain its congruence when certain members are forced to leave in order to develop certain critical skills? Hoffmeister (Chapter 7, this volume) elucidates this issue further.

As the family ecology develops, the functional effects of handicapping conditions may vary at different points in time. The mildly retarded mother, for example, may be able to provide adequate caretaking and stimulation to her children when they are infants and toddlers but may not later possess the cognitive and academic skills to provide the types of intellectual stimulation necessary to her children once they are in elementary school. How is the family ecology affected when the children become smarter, so to speak, than their mothers? Can congruence be maintained, and if so, how? How too is the children's intellectual development affected when the mother's academic skills are limited? If one is to believe data presented by Heber and Garber (1975), increasing the academic and vocational competence of intellectually limited mothers can improve the developmental outcomes in their children. While certain people have called to question these data (e.g., Page, 1975; Page & Grandon, 1981), the basic premise of Heber and Garber's proposition from a theoretical basis seems sound.

Another factor related to the effects of handicapping conditions on family ecologies is the time of onset of the handicap. Glass (Chapter 9, this volume) deals with this issue in more detail. It is important in the present context merely to raise this issue since the course of a family's ecological development may be altered significantly if a parent who has previously experienced normal function becomes handicapped. It is likely that the family will go through a period of incongruence and may have to reestablish its pattern of development. Just as the patterns of development are often quite different for persons who are disabled congenitally as compared with those who become disabled adventitiously, so too it seems reasonable to suggest that qualitative differences may occur in an ecology where handicapped individuals were present from the onset as compared with those where handicaps enter the system at a later time.

While I am sure that there are other models that might be considered in studying family ecologies that include handicapped parents, I would like to suggest that degree of ecological congruence at different points in time may provide an initial framework for studying these ecologies. Further, I would suggest several major factors that may affect the degree of congruence as the family ecology develops.

Ecological congruence or lack of it in handicapped parent family ecologies may depend on (1) the degree of parent competence, (2) whether one or both parents are handicapped, (3) the type of parental handicap, (4) the degree of parental handicap, and (5) the time of onset of the parental handicaps. Since this paper is meant to be speculative, it is possible that these factors are not critical in determining the developmental patterns within a family ecology, and certainly, further empirical study is necessary to verify or deny my speculations. It is also my contention, and I think a more widely accepted one, that the ontogenetic development of a child is a function of the ecology in which the child participates. The ultimate effect on the child with a handicapped parent may well be a function of (1) the degree of congruence within the family ecology at any point in time, (2) the developmental status of the family ecology, and (3) the particular developmental status of the child at some point in time. Thus, I submit that to understand the effects of having a handicapped parent we must first be able to adequately define, assess, and codify these three factors. As of now our ability to delineate the status of an individual child's development seems to far outstrip our ability to delineate either the degree of congruence within or the developmental status of particular family ecologies.

CONCLUSION

From this brief discussion, it can be seen that a number of different factors can combine that may account for the developmental status of a family with handicapped parents. It is necessary to begin to design research studies that can incorporate these factors. It is my contention that these studies must grow from initially descriptive studies of how nonhandicapped families develop as ecological systems. Unfortunately, I am not convinced that data exist that have adequately described the ecological development of nonhandicapped families so as to provide a basis for reasonable comparison with handicapped families. The study of various levels of congruence in families at different points in time and the delineation of the necessary and sufficient conditions to explain these levels may provide us a means of understanding the developmental unfolding of these critical ecologies.

REFERENCES

Als, H., Tronick, E., & Brazelton, T. B. Stages of early organization: The study of a sighted infant and a blind infant in interaction with their mothers. In T. M. Field (Ed.), *High-risk infants and children: Adults and peer interactions.* New York: Academic Press, 1980.

Ambrose, A. The ecological perspective in developmental psychology. In H. McGurk (Ed.), *Ecological factors in human development.* Amsterdam, The Netherlands: North-Holland, 1977.

Barker, R. G. *Ecological psychology.* Stanford, CA: Stanford University Press, 1968.

Bell, R. Q. A reinterpretation of the direction of effects in studies of socialization. *Psychological Review, 1968, 75,* 81–95.

Bixler, R. H. Nature versus nurture: The timeless anachronism. *Merrill-Palmer Quarterly, 1980, 26,* 153–159.

Bronfenbrenner, V. The ecology of human development in retrospect and prospect. In

H. McGurk (Ed.), *Ecological factors in human development.* Amsterdam, The Netherlands: North-Holland, 1977.

Farber, B. Effects of a severely mentally retarded child on family integration. *Monographs of the Society for Research in Child Development,* 1959, *24* (Whole No. 71).

Heber, R., & Garber, H. The Milwaukee Project: A study of the use of family intervention to prevent cultural–familial mental retardation. In B. Z. Friedlander, G. M. Steritt, & G. E. Kirk (Eds.), *Exceptional infant: Assessment and intervention* (Vol. 3). New York: Brunner/Mazel, 1975.

Kogan, K. L., & Tyler, N. Mother–child interaction in young physically handicapped. *American Journal of Mental Deficiency,* 1973, *77,* 492–497.

Kogan, K. L., Wimberger, H. C., & Bobbitt, R. Analysis of mother–child interaction in young mental retardates. *Child Development,* 1969, *40,* 799–812.

Lewis, M., & Feiring, C. The child's social network: Social object, social functions, and their relationship. In M. Lewis & L. A. Rosenblum (Eds.), *The child and its family.* New York: Plenum, 1979.

Lewis, M., & Rosenblum, L. A. (Eds.). *The effect of the infant on its caregiver.* New York: John Wiley, 1974.

Lewis, M., & Starr, M. D. Developmental continuity. In J. D. Osofsky (Ed.), *The handbook of infant development.* New York: John Wiley, 1979.

McCall, R. B. Qualitative transitions in behavioral development in the first two years of life. In M. H. Bornstein & W. Kessen (Eds.), *Psychological development from infancy: Image to Intention.* Hillsdale, NJ: Lawrence Erlbaum Associates, 1979.

McCall, R. B., Applebaum, M., & Hogarty, P. S. Developmental changes in mental performance. *Monograph of the Society for Research in Child Development,* 1973, *38* (Whole No. 150).

McCall, R. B., Eichorn, D. H., & Hogarty, P. S. Transitions in early mental development. *Monographs of the Society for Research in Child Development,* 1977, *42* (Whole No. 150).

McCall, R. B., Hogarty, P. S., & Hurlburt, N. Transitions in infant sensorimotor development and the prediction of childhood I.Q. *American Psychologist,* 1972, *27,* 728–748.

Moos, R. H. The human context: Environmental determinants of behavior. New York: John Wiley, 1976.

Page, E. B. Miracle in Milwaukee: Raising the I.Q. In B. Z. Friedlander, G. M. Sterritt, & G. E. Kirk (Eds.), *Exceptional infant: Assessment and intervention* (Vol. 3). New York: Brunner/Mazel, 1975.

Page, E. B., & Grandon, G. M. Massive intervention and child intelligence: The Milwaukee Project in critical perspective. *Journal of Special Education,* 1981, *15,* 239–256.

Piaget, J. The origins of intelligence in children (2nd ed.). New York: International Universities Press, 1952.

Platt, J. R. Strong inference. *Science,* 1964, *146,* 347–353.

Proshansky, H. M., Ittelson, W. H., & Rivlin, L. G. (Eds.), Environmental psychology. Holt, Rinehart and Winston, 1970.

Sameroff, A. J., & Chandler, M. J. Reproductive risk and the continuum of caretaking casualty. In F. D. Horowitz, M. Hetherington, S. Scarr-Salapatek, & G. Siegel (Eds.), *Review of child development research* (Vol. 4). Chicago: University of Chicago Press, 1975.

Simmons, J. L. *Deviants.* Berkeley, CA: Glendessary Press, 1969.

Thurman, S. K. The congruence of behavioral ecologies: A model for special education programming. *Journal of Special Education*, 1977, *11*, 329–333.

Thurman, S. K., & Widerstrom, A. H. *Young children with special needs: A developmental and ecological Approach.* Newton, MA: Allyn & Bacon, 1985.

Turvey, M. T., & Carello, C. The view from ecological realism. *Cognition*, 1982, *10*, 313–321.

Vietze, P. M., Abernathy, S. R., Ashe, M. L., & Faulstick, G. Contingent interaction between mothers and their developmentally delayed infants. In G. P. Sackett (Ed.), *Observing behavior: Vol. 1. Theory and applications in mental retardation.* Baltimore: University Park Press, 1978.

4

Effects of Parental Emotional Handicap on Early Child Development

ARNOLD J. SAMEROFF, RONALD SEIFER, and MELVIN ZAX

Handicaps are defined as conditions that limit the behavior of affected individuals. Physical and perceptual handicaps are readily apparent, and the causal connections with specific restrictions in activity are fairly clear. For example, motor impairments affect the ability to locomote and manipulate the environment, and visual handicaps affect the ability to see. However, when one moves into the realm of mental handicaps, such clear connections are not evident. The effects of emotional handicaps on the ability of parents to raise children is the topic of this chapter.

There are many ways in which parents influence the development of their children, some quite obvious and direct, others quite subtle and elusive. Socialization and educational practices produce a diversity of human cultural differences in fairly straightforward ways. However, the way in which individual differences that characterize mental illness are transmitted is far from clear.

Schizophrenia, of all the mental disorders, has generated the most interest. Whereas most other disorders can be viewed as extreme variations of normal psychological characteristics, schizophrenia has been striking in its seeming abnormality, its alienation from typical modes of functioning. As research on this disorder multiplied, clear familial influences were found, with apparent hereditary transmission (Kallmann, 1938): Large numbers of the offspring of schizophrenic parents were found to have mental disturbances.

While the rate of schizophrenia in the general population is about 1%, about 10% of children with a single schizophrenic parent became schizophrenic (Hanson, Gottesman, & Meehl, 1977). However, schizo-

phrenia is not the only outcome risk to which the offspring of schizophrenic parents are vulnerable. For example, Higgins (1976) found 76%
of these children to have one or another form of psychiatric disturbance.

The early studies of the transmission of schizophrenia used adult
psychiatric diagnoses as their outcome measure. In contrast, studies
of the outcomes of children of parents with nonpsychotic mental disturbances have centered on symptomatology during childhood and did
not address the issue of ultimate psychiatric outcome (Buck & Laugh-
ton, 1959). More recently, research on the offspring of schizophrenics
has come to deal directly with the developmental progress of these
high risk children (see Garmezy, 1974, for a summary).

HEREDITY STUDIES OF SCHIZOPHRENIA

The biological approach to familial transmission received significant
support from the early studies of Kallmann (1938, 1946). Kallmann's
original surveys reported high concordance rates for identical twins;
that is, if one twin was schizophrenic, the other was as well. These
studies have undergone considerable reassessment. Rosenthal (1962,
1970) pointed out that Kallmann's studies included primarily chronic
schizophrenics because they were based on resident state hospital populations. Furthermore, Gottesman and Shields (1966) and Rosenthal
(1970) have raised questions about Kallmann's broad diagnostic criteria. When Gottesman and Shields established careful diagnostic procedures in a study of consecutive hospital admissions, they were able
to show far lower, but still impressive, concordance rates for schizophrenia among identical twins than did Kallmann.

While twin studies supported a genetic hypothesis, they were not
free of criticism from environmentalists. Jackson (1960) led an early
assault on the value of the twin studies charging that in virtually all
such studies the twins shared the same psychological environment for
a significant portion of their lives. The finding that identical twins had
higher concordance rates than fraternal twins was attributed to the
more similar environment of the identical twins. For example, they
are more often mistaken for each other than are fraternal twins (see
Loehlin & Nichols, 1976). Further, fraternal twins have consistently
showed higher concordance than full sibs, even though these concordance rates should be identical under a genetic hypothesis (Kringlen,
1976).

Several studies have used an ingenious technique to separate constitutional from environmental etiological factors. By studying off-spring of schizophrenics and nonschizophrenics adopted by schizophrenics and nonschizophrenics, and therefore removing the confounding of genes and environment, one could determine which was the dominant influence—a schizophrenic heredity or a schizophrenic environment.

Heston (1966), using a U.S. sample, and Rosenthal, Kety, Wender, Schulsinger and their associates (Kety, Rosenthal, Wender, Schulsinger, & Jacobson, 1975; Rosenthal, Wender, Kety, Welner, & Schulsinger, 1971; Wender, Rosenthal, Kety, Schulsinger, & Welner, 1974), using Danish samples, found higher proportions of schizophrenia among offspring of schizophrenics who were adopted by nonschizophrenics than among adopted-away offspring of nonschizophrenics who were reared by nonschizophrenics. The Danish research group also found more schizophrenics in the biological families of adopted-away children who became schizophrenic than in control biological families of adopted-away children who did not suffer from schizophrenia. Both sets of findings were interpreted to support theories of biological transmission.

In our study of the children of emotionally disturbed women, we were able to throw some additional light on the results of these adoption studies (Sameroff & Zax, 1979). Of the infants in our study, six were given up by their mothers during the neonatal period for either adoption or foster placement. An analysis of these six cases is of interest to the interpretation of the studies that have shown higher rates of psychopathology in the adopted offspring of schizophrenic women when compared to the adopted offspring of normal women.

The six infants given up in our study all came from schizophrenic women. Comparisons were made between the characteristics of the schizophrenic mothers who kept their infants and the schizophrenic mothers who gave up their infants for placement in either adoptive or foster homes.

The placement mothers were significantly older and of lower socioeconomic status (SES) than those keeping their children. Neither birth order nor race were reliably different for the two groups. Not unexpectedly, a greater proportion of the placement mothers were either single, separated, or divorced than home-rearing mothers. Comparisons of the home-rearing and placement groups on mental-health measures indicate that the six placement mothers were more socially incompetent, were judged to have been more anxious and severely disturbed when interviewed in their last month of pregnancy, and had longer histories of emotional disturbance than home-rearing mothers.

The prenatal and newborn condition of the infants given up for placement was compared with the condition of the home-reared infants. The course of the pregnancy and the condition of the infants were worse for the placement group: The mothers had significantly more illness during pregnancy, and the infants had more problems after birth and were of significantly lower birth weight. Not one of the six placement babies was over 2,800 grams at birth, while four of the six spent the newborn period in the special-care nursery.

These findings indicate that schizophrenic mothers who gave up their infants for adoption or foster placement were not a random sample of schizophrenic mothers, contradicting at least one basic assumption of adoption studies. Rather, they were a selected sample of severely and chronically ill women who were older and less likely to be in an intact marriage than those schizophrenic mothers who chose to rear their infants. In this light, the proportion of their offspring expected to show emotional disorder, based on a stress model, should be much higher than the proportion of emotionally disturbed offspring from the schizophrenics who rear their own children. Indeed, researchers in the Danish group have made a similar point about their own control sample. They have grown suspicious that there is a far higher degree of pathology among mothers giving their children up for adoption, even though they are not schizophrenic, than among mothers in general (Wender et al., 1974).

Not only are the schizophrenic mothers who gave up their infants for placement not a random sample of schizophrenic mothers, but their offspring are not a random sample of schizophrenic offspring, contradicting another basic assumption of adoption studies. In our sample, these infants were more often premature and had more physical problems than the home-reared sample. Wender et al. (1974) previously found that children who were somehow deviant, such as being weak, difficult, or small, prior to adoption showed higher incidence of later mental illness, further highlighting the need to document the joint status of mothers and infants in adoption research. The adopted infant of a schizophrenic biological parent was thought to bring nothing to its new family other than its schizophrenic genes. Sameroff and Zax (1973) suggested that the infant might bring other things as well, such as a difficult temperament. The adoption data from the current study, although derived from a small sample, suggest that the infant may bring far more concrete evidence of deviancy than schizophrenic genes. Along with these genes may come an underweight, tiny body, which places extra caretaking demands on the adoptive parents. These extra caretaking demands and deviant physical appearance have been demonstrated to affect mother–infant interaction (Field, 1980), and have the potential of beginning a negative chain of transactions that could produce a deviant outcome irrespective of whether the infant carried schizophrenic genes (Sameroff, 1975).

From our small sample of six placement babies, one cannot generate strong conclusions, despite the highly significant difference we found. What can be said is that generalizations from other studies of schizophrenia that use adoptees must also limit their conclusions, since both the mothers and the children associated with adoption appear to be unusual and special samples.

ENVIRONMENTAL STUDIES OF SCHIZOPHRENIA

While psychiatric tradition has fostered a focus on the etiology of individual disorders that can be easily meshed with genetic orientations, the number of schizophrenic individuals with schizophrenic relatives is only a small proportion of the total number of schizophrenics. Other more sociologically based orientations have sought the roots of schizophrenia in the environment, conceived either broadly in terms of social class or narrowly in terms of specific forms of family interaction patterns.

Social Class and Schizophrenia

From a epidemiological perspective the data on schizophrenia and social class is overwhelming. Hollingshead and Redlich (1958) found in their New Haven study that the prevalence rate for schizophrenia is eight times as high in the lowest social class as compared to the highest (895 per 100,000 as compared with 111 per 100,000 population). Based on this New Haven data, for every 100,000 people there will be 279 schizophrenics from the top three classes on the Hollingshead (1957) scale and 1,195 from the lowest two social classes. These figures are based on individuals receiving treatment during a six month period.

The basic literature concerning the relationship between SES and schizophrenia has been reviewed by Kohn (1969, 1973). Studies of hospital admission rates show a strong relation between schizophrenia and social class in large urban areas, smaller, less linear relations in moderate-sized urban areas, and little or no relation in small towns and rural populations.

Kohn (1973) evaluated several competing explanations for the observation that lower class life is conducive to the development of schizophrenia. One hypothesis is that genetic drift over many generations has resulted in a disproportionately large amount of schizophrenia genes in the lower class gene pool. Although there is no data on multigenerational patterns, Kohn concluded from data on schizophrenics and their parents that there was not enough downward drift to support this position. A second hypothesis is that the increased stress of lower class life produces increased levels of schizophrenia. Again, Kohn rejected this hypothesis. He noted that it is not the absolute levels of stress that differentiated the social classes, but poor coping abilities of lower SES individuals that increased their susceptibility to schizophrenia when experiencing stress.

Kohn proposed that it is the basic conditions of life built into lower class existence that explain the relationship between schizophrenia and social class. He suggests that lower class families impart rigid and conforming orientation systems to their children. This conformity does not allow individuals effectively "to perceive, to assess, and to deal with complexity and stress" (Kohn, 1973, p. 73). Kohn's emphasis is that the family conditions that promote the development of schizophrenia are not unique to those families where an individual breaks down, but are conditions that characterize a vast segment of society. From Kohn's analysis that focuses on the deficient coping skills fostered by lower class life it is but a short step to those theories of the etiology of schizophrenia that focus on family process. Family interaction patterns are major contributors to the development of adequate coping abilities.

Family Studies of Schizophrenia

Several hypotheses have been advanced for the etiology of schizophrenia based on the study of families of diagnosed individuals. Early theories of family conflicts (Lidz & Lidz, 1949) and "double-bind" (Bateson, Jackson, Haley, & Weakland, 1956) attained wide recognition. Lidz and his associates (Lidz, Corelison, Fleck, & Terry, 1947) further defined the conflict model to include marital relationships characterized by schism (the isolation of individuals within the family) and skew (the formation of opposing family coalitions), both of which were thought to undercut the development of healthy family relations. More recent formulations have discussed social organization and communication deviance within families (Goldstein & Rodnick, 1975; Singer, Wynne, & Toohey, 1978).

Early research in family process concentrated on families where one offspring had been diagnosed as schizophrenic. In several studies, higher levels of communication deviance were found in families with a schizophrenic member. However, the etiological significance of such findings is unclear; the deviant behavior may be a causative factor or the result of the pathology brought by the schizophrenic member to the family (Goldstein & Rodnick, 1975). A similar body of research on family role relationships has documented poorly articulated, highly permeable role boundaries, but it suffers from the same methodological drawbacks as the communication deviance studies (Liem, 1980).

ETIOLOGICAL MODELS

While broadly conceived constitutional and environmental studies on schizophrenia have produced impressive statistics supporting their positions, they have not dealt with the specific etiologies that are of concern if one is fully to understand the disorder. Taken alone, these two perspectives are not thought to have much explanatory power (Rosenthal, 1970). A variety of more complex models have been proposed by Sameroff and Zax (1978; see Table 4.1).

Five possible models need to be considered for understanding the development of a schizophrenic disorder, two with specific constitutional factors, two with specific environmental factors, and the last with neither specific constitutional nor specific environmental factors. The single-factor views posit a condition that produces schizophrenia in all individuals having that condition. A single-factor constitutional view (Model 1) would be that one, or several, genes produces schizophrenia in any carrier of those genes. In the environmental form (Model 2), a single-factor view would be that certain schizophrenogenic social situations, like family conflict, would produce schizophrenia in any child raised in that situation.

There is insufficient evidence today to support either of these single-factor views and most investigators now assume a multifactor position. In two of the multifactor positions (Models 3 and 4) schizophrenia can still be clearly specified to result from a specific constitutional or environmental cause, but the cause is more predisposing than disposing; defects in either a child's nature or nurture may produce schizophrenia, but each requires fertile soil for its development.

In the constitutional multifactor view (Model 3), the defects may reside in a genetic diathesis or a specific area of induced brain damage (Rosenthal, 1970). Individuals with these defects need not become

Table 4.1
Etiological Models of Schizophrenia

| | Component causes | |
Views	Constitution	Environment
A. Single-factor		
Model 1. Constitutional	Schizophrenia	Irrelevant
Model 2. Environmental	Irrelevant	Schizophrenogenic
B. Multi-factor		
Model 3. Constitutional	Specific predisposition	Nonspecific stress
Model 4. Environmental	Nonspecific vulnerability	Special disposition
Model 5. Transactional	Nonspecific vulnerability	Nonspecific stress

schizophrenic if they grow up in an environment with low stress levels. Only when their resistance is stressed above a certain threshold do they "catch" schizophrenia. On the environmental side (Model 4) the multifactor position is that the germ resides in some part of the caretaking environment, such as the family. Not every child subject to these environments would become schizophrenic; some form of constitutional vulnerability would be required. Such general vulnerabilities might consist of physical deviancies resulting from delivery complications, temperamental variations, or perceptual hypersensitivities.

The hallmark of these two multifactor positions is that they are additive; the outcome of schizophrenia is predicted when the characteristics of individuals and environments are combined. When a particular threshold level of the interacting variables is surpassed, a mental disorder becomes apparent. Of particular importance is that each of the different factors is presumed not to substantially influence the development of the remaining factors. For example, an individual continues to carry schizophrenia genes regardless of whether the environment is stressful or not. Conversely, family life can be stressful regardless of whether or not a particular child has some special constitutional problems.

The difference between the first four models and the transactional view (Model 5) is that each of the former posit a specific cause or contributing factor for a schizophrenic outcome. In the transactional model there is no specific developmental precursor, either constitutional or environmental. Rather, schizophrenia is treated as one of a full range or potential normal outcomes of development. The use of the word "normal" here may seem out of place, but from a developmental point of view, normality resides in the ability of the organism to adapt to its environment (see Kringlen, 1976). To the extent that a schizophrenic outcome is the result of the transactions between a specific child coping with his or her own specific environment, an outcome that permits functional survival within that environment can be considered both adaptive and normal.

The defining characteristic of the transactional model is that all elements in the system do, in fact, influence the development of all other elements. The elements do not merely sum or multiply to achieve a particular threshold level, rather the social–psychological system undergoes fundamental change through the course of development. For example, the birth of a child with some genetic or perinatally induced defect, or even a child at the difficult end of normal variation, may increase stress levels, leading to conflict in a family that could cope with a normal or easy child. This conflict in turn may affect the personality development of the child, which in turn would make the family situation worse, and so on. The results of adoption studies discussed earlier provide an example of such transactions.

The five models reduce to two foci for research investigation. When one conceives of a constitutional factor as producing some form of schizophrenia in every carrier or merely predisposing the carrier toward schizophrenia, one must be able to identify some unique difference between such individuals and their peers. Similarly when one considers an environmental factor as producing schizophrenia in any individual raised in that environment or merely acting as a predisposing agent, one must be able to identify some unique characteristic of that environment. From a transactional view the analysis requires the specification of constitutional characteristics of individuals, functional characteristics of the environment, and the development of these elements in a unified system.

HIGH-RISK RESEARCH MODELS

Two studies begun in the 1950s provide the methodological foundation upon which studies that currently examine the effects of a mentally ill parent are based. In a study conducted by Mednick and Schulsinger (1968), a sample of children born to schizophrenic parents in Denmark was compared with a matched group of no–mental-illness controls. The sample was initially studied during adolescence and follow-ups continue through adulthood. Adolescence was chosen as a starting point since it was hoped that the entire risk period for schizophrenia (approximately 18 to 45 years of age) would be passed during the lifetime of the investigators. The main focus was on measures of psychophysiology and cognitive performance in a search for a constitutional marker for later schizophrenia.

A study by Fish and Alpert (1962) was more clinical in focus and employed a much smaller sample of children who were followed from birth. But, as in the Mednick and Schulsinger study, infants in the high-risk group were chosen because they had a schizophrenic parent, and a single no–mental-illness control group served as a contrast. Fish and her associates searched for a constitutional marker in the realm of muscular and neurological integration during the first two years of life.

These two early studies have some qualities in common. First, high-risk samples were compared with a single control group of families with no specific mental health problems. Second, the focus was on isolating one, or several, constitutional characteristics of the high-risk children as markers for vulnerability to schizophrenia. Third, both studies followed their samples into the risk period for schizophrenia (Fish, 1984; Schulsinger, 1976).

While such a design has merit if one assumes a primarily biological transmission of schizophrenia, it does not deal well with a variety of environmental factors that are associated with schizophrenia. For example, schizophrenia is found disproportionately in lower SES populations, it is a severe mental illness, and it is a condition with chronic, long-term effects. If a research design does not control for all of these influences, the presence of significant differences between groups may inappropriately be attributed to schizophrenia, when some other factor, such as social class or general mental illness, is responsible.

The age at which children are studied is an important factor in these studies. From a simple constitutional perspective, the only purpose for beginning a study with young infants would be in the service of earlier detection. On the other hand, if one has concerns about environmental etiological factors, finding group differences in adolescence would reveal little about the development of those differences. They could be a function of some constitutional variable or the consequence of living with deranged parents for an extended time period. If one were to elucidate fully the relevant contributors of both constitution and environment, one would have to begin the research effort when the children are as young as possible. In most cases this would be the period of infancy.

RECENT STUDIES OF MENTALLY ILL PARENTS

Following the work of Fish, and Mednick, and Schulsinger, many studies were begun that were extremely varied regarding the criteria used for selecting schizophrenic families, the types of control groups used, the age range of the children, the methodology employed, and the psychological constructs that were of primary interest (Garmezy, 1974). Four areas of research have been prominent in these studies: biological factors (Kety, 1978), attentional processes (Garmezy, 1978), general behavioral competence (Watt & Lubensky, 1976), and social process (Goldstein & Rodnick, 1975; Kohn, 1973; Liem, 1980). Biological risk factors that have been studied include obstetric complications (McNeil & Kaij, 1978; Mednick & Schulsinger, 1968; Sameroff, Seifer, & Zax, 1982; Sameroff & Zax, 1973), newborn neurological status (McNeil & Kaij, 1984), newborn heart rate (Schachter, Kerr, Lachin, & Faer, 1975), and neurological status during the first 4 months (Marcus, Auerbach, Wilkinson, & Burack, 1981) and first 7 years (Fish, 1984; Rieder & Nichols, 1979). Although studies of attention have been prominent in the literature on adults and older high-risk children, few studies have been done with younger children (Gamer, Gallant, Grunebaum, & Cohler, 1977). Other studies have used a variety of behavioral measures. These include temperament and language assessments (McNeil & Kaij, 1984; Sameroff et al. 1982), cognitive and psychomotor developmental tests (Hanson, Gottesman, & Heston, 1976; Sammeroff et al. 1982), and parent–infant interaction and attachment (McNeil & Kaij, 1984; Sameroff et al. 1982).

The surprising result of all these studies assessing a wide variety of measures was that few differences among children of parents with varying psychiatric diagnoses could be directly related to the diagnoses. Where differences were found between offspring of schizophrenics and others, they were in studies that used only children of normal women as a control group. Where other psychiatric groups were also compared in the studies, the offspring of schizophrenics did not differ.

In studies using school age children a similar pattern of findings was found. Where children of schizophrenics were only compared to children of healthy parents, they differed on a variety of behavioral dimensions. When children of parents with other diagnoses were included, all risk groups differed from children of healthy mothers but not among each other (e.g., Sameroff et al. 1982).

One area where there is promise of finding unique differences between school age offspring of schizophrenics and offspring of other parents with psychiatric disturbances is in studies of attentional processes (Harvey, Winters, Weintraub, & Neale, 1981). However, in a review of the findings of current high-risk studies of schizophrenia, Watt (1984) was led to note that even where differences have been found between offspring of schizophrenics and other children, few of these have been replicated by other research groups.

Despite the epidemiological research cited earlier implicating social factors as major correlates of mental illness, these variables are conspicuously absent from high-risk studies. These easily identifiable characteristics of families have been shown to be powerful factors in almost all aspects of development, for example, psychometric test performance (Golden & Birns, 1976), mother–infant interaction (Tulkin & Kagan, 1972), and parental attitudes (Kohn, 1969), but they have not been included in developmental research on young children in high-risk categories.

NORMATIVE APPROACHES
TO EARLY DEVELOPMENT

The high-risk studies reviewed above used as target variables measures thought to have some relationship to the adult manifestations of a schizophrenic disorder. As younger and younger children are studied, it becomes more difficult to make hypothesized connections between the behaviors that can be conceptualized and measured during infancy or early childhood and the behaviors of mentally ill adult patients. For example, the thought disorder that characterizes a diagnosis of schizophrenia is difficult to assess in a child or infant who is just beginning to think. Similarly, social competencies are difficult to assess in young children for whom parents provide the interface between the child and the rest of the environment.

The 1960s and 1970s have produced a variety of new measures and approaches for examining the behavior of young children. Many of the infant behaviors currently of interest were not recognized as being at all relevant until this period. Examples of these measures are the Neonatal Behavioral Assessment Scales (Brazelton, 1973), the "strange" situation of Ainsworth (1973), and new intellectual assessments (Uzgiris & Hunt, 1975). Family interaction variables had long been implicated in the study of schizophrenia (Goldstein & Rodnick, 1975), but only recently have such studies become common for young infants and their families (Moss, 1967; Osofsky & Connor, 1979). Even such areas as personality and adaptive behavior have been extended downward in the work on temperament of Thomas, Chess and Birch (1968), and competency assessments (Seifer, Sameroff, & Jones, 1981).

These developments, which enlarge the possibility for assessing early behavior of all children, offered special opportunities for detecting vulnerabilities in special populations such as the risk children considered here. From these measures it was possible to assemble a set of variables that could be used to examine characteristics of the child and the caretaking environment as well as the interaction between the two through early development.

SOCIAL STATUS

An important determinant of parental behavior is the social and cultural context of the family. The normative literature on development and the epidemiological literature on mental illness suggest that this would be an essential factor to examine. Sameroff and Chandler (1975) have emphasized the importance of SES in the development of children with constitutional risk factors associated with obstetrical complications. Also, Kohn (1969, 1973) has reviewed the importance of SES in the development of schizophrenia.

Available evidence shows that social status has an impact early in development. First, parents from different SES groups bring different attitudes, values, standards, and methods for raising their children (Becker & Krug, 1965; Kohn, 1969; Sameroff & Feil, 1984). Second, families in different social strata vary as to the frequency with which a variety of problematic events occur. For example, poor prenatal care and obstetrical complications (Birch & Gussow, 1970; Kopp & Parmelee, 1979), single-parent families and teenage pregnancy (Baldwin, 1980), and child abuse (Gabriano, 1976) are more common in lower SES families. More importantly, these differences translate into differences in the development of children from these different social groups.

Golden and Birns (1976) concluded from their review of the literature on assessments of infant intelligence that lower-SES infants show consistent deficits by their second birthday. These differences may be related to the ways that mothers and infants interact in different social groups. Tulkin and Kagan (1972) found that middle class mothers of 10-month-olds were more vocal, interactive, and playful, with quicker response to distress, and engaged in more en face contact than working class mothers. The middle class infants had more opportunity to explore, more toys, and less extraneous stimulation. Tulkin (1973) has also demonstrated that middle class infants, but not lower class infants, responded differently to the voice of their mother and a stranger. Lewis and his co-workers (Lewis and Wilson, 1972; Messer & Lewis, 1972) have also found SES differences in younger infants in a variety of home and laboratory observations.

ROCHESTER LONGITUDINAL STUDY

In the context of high-risk research described above, we have been conducting a longitudinal study since 1970 that investigates the role of parental mental illness, social status, and other family cognitive and social variables that might be risk factors in the early development of children from birth through 4 years of age. The Rochester Longitudinal Study (RLS) (Sameroff et al., 1982) was one of many studies begun in the last 20 years that were explicitly concerned with the impact of parental schizophrenia on the development of children. The RLS differed from most of these other studies in three ways. First, the age range of children studied was younger; most other studies focused on school-age children while we were concerned with infants and preschool children. Second, in addition to schizophrenics, a variety of other diagnosis groups were studied to explore issues related to mental illness, in general, as well as schizophrenia, in particular; most other studies had only normal controls or only a single mental illness control group. Third, the sample was heterogeneous for many family variables, in particular SES and race; the strategy of almost all other high-risk schizophrenia studies had been to control race or social class factors out of their designs by matching subject groups or choosing subjects from limited social status samples.

CONSEQUENCES OF HAVING
A SCHIZOPHRENIC MOTHER

The results of the study to date were that the offspring of women with severe and chronic mental disturbance suffered from a variety of deficits in social, emotional, and cognitive functioning. These deficiencies, however, could not be related to any specific maternal psychiatric diagnosis, especially schizophrenia.

For the analyses of the effects of a schizophrenic mother on the development of her child, four groups were formed out of a larger total sample as the basis for a diagnostic comparison: (1) a schizophrenic group, (2) a neurotic–depressive group, (3) a personality-disordered group, and (4) a no–mental-illness group that was matched to the other groups on the basis of age, race, SES, number of children, education, and sex of child.

As newborns, the offspring of schizophrenic women were nearly indistinguishable from the matched no–mental-illness control group on almost all evaluations of infant characteristics except birthweight. Although the schizophrenic group had the lowest birthweight, they did not differ significantly from newborns in other psychiatric groups. At 4 and 12 months the offspring of schizophrenics had slightly lower Bayley scores but showed no differences in behavior during home observations or on temperament assessments. The early Bayley differences had disappeared by the time the infants were 30 months old.

Parenthetically, if one were to seek a maternal diagnostic group where children were at most risk, it would be depression rather than schizophrenia. These infants had by far the worse obstetric status including a number of neonatal deaths. However, even for the neurotic depressive group, unique behavioral differences had almost all dissipated by the 30th-month assessment.

When diagnostic category was ignored and comparisons made between offspring of mothers with varying degrees of mental symptoms, the demonstrable effect on the child was much clearer. Scores on general dimensions of mental illness were determined for the chronicity and severity of the mothers' illness. The severity of mental illness dimension had four categories ranging from no symptoms to many clinical symptoms that were scored from psychiatric interviews. The chronicity of mental illness also had four categories ranging from no illness to long-term hospitalization and was based on information from both the interviews and a mental health registry.

The effects of the severity and chronicity of maternal mental illness on the children were ubiquitous throughout the study. Children of severely or chronically ill mothers had lower birthweights, poorer obstetrical status, poorer performance on newborn measures, lower Bayley scores, and more difficult temperaments at 4 months of age, were less spontaneous and responsive in home and laboratory at 12 months and 30 months and had much poorer adaptive behavior scores.

From these analyses we concluded that among the mental illness measures, severity and chronicity of disturbance were better predictors than specific psychiatric diagnoses. Through these mental illness comparisons, we became aware that social status was a major factor in our results. Particularly striking was that the differences found between children with mentally ill mothers and those with normal mothers were frequently paralleled by differences between children from lower and higher social status homes. One way of separating the effects of mental illness and social status was to do a developmental analysis of the data.

A good example of the results of a longitudinal analysis can be found in the assessment of the social and adaptive competence of the children in the RLS. Seifer, Sameroff, and Jones (1981) compared groups from families that differed on mental illness and social status dimensions when the children were 30 and 48 months old. The measure used was the Rochester Adaptive Behavior Inventory (RABI), a parental interview that assesses global social–emotional competence of the child, in addition to adaptive behavior, on a number of specific dimensions that reflect symptomatic behavior. At 30 months, children from families with mentally ill mothers differed from children from families with no parental mental illness, and children from lower social status families differed from children from higher social status families. Both groups of risk children were less cooperative, more timid, more fearful, more depressed, and engaged in more bizarre behavior than their comparison groups. However, at 48 months there was a separation between the risk group behaviors. The children of mentally ill mothers continued to show the same deficits they had at 30 months compared with children of healthy mothers, but many of the differences among children in different social status groups became less pronounced. The effects of having a parent with social–emotional problems on preschool children's social–emotional functioning seemed to be more pervasive and long lasting than the effects of having a low social status parent. If the children had been assessed only at one point in time, one would have reached far different conclusions than when the evaluations were made at both 30 and 48 months. The data from 30 months, when viewed alone, suggest equal impacts of mental illness and social status. On the other hand, the 48th-month data alone suggest a greater role for mental illness than for social status. It was only when multiple assessments were made that developmental changes became apparent.

Another caution in the analyses of data from high-risk studies such as the RLS is that while one can attempt to separate the effects of social status and mental illness in experimental designs, the two factors are correlated in the real world (Hollingshead & Redlich, 1958). When women were recrutied as lower social status controls in the Rochester study, one fourth of those randomly selected from an obstetric clinic showed emotional disturbance during a psychiatric interview.

In contrast to the declining independent contribution of social status to the *social–emotional* competence of the child with age, there was an increasing impact of social status on the *cognitive* competence of the child. Child mental development was assessed at 4, 12, and 30 months of age using the Bayley Scales of Infant Development and at 48 months using the WPPSI. Comparisons were made between three groups of subjects: whites from SES levels I, II, and III (Hollingshead, 1957), whites from SES levels IV and V, and blacks from SES levels IV and V. At 4 and 12 months there were no differences in the group means. By 30 and 48 months there were large differences. Golden and Birns (1976) found a similar lack of differences between racial groups before the second year in both standardized and Piagetian cognitive tests, with major differences thereafter. In Broman, Nichols and Kennedy's (1975) report of the Collaborative Perinatal Project sample of over 20,000 children, there were only small correlations between Baylew MDI scores and SES at 8 months of age, but at four years the relationships were very strong.

The data from these studies indicate that social status has an impact on the development of intellectual growth after the first year. As children grow older, those from higher SES families are thriving more and more, while lower SES children are becoming more stifled.

CONCLUSIONS

Our investigation was an attempt to identify variables in mentally ill mothers that place children "at-risk" for the later development of mental disorder. The target population was the offspring of schizophrenic women, who have been shown to have more than 10 times the risk for developing schizophrenia as offspring of nonschizophrenic women. The variables that define risk were conceptualized in a series of models that differentially emphasized constitutional and environmental factors. From the constitutional perspective, we were interested in identifying characteristics of the child's behavior uniquely associated with having a mentally ill mother. From the environmental perspective, we were interested in identifying characteristics of the child's caretaking context associated with having a mentally ill mother.

To test if these constitutional or environmental characteristics were specific to one or another psychiatric diagnosis, we included a variety of control groups. For example, since schizophrenia is a severe and chronic mental illness found predominantly in lower social status groups, we included, as controls, mothers who had severe and chronic mental illnesses other than schizophrenia and mothers with no evidence of mental illness who came from lower social status groups.

In the course of our studies, we have become convinced that our questions about the effects of having a mentally ill parent must be embedded in an analysis of the general risks to which young children are subject and the range of outcomes associated with such risks.

Our results lead us to two conclusions on the issue of schizophrenia. The first is that the offspring of schizophrenic women as a group have many developmental problems. The second is that these problems do not appear to be the simple result of maternal schizophrenia. If one compares the offspring of schizophrenic women in our study with a group of offspring of middle-class, white mothers with no mental illness, the children of the schizophrenics have lower cognitive, linguistic, and motor performance scores, poorer emotional behavior, poorer adaptive behavior in the home, and worse behavior in the testing situation. However, when nonschizophrenic women with similar social status, severity, and chronicity of mental disturbance were compared to the schizophrenics, similar deficiencies were found.

These differences did not appear to be the result of the maternal diagnosis of schizophrenia, but rather the effect of suffering from a serious and chronic mental disorder. Moreover, a high proportion of these women lived in poor economic circumstances, which would impede their own adaptive behavior. It would not be surprising to us that children from such backgrounds who get off to a bad start eventually become emotionally disturbed themselves and on occasion develop schizophrenia (see Rutter, 1966).

The ways in which personality might be passed from generation to generation, though long studied, is still little understood. An examination of the transmission of extreme patterns of behavior, such as those found in mental illness, was thought to be a reasonable strategy for illuminating the transmission of more typical psychological characteristics. Most of the research in this area has centered on the offspring of schizophrenics, since this group is a potential model for both biological and social heredity. The work we have reported has been in this area.

To summarize the results of our longitudinal study to date, we have not found that offspring of schizophrenic women are a healthy, happy, intelligent lot. Our measures have shown that they have high levels of illness, fearfulness, sadness, retardation, and social maladaptiveness. However, this does not make them uniquely different from the offspring of women with other severe or chronic mental disorders or even children of psychiatrically normal women from the lower socio-economic strata of our society. Without the appropriate control groups built into our study, we might have been led into the error of attributing these differences to the effects of a schizophrenic heritage alone.

In short, caretaking environments in which high levels of stress exist, whether through economic or emotional instability, produce young children with high levels of incompetent behavior. Whether or not these early manifestations of aggressiveness or fearfulness will express themselves in later mental illness will only be determined by further longitudinal research. In the interim, our findings have identified a population of vulnerable children toward which early intervention studies might fruitfully be directed.

REFERENCES

Ainsworth, M. D. S. The development of infant–mother attachment. In B. Caldwell & H. Ricciuti (Eds.), *Review of child development research* (Vol. 3). Chicago: University of Chicago Press, 1973.

Baldwin, W. H. Adolescent pregnancy and childbearing: Growing concerns for Americans. *Population Bulletin,* 1980, *31(2),* 1–37.

Bateson, G., Jackson, D., Haley, J., & Weakland, J. Toward a theory of schizophrenia. *Behavioral Science,* 1956, *1,* 251–264.

Becker, W. C., & Krug, R. S. The parent attitude research instrument: A research review. *Child Development,* 1965, *36,* 329–365.

Birch, H. G., & Gussow, J. D. *Disadvantaged children.* New York: Harcourt, Brace, and World, 1970.

Brazelton, T. B. *Neonatal behavioral assessment scale.* London: Heinemann, 1973.

Broman, S. H., Nichols, P. L., & Kennedy, W. A. *Preschool IQ: Prenatal and early developmental correlates.* New York: Erlbaum, 1975.

Field, T. M. Interactions of preterm and term infants with their lower-and middle-class teenage and adult mother. In T. M. Field, S. Goldberg, D. Stern, & A. M. Sostek (Eds.), *High-risk infants and children: Adult and peer interactions.* New York: Academic Press, 1980.

Fish, B. Characteristics and sequelae of neurointegrative disorder in infants at risk for schizophrenia (1952–1982). In N. Watt, E. J. Anthony, L. C. Wynne, & J. Rolf (Eds.), *Children at risk for schizophrenia: A longitudinal perspective.* New York: Cambridge University, 1984.

Fish, B., & Alpert, M. S. Abnormal states of consciousness and muscle tone in infants born to schizophrenic mothers. *American Journal of Psychiatry,* 1962, *119,* 439–445.

Gabriano, J. A preliminary study of some ecological correlates of child abuse: The impact of socioeconomic stress on mothers. *Child Development,* 1976, *47,* 178–185.

Gamer, E., Gallant, D., Grunebaum, H. U., & Cohler, B. J. Children of psychotic mothers. *Archives of General Psychiatry,* 1977, *34,* 592–597.

Garmezy, N. Children at risk: The search for the antecedents of schizophrenia: Part 1. Conceptual models and research methods. *Schizophrenia Bulletin,* 1974, *8,* 14–90.

Garmezy, N. Attentional processes in adult schizophrenia and in children at risk. *Journal of Psychiatric Research*, 1978, *14*, 3–34.

Golden, M., & Birns, B. Social class and infant intelligence. In M. Lewis (Ed.), *Origins of intelligence: Infancy and early childhood*. New York: Plenum, 1976.

Goldstein, M. J., & Rodnick, E. H. The family's contribution to the etiology of schizophrenia: Current status. *Schizophrenia Bulletin*, 1975, *14*, 48–63.

Gottesman, I. I., & Shields, J. Schizophrenia in twins: 16 years' consecutive admissions to a psychiatric clinic. *British Journal of Psychiatry*, 1966, *112*, 809–813.

Hanson, D. R., Gottesman, I. I., & Heston, L. L. Some possible indicators of adult schizophrenia inferred from children of schizophrenics. *British Journal of Psychiatry*, 1976, *129*, 142–154.

Hanson, D. R., Gottesman, I. I., & Meehl, P. E. Genetic theories and the validation of psychiatric diagnoses: Implications for the study of children of schizophrenics. *Journal of Abnormal Psychology*, 1977, *86*, 575–588.

Harvey, P., Winters, K., Weintraub, S., & Neale, J. M. Distractibility in children vulnerable to psychopathology. *Journal of Abnormal Psychology*, 1981, *90*, 298–304.

Heston, L. L. Psychiatric disorders in foster home reared children of schizophrenic mothers. *British Journal of Psychiatry*, 1966, *112*, 819–825.

Higgins, J. Effects of child rearing by schizophrenic mothers: A follow up. *Journal of Psychiatric Research*, 1976, *13*, 1–9.

Hollingshead, A. B. *Two factor index of social position*. Unpublished mimeograph, 1957. (Available from author, Sociology Department, Yale University, New Haven, CT.).

Hollingshead, A. B., & Redlich, F. C. *Social class and mental illness: A community study*. New York: Wiley, 1958.

Jackson, D. D. *The etiology of schizophrenia*. New York: Basic Books, 1960.

Kallmann, F. J. *The genetics of schizophrenia*. New York: J. J. Augustin, 1938.

Kallmann, F. J. The genetic theory of schizophrenia: An analysis of 691 schizophrenic twin index families. *American Journal of Psychiatry*, 1946, *103*, 309–322.

Kety, S. S. Biochemical approaches: Introduction. In L. C. Wynne, R. L. Cromwell, & S. Matthysse (Eds.), *The nature of schizophrenia: New approaches to research and treatment*. New York: Wiley, 1978.

Kety, S. S., Rosenthal, D., Wender, P. H., Schulsinger, F., & Jacobson, B. Mental illness in the biological and adoptive families of adopted individuals who have become schizophrenic: A preliminary report based on psychiatric interviews. In R. R. Fieve, D. Rosenthal, & H. Brill (Eds.), *Genetic research in psychiatry*. Baltimore: John Hopkins, 1975.

Kohn, M. L. *Class and conformity: A study in values*. Homewood, IL: Dorsey, 1969.

Kohn, M. L. Social class and schizophrenia: A critical review and reformulation. *Schizophrenia Bulletin*, 1973, *7*, 60–79.

Kopp, C. B., & Parmelee, A. H. Prenatal and perinatal influences on infant behavior. In J. D. Osofsky (Ed.), *Handbook of infant development*. New York: Wiley, 1979.

Kringlen, E. Twins still our best method. *Schizophrenia Bulletin*, 1976, *2(3)*, 429–433.

Lewis, M., & Wilson, C. D. Infant development in lower class American families. *Human Development*, 1972, *15*, 112–127.

Lidz, T., Cornelison, A., Fleck, S., & Terry, D. The intrafamilial environment of schizophrenic patients: II. Marital schism and marital skew. *American Journal of Psychiatry*, 1957, *114*, 241–248.

Lidz, R. W., & Lidz, T. The family environment of schizophrenic patients. *American Journal of Psychiatry*, 1949, *106*, 332–345.

Liem, J. H. Family studies of schizophrenia: An update and commentary. *Schizophrenia Bulletin*, 1980, *6*, 429–455.

Loehlin, J. C., & Nichols, R. C. *Heredity, environment and personality.* Austin: University of Texas Press, 1976.

Marcus, J., Auerbach, J., Wilkinson, L., & Burack, C. M. Infants at risk for schizophrenia: the Jerusalem infant development study. *Archives of General Psychiatry,* 1981, 38, 703–713.

McNeil, T. F., & Kaij, L. Obstetric factors in the development of schizophrenia: Complications in the births of preschizophrenics and in reproductions by schizophrenic parents. In L. C. Wynne, R. L. Cromwell, & S. Mathysse (Eds.), *The nature of schizophrenia: New approaches to research and treatment.* New York: Wiley, 1978.

McNeil, T. F., & Kaij, L. Offspring of women with nonorganic psychoses. In N. Watt, E. J. Anthony, L. C. Wynne, & J. Rolf (Eds.), *Children at risk for schizophrenia: A longitudinal perspective.* New York: Cambridge University, 1984.

Mednick, S. A., & Schulsinger, F. Some premorbid characteristics related to breakdown in children with schizophrenic mothers. In D. Rosenthal & S. S. Kety (Eds.), *The transmission of schizophrenia.* Oxford: Pergamon Press, 1968.

Messer, S. B., & Lewis, M. Social class and sex differences in the attachment and play behavior of the year-old infant. *Merrill Palmer Quarterly,* 1972, 18, 295–306.

Moss, H. A. Sex, age, and state as determinants of mother–infant interaction. *Merrill Palmer Quarterly,* 1967, 13, 19–36.

Osofsky, J. D., & Connors, K. Mother–infant interaction: An integrative view of a complex system. In J. D. Osofsky (Ed.), *Handbook of infant development.* New York: Wiley, 1979.

Rieder, R. O., & Nichols, P. L. Offspring of schizophrenics III: Hyperactivity and neurological soft signs. *Archives of General Psychiatry,* 1979, 36, 665–674.

Rosenthal, D. Problems of sampling and diagnosis in the major twin studies of schizophrenia. *Journal of Psychiatric Research.* 1962, 1, 116–134.

Rosenthal, D. *Genetic theory and abnormal behavior.* New York: McGraw Hill, 1970.

Rosenthal, D., Wender, P. H., Kety, S. S., Welner, J., & Schulsinger, F. The adopted-away offspring of schizophrenics. *American Journal of Psychiatry,* 1971, 128, 87–91.

Rutter, M. *Children of sick parents.* London: Oxford, 1966.

Sameroff, A. J. Early influences on development: Fact or fancy? *Merrill-Palmer Quarterly,* 1975, 21, 267–294.

Sameroff, A. J., & Chandler, M. J. Reproductive risk and the continuum of caretaking casualty. In F. D. Horowitz, M. Hetherington, S. Scarr-Salapetek, & G. Siegel (Eds.), *Review of child development research* (Vol. 4). Chicago: University of Chicago Press, 1975.

Sameroff, A. J., & Feil, L. A. Parental concepts of development. In I. Sigel (Ed.), *Parental belief systems: The psychological consequences for children.* Hillsdale, NJ: Lawrence Erlbaum, 1984.

Sameroff, A. J., Seifer, R., & Zax, M. Early development of children at risk for emotional disorder. *Monographs of the Society for Research in Child Development,* 1982, 47(7, Serial No. 199).

Sameroff, A. J., & Zax, M. Perinatal characteristics of the offspring of schizophrenic women. *Journal of Nervous and Mental Disease,* 1973, 157, 191–199.

Sameroff, A. J., & Zax, M. The child of psychotic parents. In S. Wolkind (Ed.), *Medical aspects of adoption and foster care. Clinics in developmental medicine* (No. 74). London: Heinemann, 1979.

Sameroff, A. J., & Zax, M. In search of schizophrenia: Young offspring of schizophrenic women. In L. C. Wynne, R. L. Cromwell, & S. Matthysse (Eds.), *The nature of schizophrenia: New approaches to research and treatment.* New York: Wiley, 1978.

Schachter, J., Kerr, J., Lachin, J. M., & Faer, M. Newborn offspring of a schizophrenic parent: Cardiac reactivity to auditory stimuli. *Psychophysiology*, 1975, *12*, 483–492.

Schulsinger, H. A. A ten year follow-up of children with schizophrenic mothers. *Acta Psychiatrica Scandinavica*, 1976, *63*, 371–386.

Seifer, R., Sameroff, A. J., & Jones, F. H. Adaptive behavior in young children of emotionally disturbed women. *Journal of Applied Developmental Psychology*, 1981, *1*, 251–276.

Singer, M. T., Wynne, L. C., & Toohey, M. L. Communication disorders and the families of schizophrenics. In L. C. Wynne, R. L. Cromwell, & S. Matthysse (Eds.), *The nature of schizophrenia: New approaches to research and treatment.* New York: Wiley, 1978.

Thomas, A., Chess, S., & Birch, H. *Temperament and behavior disorders in children.* New York: New York University, 1968.

Tulkin, S. R. Social class differences in infants' reactions to mother's and stranger's voices. *Developmental Psychology*, 1973, *8*, 137.

Tulkin, S. R., & Kagan, J. Mother–child interaction: Social class differences in the first year of life. *Child Development*, 1972, *43*, 31–41. Uzgiris, I., & Hunt, J. McV. *Assessment in infancy: Ordinal scales of psychological development.* Urbana, IL: University of Illinois Press, 1975.

Watt, N. F. In a nutshell: The first two decades of high-risk research in schizophrenia. In N. Watt, E. J. Anthony, L. C. Wynne, & J. Rolf (Eds.), *Children at risk for schizophrenia: A longitudinal perspective.* New York: Cambridge University, 1984.

Watt, N. F., & Lubensky, A. W. Childhood roots of schizophrenia. *Journal of Consulting and Clinical Psychology*, 1976, *44*, 363–375.

Wender, P. H., Rosenthal, D., Kety, S. S., Schulsinger, F., & Welner, J. Crossfostering: A research strategy for clarifying the role of genetic and experiential factors in the etiology of schizophrenia. *Archives of General Psychiatry*, 1974, *30*, 121–128.

5

Diversity, Shared Functioning, and the Role of Benefactors: A Study of Parenting by Retarded Persons*

ANDREA G. ZETLIN,
THOMAS S. WEISNER,
and RONALD GALLIMORE

In the past, being mentally retarded often meant restrictions in the life chances available to the individual. With the recent trend toward normalization, retarded persons can succeed in living their lives as normally as they are able to (Wolfensberger, 1972). This includes the right to take normal risks, to make consequential decisions, to come and go as they please, and to experience normal societal relationships (Kernan, Turner, Langness, & Edgerton, 1978). It is now recognized that healthy social and sexual relationships are basic to an individual's successful adaptation in community life (Koegel & Whittemore, 1983). Historically, however, the sexuality of retarded adults has been both feared and denied, resulting in the implementation of strict controls (i.e., sterilization and segregation), justified in terms of the safety of the retarded individual and the good of society.

It is only in recent years that marriage and parenting have been viable considerations for retarded adults. Still, there is much apprehen-

*This study was part of a larger investigation of personal and social adjustment of retarded persons living in community settings. The research was supported by NICHD Grant HD 11944 to the Socio–Behavioral Research Group, Mental Retardation Research Center, UCLA. We gratefully acknowledge the contributions of Lesley Winik, Regina Love, Dara Vines and Paul Koegel to the collection of data and the helpful comments of Jim Turner and Gelya Frank during the writing of this chapter.

sion over the possibility of retarded persons becoming parents. Bass (1963) suggested that retarded persons be permitted to marry only if they have been sterilized. Johnson (1969) contended that while the deprivation of close human relations is inexcusable as a policy, parenthood is not the automatic right of all human beings and the rights of the child must be considered. Similarly, the 1976 President's Committee on Mental Retardation qualified its statement that marriage and reproduction are rights, not privileges, for retarded individuals, by emphasizing the rights of children to an adequate home environment that prepares them both cognitively and emotionally for entry into school.

In general, discussions of retarded persons as parents have focussed on three issues: (1) The effect of the parents' retardation on the child's cognitive and behavioral profile—for example, Will retarded persons produce handicapped offspring? What problems in self-esteem maintenance will arise when the child becomes aware of his or her parents' handicap? (2) The retarded persons' competence as parents—Are they capable of setting adequate child-rearing goals, providing a suitable environment, and sustaining appropriate practices? (3) The effect on their self-maintenance skills of the additional burden of parenting—Will parenting be too much for the retarded person to cope with, resulting in their offspring becoming a burden to society?

Hall (1974) compared a number of studies that examined the likelihood that retarded persons would produce retarded children and found that estimates vary tremendously depending on the sample surveyed. The studies reviewed did indicate, however, that while the reproductive rates of retarded persons are lower than those of nonretarded people, the relative risks of retardation are much higher for the offspring of retarded parents. In response to such evidence, the fear that mentally retarded parents will beget mentally retarded children has resulted in the legal involuntary sterilization of mentally retarded adults in 26 states and the passage of laws prohibiting the marriage of retarded adults in all but 10 states and the District of Columbia (Winik, 1981).

The second issue, the adequacy of retarded persons as parents, is by no means a simple matter. The skills that constitute adequacy of any parents have yet to be agreed upon. However, studies have attempted to explore the competence of retarded persons as parents and in general have found them to be satisfactory parents; their children are reasonably clean, are within the normal range of intelligence, and exhibit no unusual behavior problems in school (Whittemore & Koegel, 1978; Winik, 1981). When inadequacy was detected, it could be accounted for by factors other than retardation, such as family size, socioeconomic status, marital status, and the harmoniousness of the marital relationship (Mickelson, 1947; Scally, 1973; Winik, 1981).

Johnson (1981) contends that these families appear incompetent and their home environments deprived because we tend to judge them using middle class standards of orderliness and efficiency.

> If a retarded mother is careless in keeping her children clean, if she does not prepare nutritious meals, if her children are sent to school in secondhand clothing, or if her children have minor bruises from playing, the mother is much more likely to be suspected of incompetence or neglect than a mother who does not have a history of retardation. (p. 3)

Both Winik's (1981) intensive study of two families and Johnson's (1981) observations of six families concluded that none of the families could be considered abusive or neglectful of their children. And although certain problems (e.g., bureaucratic tangles or marital conflicts) were experienced, which tended to overwhelm the families and caused them to become temporarily less conscientious about their childcare responsibilities, the availability of an extensive amount of support aided them in coping with the pressures of self-maintenance and child care.

The provision of assistance from outside sources directly relates to the third concern, the potential for having to remove the child from the home. While instances of custody being denied have been reported—one infant was unwittingly bathed in water too hot, resulting in burns on his bottom, and another was left at home alone when his parents went out for the evening (Koegel & Whittemore, 1983)—when family members, benefactors, or delivery system personnel are accessible to aid in the management of everyday problems and critical incidents, there is less likelihood of poor parenting becoming an issue (Johnson, 1981; Winik, 1981).

Reports from all sources—sample members, family members, and field researcher observations—suggest a relationship between family provision of support and the perception of adequate or competent childcare management by the retarded person as parent. When the more capable individual perceives an inability in the retarded person to carry out an activity independently, he or she either assumes responsibility for the task or provides the strategic assistance necessary for the less capable individual to organize his or her efforts in a task-appropriate manner (Vygotsky, 1978). While guided by the premise that a range of competence is possessed by our sample members, the intention of this chapter is to examine the relationship of the retarded person with family members as it relates to the issue of adequacy of parenting skills.

SAMPLE

For a number of years, the Socio—Behavioral Group of the Mental Retardation Research Center at UCLA has been investigating various aspects of the community adaptation of mildly retarded adults. More specifically, attempts have been made to identify factors responsible for facilitating or hindering these individuals' potential for normalization, particularly in independent living and competitive employment. In June 1980, a new phase was initiated with the same aim of employing naturalistic research methods to document the everyday life behaviors of mildly retarded adults. This time the sample was broadened to include black participants in addition to the original caucasian members.

During this phase of our research, 90 adults living in the greater Los Angeles area have been followed and intensely studied. All of the sample members were individuals who had been classified as mentally retarded at some point in their development, by a component of the service delivery system. From this larger sample, a subsample of those individuals with children were identified and their parenting practices examined. While IQ data were not available for all these individuals, all members of this smaller sample had been placed in special education classes during their school years and remained in them until they graduated or dropped out.

In total, 13 family units that included at least one retarded parent were identified. Three were white and 10 were black. Both parents were present in 8 of the families; in 3 of these, 1 spouse was of normal intelligence. Five families contained single or divorced mothers, 2 of whom had never had custody of their children but maintained regular contact with them. Eight of the families lived in their own apartment, 7 of them in close proximity to their own parents or other family members. Four families lived in the same house as their own parents; and one woman, who did live with her children, resided in a board and care facility. Additional details of age, IQ (when available), age and sex of the children, and source of income are presented in Table 5.1 (pp. 74–75).

No case is made for this being a representative sample; there simply are no figures available on the universe of mentally retarded individuals in the role of parent nor the retarded adult in the community. However, the heterogeneity of the sample permits at least preliminary examination of the effects of a number of factors such as marital status, family size, age of the children, and availability of support, on the child-rearing practices of retarded persons.

METHOD

Sample members were located through a variety of sources. Regional Centers, residential facilities, sheltered workshops, social groups, and training programs were contacted; and a pool of potential sample members was identified. These individuals were then approached by the various agencies; an explanation of our research was given; and if interest was shown, permission was asked for them to be contacted by us. Other potential sample members were nominated by individuals already contacted or, in some cases, by their own parents.

Once a potential sample member agreed to become involved in the research, participant observation began. The technique of participant observation allows for the field researcher and sample member to engage in intensive interaction over a prolonged period of time during which discussions take place and observations are made as the sample member engages in various typical activities. Given the constant and long-term nature of the contact, close relationships developed between researcher and sample member, allowing for intimate conversations on a range of topics such as personal feelings, past events, and hopes or fears for the future.

A field researcher was assigned to each sample member, and visits were made approximately once a month. Over the course of the study, these meetings took place in the homes of the sample members as well as in less familiar settings (e.g., a relative's home, a neighborhood park, Disneyland, or a department store) to observe how they handled themselves and their children under different conditions.

Extensive fieldnotes were made after each contact, which serve as a record of the field researcher's observations of the sample member. They provide an account of everyday behaviors and skills as observed over time across different situations and have become extremely detailed, allowing us to examine a number of features, such as parenting practices and self-maintenance skills, of the sample members' lives.

RESULTS AND DISCUSSION

Case study accounts of four family units are presented below. These four families were chosen for intensive description because their lives provide a sense of the range of competence–incompetence displayed by the sample members as they cope with the demands of parenthood. Issues related to adequacy in parenting, which are apparent in these

Table 5.1

Bio-Demographic Data for 13 Families

Sample member	Marital status	Ethnicity	Age	IQ	Residence	Sex & age of Child	Intelligence of children	Source of family income
1. Faith	Married	Caucasian	28	78	Own apt.	M-5 (F-newborn)[c]	IQ = 90	SSI + AFDC + workshop salary
Roy		Mex.-Amer.	32	<69[b]				
2. Marilyn	Married	Caucasian	34	85	With parent	F-4 F-3 F-2	Normal Normal/lang. delayed Normal/lang. delayed	SSI + AFDC + workshop salary
Rich		Caucasian	40	67				
3. Chrissy	Married	Caucasian	35	<69[b]	Own apt.	M-1	Normal	SSI + AFDC + competitive employ.
Lonnie		Caucasian	30	<69[b]				
4. Debbie	Single/married[a]	Black	20	55	With parent/own apt.	M-1	Normal	SSI + AFDC + competitive employ.
Michael		Black	20s	Normal				
5. Ken	Married	Black	24	46	Own apt.	M-2½ M-1½ F-infant	Ment. ret. NA NA	SSI + AFDC + workshop salary
Arlene		Black	26	50				

Name	Marital status	Race	Age	IQ	Residence	Children	Child status	Income
6. Dan	Married	Black	27	55–60	Own apt.	F-2 (F-newborn)[c]	Normal	SSI + AFDC
Laura		Black	24	NA			NA	
7. Manny	Married	Black	22	60	With parent	F-infant	Normal	SSI + AFDC + workshop salary
Stacey		Black	22	<69[b]				
8. Marlinda	Engaged	Black	27	<69[b]	Own apt.	F-infant	Normal	Unemployment ins. + inheritance
Mike		Black	20s	Normal				
9. Alene	Divorced[a]	Black	32	62	Own apt.	F-13	Normal	Competitive employ.
10. Mary	Divorced	Black	31	58	With parent	F-6	Ment. ret.	SSI + AFDC
						F-4	Ment. ret.	
						M-2	NA	
11. Sandy	Single	Black	21	51	With parent	M-5	Ment. ret.	SSI + AFDC
						F-4	Lang. del.	
						M-3	Ment. ret.	
						M-1	NA	
12. Willa	Single	Black	26	69	Own apt.	F-9[d]	Normal	SSI
13. Penny	Divorced[a]	Black	31	63	Board & care	M-10[d]	Ment. ret.	—
						M-NA	Ment. ret.	
						F-NA	Ment. ret.	

[a] Not the natural father.
[b] Official records indicate IQ is below 69.
[c] Data was collected when only one child was present in the home.
[d] Children do not reside with mother.

more detailed accounts, such as judgments of competence by close
family members, the relationship of familial support to those judge-
ments, and the identification of factors related to the maintenance of
a child care environment, will then be clarified further with data from
the remaining families.

Debbie and Michael (Case No. 4)

Debbie, age 20, was first contacted when her son, Danny, was 10
months old. He was born out of wedlock, and the father, a steady boy-
friend, refused to acknowledge Danny as his child. During the pregnancy, Debbie lived with her grandmother and after the birth, with
her parents. While pregnant, she had been concerned that her handicaps—deafness in one ear and mental slowness—might be passed on
to her child. This did not occur.

She recently married Michael, a normal man, who assumed support
of and coresponsibility for Danny. They moved into their own apartment, but the marriage was shakey from the start as he started beating
her and involving himself with another woman. She finally left him
and went back to live with her parents but admitted to feeling bad
about having separated Michael and Danny, who cared strongly for each
other. At last contact, they had reconciled their differences and planned
to move back together.

Debbie has always assumed complete responsibility in caring for
Danny, whether she lived at home with her parents or in an apartment
with Michael. She is, in fact, resentful when others try to interfere and
to give advice without being asked. All those around her acknowledge
that she takes good care of Danny and receives only minimal assistance from family members, mostly in the form of babysitting. She
recognizes that others can be approached for advice and has sought
their assistance when experiencing problems with Danny. For example, her frustration at not being able to toilet train Danny after repeated
tries led her to ask her mother, Michael, and even Michael's boss for
advice. Another problem, Danny's frequent masturbating, was discussed with an experienced aunt when he resisted attempts to discourage the behavior. Her aunt speculated that he might have a rash,
but Debbie checked and, having found none, next sought help from
the doctor.

Debbie has some definite ideas about how she wants to raise Danny.
She pointed out that many people raise their children in the same manner in which they were raised. She, however, intends to improve on

her experience. She described how her father used to beat her for not doing well in school and how she resented him for thinking she wasn't learning because she was lazy. She says, "I'm sure not gonna try to beat any knowledge into Danny when he has trouble in school. I'm gonna take time with him and if I can't, I'm gonna get someone else to tutor him."

She actually puts this philosophy into practice. When she and Michael were in the market buying food for dinner, Debbie wanted to buy eggs for Danny. Michael objected, saying they didn't have enough money and Danny could eat tacos along with them. Debbie argued that she didn't want to feed her baby "junk food," to which Michael responded that there were times when he, as a child, had to eat junk food for breakfast. Debbie insisted that she is "not gonna stand for him to raise Danny like he was raised and that families should always try to do the best they can for their children." When she threatened to go to her mother for eggs, Michael finally consented.

Debbie's ability to think in terms of future outcomes is evident in other areas as well. She currently receives tutoring in reading and math (i.e., learning to count money) and plans to find work when the tutoring ends. She is also one of the few sample members who regularly uses birth control. And although Michael keeps pressuring her to have another child, she is reluctant to do so at this time.

Debbie's biggest concern right now is getting Danny to mind her. She is disturbed that her yelling and spanking have little effect. Nonetheless, she adores her son and shows him a great deal of warmth and affection even when disciplining him. For example, when the field researcher accompanied Debbie and Danny shopping, Debbie was observed to be quite responsive to Danny's needs. When they entered the store he was given a toy from the shelf to play with. As they prepared to leave, the toy was replaced and Danny began crying. Debbie tried comforting him and finally resorted to picking him up and carrying him to the car as she firmly explained, "How come you so bad? You think every time you go into the store you suppose' to get something." After a short while he calmed down and she began playing with him, tickling him, and enjoying his laughter.

Faith and Roy (Case No. 1)

Faith, age 28, and Roy, age 32, have been married for 6 years. They met while working at Goodwill Industries, a sheltered workshop, and married 9 months later against the advice of both sets of parents.

They have always lived in their own apartment and are supported by Social Security Insurance (SSI), Roy's workshop salary, and Aid to Families with Dependent Children (AFDC).

Both Faith and Roy admit to being handicapped, and Faith recognizes that she is the more competent of the two. She has assumed responsibility for managing financial matters and running the household as well as for the maintenance and safety of her four-year-old son, John, and her husband. She is an immaculate housekeeper and prepares all the family meals, being careful to include meat as well as vegetables and starch. Occasionally they eat out, mostly pizza or hot dogs, which is recognized as junk food.

Faith is the primary caretaker of John and she receives only a minimal amount of support from others. Her parents and siblings live out of state as do Roy's parents. Faith remains very close to her family. Her mother was there initially after John's birth to lend a helping hand, and Faith telephones her sister once a week to chat and seek advice.

Faith's formula for raising a child includes two essential ingredients: love and supervision. Children, she feels, must know there are limits and be disciplined if they exceed them; but above all, they must know they are well loved all of the time.

Her handling of John reflects this philosophy. She deals with him in a patient and loving, but firm, manner and is an attentive parent. She takes him to the park regularly, sees that he gets his daily afternoon nap, takes him to children's movies, and carefully watches over him when they are close to traffic. She is careful about planning for his future; when he reached preschool age, she spent time searching for a good school to be paid for by money carefully saved. Having attended private school herself, she was unaware of the possibility of public education from six years and up and so was quite prepared to pay for 13 years of private schooling as well. And in terms of John's development, fearful that Roy's or her handicap might have been passed on, requested that John be evaluated to make sure he was developing normally.

She believes that Roy, on the other hand, does not show enough of an interest in John and that when he does, does not exhibit what she feels to be good qualities in a parent. During an outing with the field researcher to an amusement park, the contrast in parental styles was quite obvious. John had earlier indicated that he wanted cotton candy and had been easily distracted by Faith with a drink and a ride. Later that day, Roy quietly decided he wanted cotton candy and disappeared for a short time only to reappear eating the candy. John immediately became upset, reminded of what he had been diverted from; and Faith glared, overtly disgusted with Roy's action. When an unhappy John approached his father with an open mouth for his share of the candy, Roy reluctantly gave him a taste, which by no means satisfied John.

Faith, by contrast, had indicated throughout the day that she was very attuned to the needs of her son. Without being overprotective, she always knew where he was and made sure that he did not wander off. She reminded him to use the bathroon from time to time and urged him to drink milk rather than coke during lunch. When John played in a playground specially designed for young children, she went in to show him some of the playground equipment he had missed.

John seems to recognize the differential care he receives from each of his parents and gives signs that he is aware of his mother's position of control. For example, he knows he has to mind her and is less likely to mind his father; he has also learned to approach his mother when he needs or wants something.

Roy's desire to have more children had been resisted by Faith for she knew the burden of caring for them would fall on her shoulders. She felt Roy liked the idea of having a lot of kids but had no idea of what was involved in raising them. She wanted to wait until John was old enough to assume some responsibility for caring for himself. When John was five and a half years old, she informed us she had given birth to a baby girl.

Ken and Arlene (Case No. 5)

Ken, age 24, and Arlene, age 26, met in a sheltered workshop and married shortly after Arlene became pregnant. Arlene had given birth to twins before having met Ken but was not allowed custody of them and had had no contact with them since birth. Ken and Arlene now have three children: two boys, Ken, Jr., 2, and Clifford, 1, and an infant daughter, Shannon. They lived with Ken's parents after the marriage and continued to live with them until the third baby was due. Arlene's poor skills in caring for herself, the house, and her family were the main reason for their moving out, as her mother-in-law could no longer tolerate the situation.

Ken's parents still assume the bulk of responsibility for caring for Ken, Arlene, and the children; they handle all their money, depositing their SSI and AFDC payments, paying their bills, doing the major shopping for the family, and until recently, doing the laundry. Arlene assumes most of the housekeeping and childcare responsibility in their own home. Ken does not help much and is considered by both Arlene and his mother to be lazy.

Neither Arlene nor Ken will talk much about their handicaps. Arlene has referred to the teasing she experienced when in school, and Ken also is sensitive to teasing. No reference has been made by either of them to Ken, Jr.'s handicap—he has been diagnosed as retarded— although they do recognize his slowness in comparison to his younger brother.

Ken's mother is concerned that the children are not being well cared for or being provided a very good environment. She feels that Ken, Jr., might not be so slow if he had been raised by someone other than Ken and Arlene. She thinks had they had just one child it would possibly have been all right, but three is too much for them to handle. She has temporarily assumed responsibility for caring for Shannon, at the doctor's suggestion, and will continue to do so until the baby is older and less demanding. She admits that "there's just so much I can do" but hopes at least to make sure that the physical needs of the children are taken care of.

Ken's mother insists that Ken and Arlene really do not know how to discipline their children. Ken makes a lot of threats but takes no action, preferring to defer to Arlene. Arlene resorts to yelling and spanking them, often complaining that her throat is sore from having to yell so much. Her mother-in-law has suggested an alternate method of discipline—sending them to bed if they don't do as they're told— which Arlene has ignored. In general, their discipline tends to be inconsistent and sometimes extreme. For example, for having ripped up his mother's cigarettes that had been lying around, Clifford got his "ass whipped," a beating considered unnecessarily harsh by Ken's sister, who witnessed it.

Most striking about Ken and Arlene is their expectation that others will provide assistance, such as caring for their children, even when they are present. Moreover, they have come to take this support for granted whether it be from family members, friends, or service delivery system personnel. In turn, these extended care-providers fully recognize Ken and Arlene's need for help and their inability to care for themselves or their children and respond with whatever help they can offer. For example, Arlene and the field researcher were seated in the house when Ken, Jr., caught his finger in the door and began shrieking in pain. Arlene remained seated even after the field researcher informed her that his finger, which was in plain view, was still caught in the door. Arlene continued to show no initiative to move and finally the field researcher got up and freed his finger. During another visit, the field researcher, Arlene, and her sister-in-law were out on the porch when Ken's brother came out to strongly suggest that Ken, Jr., who was covered from head to toe with filth and smelling of urine, be bathed. He also pointed out that the boy had a bowel movement in his pants and that if it was not tended to immediately, it might wind up on the carpet. Arlene remained seated and simply replied that he had on rubber pants, which would prevent such an occurrence. At that point, her sister-in-law got up and escorted Ken, Jr., into the house, announcing that she would give him a bath.

Family members other than Ken's parents assume a large role in caring for the children. Ken's two sisters planned to take the two boys to live with them and raise them for a while, presumably to give Arlene a rest. Ken's brother and sister-in-law moved in with Ken and Arlene for a short period to help out and to take a firm hand with the boys. And when Arlene returned to her job at the sheltered workshop, arrangements were made with a cousin to come by every morning to get the two boys ready for nursery school.

At last contact, Ken, Arlene, and the boys had moved out of their home and had returned to live with Ken's parents.

Marilyn and Rich (Case No. 2)

Marilyn, age 34, and Rich, age 40, met while working at a sheltered workshop and married shortly afterward. They moved into Rich's mother's house and have continued to live with her except for a brief period after the birth of their first child. Although Rich's family had advised them not to have children, after five years of marriage they have three daughters, Janice, 4, Marion, 3, and Melody, 2. Rich's mother admits that "they had been able to manage one baby, taking good care of her and keeping up the house, but after the second and then the third, things became more and more difficult for them to handle." After the birth of their third child, Rich was persuaded by Marilyn and his mother to have a vasectomy, an idea he initially resisted because he wanted a son.

Both Marilyn and Rich admit to being slow but reject the label "retarded." Marilyn had been concerned that Marion was slow in talking and so had all three girls evaluated. The assessments revealed normal intelligence, but indicated Marion and Melody were each a few months behind in their language development.

Marilyn is the more capable of the two and assumes most of the responsibility for the girls and the housekeeping. Rich generally eats, sleeps, and works, and when he is home spends most of the time yelling at the girls or being involved with his hobby. Rich's mother shares a lot of the childcare and household responsibilities with Marilyn, including cooking, cleaning, shopping, paying the bills, chauffeuring the family, and tending to the girls' needs. Her efforts, however, are largely unacknowledged by Marilyn, who complains her mother-in-law does not help enough.

The Mormon church is another source of support for Marilyn and Rich. They purchase their food from the bishop's storehouse and members of the church act as handymen, provide transportation, and babysit for the girls. When Rich's mother was out of state for a prolonged period, Marilyn experienced trouble handling the family's bills, and the bishop assumed responsibility.

The major problem that preoccupies the family is getting the children to mind their parents. Things are generally out of control in their home. The children are always running from room to room, fighting over their toys, and creating quite a commotion. All three girls have minds of their own, which is all the more evident as they grow older. Attempts to bring things under control by Rich or Marilyn are usually ineffective. Rich typically begins by requesting that the girls stop what they're doing, then pleads with them, and finally escalates to threatening them. He almost never follows through on any of his threats but occasionally resorts to hitting them. Marilyn usually raises her voice but sometimes, when unable to cope with the situation, locks the girls in their bedroom.

A real fear among family members is that Rich, in desperation, may abuse the children. Marilyn's sister observed during a visit that Rich was much too hard on the girls, yelling and hitting them in a manner too harsh for their age. Rich's mother and Marilyn agree that the children are really too much for Rich and that he does not know how to handle them. Rich, himself, admits that the situation is driving him crazy.

On two different occasions Rich has actually been suspected of child abuse, and the last time the girls were temporarily removed from the house. Rich was so full of remorse he even offered to leave the home, if required, so as to permit the court to return the girls to Marilyn and his mother. The children were eventually returned, and at the court's recommendation, Rich and Marilyn enrolled in counseling at the Children's Institute and in a parent education class at UCLA.

Rich's sister has urged the family to move to Utah, close to her, so she can help manage things. She is concerned that if the girls continue to be raised by Marilyn and Rich "they won't have a chance for a normal life." Rich and Marilyn, after much consideration, rejected her offer, deciding to remain in Los Angeles, independent of her supervision.

Chaos continues in their home and at last contact Rich's mother planned to retire from work in a few weeks and hoped to be around during the day to provide additional support for Marilyn and the girls.

RELATIONSHIP OF FAMILY MEMBERS
TO RETARDED PARENTS

The four families described illustrate the differing levels of awareness and competence in parenting ability possessed by our sample members and the corresponding responsiveness of extended family members to their realized needs.

Debbie, whether single and living with her parents or married and living with Michael, assumed the position of control, making all the decisions pertaining to Danny's care and taking responsibility for seeing things through. Moreover, she displayed a sense of the future, which was evident in her parenting philosophy and her own life goals.

Family members were available when needed and provided assistance when called upon to do so. For example, Debbie was permitted to return to her parent's home when she separated from Michael. While appreciative of the assistance of others, as in the case of toilet training Danny or supporting Danny's need to eat well, Debbie resented any uninvited attempts by others to intervene in her life. She was confident of her ability to take care of her own and Danny's needs and was offended by others' interference, seeing it as lack of confidence in her competence.

Faith also assumed the burden of care for her child as well as her home and did a remarkable job. Her son was well cared for, their home well managed, and their money carefully budgeted. Her husband was recognized as being less competent than she and, therefore, was not expected to share most responsibilities with her. Faith accepted his need to depend on her and realized that she in turn had to do certain things that a husband might normally do.

For the most part, Faith functioned as an independent person who usually handled problems on her own. However, she was not unwilling to seek help when the situation was beyond her ability. She was close with family members, who came to her assistance when called upon. Her mother, while living out of state, came to help when John was born, and her sister provided advice on marital and parental concerns when consulted during weekly phone conversations.

In the cases of Ken and Arlene and Rich and Marilyn, as in that of Faith and Roy, the wives assumed more of the responsibility for the children and the home. In both of these cases, however, the situation was so out of hand that extended family members stepped in to actively help out.

Ken and Arlene's lives were very closely supervised by family members whether they lived on their own or with Ken's parents. They were allowed little autonomy to the extent that even the amount of time spent with friends was regulated by Ken's mother. Relatives were taking care of all their money, their bills, their shopping. Ken's sisters, brother, and cousin aided in the day-to-day care of the boys. And Ken's mother, cognizant of the difficult enough time they were having managing two children, assumed total care of their infant daughter. While aware of their extensive dependence on Ken's family for support in almost every area of their lives, Ken and Arlene showed little initiative to assume more responsibility for their own lives. Rather, they seemed to accept the way things were carried on accordingly.

For Rich and Marilyn, while the management of one child was within their capability, coping with three children, all under the age of five, in addition to the strain of running a household, proved too difficult a load for them to handle. With the presence of Rich's mother, the family seemed to be coping somewhat better. She shared responsibility for some tasks, such as cleaning, cooking, and providing discipline and routine care for the girls, and assumed sole responsibility for other tasks, such as paying the bills. However, even this was not sufficient, and other family members, such as Rich's sister, church members, and service delivery system personnel, recognized the need for additional support and acted to make such assistance available.

The cooperative relationship that evolved between family members and the retarded parents seems to have been determined by the surrounding support systems' assessment of the retarded individual's adequacy in parenting. In all these instances, the extended family has adapted to the perceived needs of the retarded persons. They have their own standards for judging adequacy, which are based on personal, cultural, and social class experience rather than some general normative criteria; and these standards are applied in distinguishing the need to support from the need to intervene. In those homes in which responsibilities were considered satisfactorily handled, minimal support was provided. When incidents arose that warranted additional assistance, for example, Debbie's need to return home after her separation, appropriate accommodations were made. And when the situation necessitated intensive intervention, as in the cases of Ken and Arlene and Rich and Marilyn, extended family members responded accordingly.

Such is the case with other sample members as well. In those extreme cases, when mothers were judged by family members to be incapable of providing adequate care for their children, as with Penny (case no. 13) and Willa (case no. 12), custody was not permitted. Penny's three children, all severely retarded, were immediately institutionalized or placed in foster care. In Willa's case, her parents assumed responsibility for the child and even now after 10 years, dismiss the possibility of Willa ever caring for her.

In those instances in which sample members reside with their parents, even within this supportive environment, differing levels of assistance are perceived necessary and subsequently provided by the parents. In the case of Sandy (case no. 11), her mother assumes most of the responsibility for caring for Sandy and her four children, including handling her money, overseeing the care of the children, and dictating who she can and cannot socialize with. She believes Sandy is a good mother when she wants to be but frequently needs to be reminded to do routine things like dress and feed the children. Her mother has stated that while she hopes Sandy will marry some day, she has no intention of allowing her to take the children with her, as she does not believe she will take proper care of them on her own.

In the case of Mary (case no. 10), her relationship with her mother is somewhat different. While her mother responds to her need for help with financial matters and in making decisions pertaining to her three children, she discourages Mary from being too dependent and tries to minimize the amount of assistance she provides. She intervenes only when Mary has been too lenient or has forgotten to do something with regard to the children (e.g., to give her son his daily dosage of medicine) or shows poor judgment when other people try to take advantage of her. She looks forward to the day when Mary will no longer be a burden to her and wants Mary to return to school to learn more skills to prepare for living on her own.

For some sample members, for instance, Manny and Stacey (case no. 7), the provision of a suitable place to live in their parent's home and assistance in money management are the only areas in which intervention is perceived necessary by the parents and thus provided. Child-care is performed totally by the sample members and is apparently considered sufficient, as no intervention is deemed necessary.

Similarly for sample members living on their own, when specific deficiencies in self-management are detected by family members, assistance is provided. In the case of Alene (case no. 9), her mother recognized the difficulty she was experiencing in handling money and assumed responsibility for managing her banking and paying her bills. The same is true for Dan and Laura (case no. 6). Both their mothers agree they are wasteful and frivolous with what little money they have and on different occasions have had to step in and pay overdue bills and purchase necessities for their grandchildren.

In the case of Chrissy and Lonnie (case no. 3), Chrissy's mother acknowledges that neither are good managers and so has taken over the task of budgeting their money for them. She also visits three or four times a week, drives Chrissy shopping, as she complains of the difficulty of managing groceries and her toddler son on the bus, and is available for the numerous phone calls she receives from Chrissy or Lonnie seeking advice. Nonetheless, the mother views Chrissy and Lonnie as capable, attentive parents and contends that if they were not, she would immediately assume responsibility for her grandson's care.

And finally for Marlinda (case no. 8), who like Faith and Debbie is considered resourceful and self-sufficient, family members respect her independence and are available for companionship and occasional advice.

FACTORS RELATED TO PROVISION OF ADEQUATE CHILDCARE

It remains now to identify the factors that are related to the ability of these retarded individuals to cope with the responsibility of parenthood as well as the factors that influence judgments of adequacy by close family members.

While the relative intelligence level of the retarded person might be assumed to be a contributing factor, our data do not support this notion. The IQs of the three mothers who were denied custody of their newborns, Arlene, Willa, and Penny, ranged from 50 to 69. Moreover, Faith, whose IQ was 78, and Debbie, with an IQ of 55, were viewed as managing admirably, while Marilyn, who scored 85, and Arlene, whose IQ was 50, were seen as incapable of coping with their situation.

Family size and birth spacing seemed to account for some of the ease or difficulty experienced by our parents. In those homes in which one child was present, parents were able to handle the routine care of their child with a minimal amount of assistance. When a second child was expected, grandparents expressed concern as to what effect this additional burden would have on their retarded children's parenting skills as in the case of Dan and Laura. Both Debbie and Faith were aware of the amount of work involved in raising a child and so wisely planned to allow a sufficient amount of time to pass before considering a second pregnancy.

In those homes in which three or four children very close in age were being reared, extensive intervention by grandparents was a necessity. In all these instances, while the grandparents recognized their retarded child's desire for a child and thought they could possibly handle the responsibility for one child, all were concerned over the multiple pregnancies, especially so closely spaced. Sandy's mother had suggested a tubal ligation after the first child, and again after the second and third; sterilization was finally arranged after the fourth child was delivered. In the case of Rich and Marilyn, both Rich's mother and Marilyn realized three children were enough, if not too much, for the couple to handle and encouraged Rich's vasectomy. Arlene's and Mary's family also insisted that three was enough, and tubal ligations were subsequently performed.

Finally, a most crucial element to the success of these individuals appears to be the willingness and sensitivity of their parents to react to the demonstrated or perceived needs of their retarded offspring and grandchildren. By carefully matching assistance with need, specifically in those areas that warrant intervention, the parents are able to ensure that both their retarded offspring and grandchildren will be maintained at an acceptable level of adequacy. Judgments as to needs are based on implicit standards that the family members have developed from cultural and/or social class experience, which serves as mechanisms for judging behavior as falling within or outside what they consider to be an acceptable range.

The result is a pattern of the assumption of responsibility by grandparents that parallels the informal adoption observed in other societies, for instance, in Polynesia (Gallimore, Boggs, & Jordan, 1974; Levy, 1973) and among blacks in some American samples (e.g., Stack, 1974). In Tahiti and Hawaii it is quite common for members of the extended kin, as well as nonrelated families, to take full or partial responsibility for the rearing of children. Typically this occurs when a child is born to adolescent parents who may or may not be legally married and who either will not or cannot assume responsibility for parenting. In Hawaii this may range from a change of residence for the infant or child to the taking up of residence by the mother, child, and sometimes the father in the grandparent's home. The variations in support by parents and grandparents are as diverse as those described by the retarded parents in our sample.

Just as in the case of the retarded families, the most typical pattern in these Hawaiian households is the assumption by grandparents of primary responsibility for functions, such as the provision of resources and shelter, with more or less responsibility for tasks, such as routine childcare, being assumed by the parents. In Hawaii, this division of responsibility represents a kind of parenting apprenticeship with the as-yet-unprepared parent gradually assuming more responsibilities.

We cannot, of course, draw a full analogy between the informal adoption in Polynesia and the circumstances of our urban families. However, though many Hawaiian grandparents may complain about the irresponsibility of their children as parents (usually the inability of the young fathers to provide a stable income), they have considerable hope that maturity will come eventually; and so it does, often in the late twenties for the males and early twenties for the females. Our data are too limited and the grandchildren too young for us to know yet whether the struggles of the grandparents and parents will lead to more self-sustaining households; although in at least one case, Alene's, this sequence of events did occur, resulting in Alene and her daughter's move out of the grandparent's home to a more self-sustaining situation. At present, only minimal support in the form of money management and babysitting is necessary from the grandparents. It is probably the case that for some families, the progression to independence will be possible; in others it seems the solution will be continued support; and in the extreme situations, as the children mature and more difficult management problems are posed, the separation of the children from their parents may be the only alternative.

ACCOMMODATIONS TO RETARDED PARENTS: A COMPARATIVE PERSPECTIVE

The adaptations seen in our sample are unremarkable when framed in a wider cultural perspective. Extended family interdependence and shared child care support are the norm as well as a sign of strength in most societies throughout the world. For the Polynesians, shared interdependence and shared function are a sign of maturity and success, while independence from family members is perceived as a sign of trouble (Gallimore, Boggs, & Jordan, 1974). It is only the context of contemporary American life, with its normative pattern of nuclear, socially, and familially isolated households, that the sometimes extensive involvement of the grandparents draws so much attention. Indeed, millions of nonretarded parents of young children in America might well envy those families whose ecologies provide for shared caretaking—a system that can support work roles of women as well as men, provide relief from daily burdens, provide consultation on child-care questions, and insure a reliable backup during times of hardship or crisis. The retarded parents may be considered fortunate in being ahead of the "culturally deprived" nonretarded counterparts, since they occupy an ecological niche that includes shared caretaking.

Most other non-Western societies would not consider our retarded parents' need for support in child care to be deviant or a sign of dependence. Rather, the kinds of ecological and subsistence pressures that trouble these retarded parents are more likely to be seen as (1) events beyond the personal control of parents and families, (2) contrasts that in any case are unrelated to self-esteem and self-worth, and (3) circumstances of family life that children can participate in amelioriating as helpers, rather than as life problems from which children are to be sheltered. In short, it is the requirements of the larger eco–cultural niche surrounding these retarded parents (time-boundedness, separated housing, etc.) that make requirements for support so problematic and troubling in the eyes of others.

The benefactors of the retarded parents (grandparents, siblings, neighbors) do not get involved in every area of the parents' lives. They appear to concern themselves selectively with certain domains and certain times of the day, week, or month more than others. The benefactors selectively mediate between the larger eco–cultural niche and the retarded parents and their children. We can better understand how effective intervention can work in the natural environment by examining these patterns and relating them to parental resources and children's ages.

We can start by contrasting different needs of retarded parents affected by their niche: (1) survival needs, such as minimum requirements for shelter, subsistence, health, and defense and security ("minimum" being open to some debate); (2) child caretaking and childcare task support needs, such as the need for personnel to help parents and to give concrete aid in the specific tasks of child rearing; and (3) the need for quality of child care, that is, provision of social–emotional support and cultural and intellectual advice on how the structure or pattern of life should be carried out. These domains are also represented in current theories of the role of childhood social ecology in influencing development; these models specify family pressures affecting survival, tasks and routines, and beliefs and ideals implemented by families during social interactions with their children (Weisner, 1984). These different levels of environmental influence require different kinds of benefactor support—differently timed, structured, and available for use.

Need I

Implementation of benefactor support occurs most often for survival and maintenance needs, next for childcare task supports and management, and last for the quality of and styles of interaction with children. One reason for this pattern is that maintenance tasks are necessary but not sufficient for quality childcare to occur at all, and retarded persons living in the community are often in difficulty precisely in this area of subsistence. Coping with money, budgets, time-contingent events, or tasks requiring literacy is not easy for retarded adults. Having children vastly complicates these already problematic matters.

Why is this a difficult area for the retarded adult? Because survival skills in our particular ecology require more developed memory abilities cued by abstract signs or by time; the ability to self-manage complex sequences of behavior; skill at planning and managing staged contingent series of events; an understanding of implicit, covert social norms concerning public behavior that need to be quickly recalled by often subtle situation cues; and at least a minimum level of literacy. All these metacognitive abilities are inherent in managing money, making sure that schedules involving outside agencies are kept, untangling bureaucratic misunderstandings, planning for nonroutine events in or out of the home, and so on; these tasks are difficult for retarded individuals to perform.

Our data indicate that all the retarded parents have help in at least some survival needs that have an impact on their family functioning: housing, food, money management, safety in travel, scheduling of events such as school and medical appointments, and so forth. Grandparents are almost always deeply involved in this kind of assistance. Indeed, it may well be that those families available to us for observation have remained intact because of the provision of aid in survival skills, while other families that either have lost or were never permitted custody of their children might have been able to provide adequate child care if critical assistance for survival needs had been available.

Need II

Given that subsistence and survival needs are met through benefactor and parent actions, direct support for childcare-related tasks can then at least be attempted. The most effective method for implementing support for retarded parents in our sample appears to be the provision of appropriate personnel at those points in the daily or weekly schedule when one or more of three events occur: (1) caretaking tasks are directly linked to survival pressures impinging on the family, (2) childcare tasks require self-managed strategic thinking or the organization of staged behavioral sequences, (3) coordination among several family members and their roles is needed. Such activities require a degree of reflectivity and empathy for others' roles as well as pragmatic planning skills (contingent on the plans of others). Many of these retarded parents have difficulties with such activities; for instance, (a) if parents run out of funds early in the month, their children may run out of needed food, diapers, and bus fares, babysitters or nursery schools may remain unpaid, and so on; (b) if parents have to plan ahead for their own and their childrens' schedules: one child must be ready at 8:00 for school, another is picked up at 9:15 except on Tuesday; one needs lunches prepared, the other does not; (c) if child care arrangements have to be made in advance or if help will not be there when parents thought it would be. The integration of different family members' routines with the requirements of institutions and others' schedules appears to be an area where benefactors and aid is typically needed. Parents themselves are often puzzled over how they have divided tasks relating to childcare and do not agree or cannot remember what they have agreed on or discussed in a different context. However, with guidance and available support at the right times, they can share these functions quite well—finish their chores, get their child to school on time, recall when their spouses will be home, and remember the bus schedule—in one sequence of events.

Need III

Finally, we come to the content of specific interactional styles within the family circle. How are children to be disciplined? Over what matters? When and at what ages? In how loud a voice and how consistently? How much television should children watch? What can and cannot be said around children? How clean should they be? Which parent should do what jobs and what should be the division of labor? Should boys be treated differently than girls? We observe that the families in our sample have handled these and the many other matters of how to relate to their children, in varied ways. We also observe that with a few exceptions, they appear, so far, to have done so in ways that have not harmed their children. We would predict this, given that needs I and II are met, that is, the parents and child have appropriate survival and management aids.

Few of our parents appear to have required extensive interventions into their styles of interaction with their children. They do hear comments and criticism and ask questions themselves. But the consistent, regular benefactor interventions required for the survival and childcare aspects of parenting are not repeated at the level of interactional styles. For these kinds of families, then, we hypothesize that continuous, direct tuition and intervention is not generally required.

Our parents appeared to have learned to respond to their children and to have adjusted their behavior as their children grew older, by using immediate models and cues, observational learning, and direct reinforcement from their children. Their children learned and adjusted in the same ways. Complex memory skills, elaborate planfulness, and literacy do not seem to be required to meet these immediate, moment-to-moment, day-to-day demands of social life within the family circle. Evolved adaptive skills of both children and parents can come into play to mutually reinforce some appropriate behaviors and discourage others. For example, child activity and hunger reciprocally interact with parent food preparation and meal organization. Such reciprocal interaction effects serve to establish boundaries around a potentially wide behavioral range and shape the retarded parents' responsiveness to their children in reasonably appropriate ways.

These parents are best able to parent in a local, controlled context with familiar cues from children, spouses, and helpers, with a minimum of situational ambiguity and variability, and without accompanying overt or implied messages labeling them as incompetent or in need of direct retraining and aid in these most personal areas of life. It appears that most of the benefactors have consciously or unconsciously followed many of the implications of this view; they provide security and caretaking aid but without the accompanying provision of direct training and intervention into the content of child rearing and interaction.

CONCLUSION

The lessons of the kind of contextualized and nondemeaning assistance described in this chapter should be carefully reviewed by those in the service delivery system whose goal it is to serve this population. At least for those families who receive support and assistance from grandparents and other family members, policies should be developed that allow service providers to be more responsive to the already-existing support system. Rather than providing an across-the-board, middle-class–oriented parent education program, which may only interfere with the well-functioning, adaptive family support system, the delivery of services should be matched to survival and managerial needs (e.g., provide personnel for respite for the grandparents and money allotments for grandparents who offer shelter). In many cases, family members already have targeted problem areas and have experimented with various solutions to insure that survival and childcare needs are met. For example, in the case of Ken and Arlene, Ken's parents first had Ken and Arlene reside in their home, then had Ken's brother and his wife live with Ken and Arlene, and finally arranged for a cousin to be present for the morning routine; these all were attempts to find a viable solution. It is time for the service delivery system to recognize the resourcefulness of the family and to begin looking to them as innovators.

The principle of normalization has led to the encouragement of mentally retarded adults to behave in a culturally normative manner. This includes the possibility of marriage, which is perceived by these adults as a meaningful status achievement, as well as parenthood, which also is viewed as a desirable social role. Our data, as others have noted before, attest to the heterogeneity in parenting competence present in this population. In some cases, family units manage quite well on their own, and extended family members remain passively in reserve. In other situations, an active unity of management is required by grandparents and retarded parents to maintain an adequate childcare environment. These data are evidence of remarkably diverse levels of ability and should give pause to those who argue for either the blanket right or the absolute denial of the right of retarded persons to have families. Rather, it is a decision to be made, at least in part, by extended family members, based on their knowledge of the retarded individual's past need for support and their anticipation of and willingness for continued involvement.

While we have primarily attempted to identify (1) whether the childrearing practices of retarded parents are judged satisfactory by extended family members, and (2) what factors are related to the maintenance of an adequate childcare environment, other questions, pertaining to outcome, still remain unanswered. For the most part, our sample members' children are quire young; and little can be said as yet about the long-term effects of parenting by retarded persons—on the child, on the retarded individual, or on extended family members. As the children mature and present more and more difficult management problems, will extended family members continue to be supportive? What effect will the sharing of childcare responsibilities have on the developing child? What will be the effect of a household dominated by grandparents and other family members? Our data show that in at least one family, the grandparent is concerned because the children tend not to pay attention to their mother since they have overheard family members describe her as "being slow and different."

There are also ethnic differences evident within even our small sample, which warrant further investigation. Preliminary data indicate that white families are more likely to prejudge their retarded offspring as being incapable of parenting and to insist that either sterilization be a prerequisite for marriage or that an abortion be performed if conception occurs. Those white retarded adults who manage to have children are generally married, in their late 20s or 30s and less tied into a family support system. Black families, on the other hand, are more likely to welcome the first grandchild and tend to become involved in the internal affairs of their retarded child only after a grandchild is born. These births tend to occur when the retarded mother is unmarried, in her teens, and living at home with family members. And most striking, while white grandparents fear being burdened by the care of their grandchild, black grandparents appear hopeful that the grandchild, when older, may in turn provide support for the retarded parent.

REFERENCES

Bass, M. S. Marriage, parenthood and prevention of pregnancy. *American Journal of Mental Deficiency*, 1963, 68, 318–333.
Gallimore, R., Boggs, J., & Jordan, C. *Culture, behavior, and education: A study of Hawaiian–Americans*. Beverly Hills: Sage Publications, 1974.
Hall, J. E. Sexual behavior. In J. Wortis (Ed.), *Mental retardation: An annual review* (Vol. 6). New York: Brunner/Mazel, 1974.
Johnson, O. R. *Mildly retarded adults as parents*. Paper presented at the 89th Annual Convention of the American Psychological Association, Los Angeles, CA, August, 1981.
Johnson, W. R. Sex education and the mentally retarded. *Journal of Sex Research*, 1969, 5, 179–185.
Kernan, K. T., Turner, J. L., Langness, L. L., & Edgerton, R. B. *Issues in the community adaptation of mildly retarded adults*. Working Paper No. 4, Socio-Behavioral Group, Mental Retardation Research Center, School of Medicine, University of California, Los Angeles, 1978.
Koegel, P., & Whittemore, R. D. Sexuality in the ongoing lives of mildly retarded adults. In A. Craft & M. Craft (Eds.), *A review of sex education and counselling for mentally handicapped people*. Baltimore, MD: University Park Press, 1983.
Levy, R. *The Tahitians: Mind and experience in the Society Islands*. Chicago: University of Chicago Press, 1973.

Mickelson, P. The feebleminded parent: A study of 90 family cases. *American Journal of Mental Deficiency,* 1947, *51,* 644–653.

President's Committee on Mental Retardation. *People live in houses: Profiles of community residences for retarded children and adults.* Washington, DC: U.S. Government Printing Office, 1976.

Scally, B. G. Marriage and mental handicaps: Some observations in Northern Ireland. In F. F. de la Cruz and G. D. LaVeck (Eds.), *Human sexuality and the mentally retarded.* New York: Brunner/Mazel, 1973.

Stack, C. B. *All our kin: Strategies for survival in a black community.* New York: Harper & Row, 1974.

Vygotsky, L. S. *Mind in society: The development of higher psychological processes* (M. Cole, V. John-Steiner, S. Scribner, & E. Souberman, Eds.). Cambridge, MA: Harvard University Press, 1978.

Weisner, T. S. The social ecology of childhood: A cross-cultural view. In M. Lewis & L. Rosenblum (Eds.), *Social connections beyond the dyad.* New York: Plenum Press, 1984.

Whittemore, R. D., & Koegel, P. *Loving alone is not helpful: Sexuality and social context among the mildly retarded.* Working Paper No. 7, Socio-Behavioral Group, Mental Retardation Research Center, School of Medicine, University of California, Los Angeles, 1978.

Winik, L. *The mildly retarded as parents: A description and explication of the parenting practices of two mildly retarded couples.* Unpublished master's thesis, University of California, Los Angeles, 1981.

Wolfensberger, W. *The principle of normalization in human services.* Toronto: National Institute on Mental Retardation, 1972.

6

Parents with Insulin-Dependent Diabetes: Impact on Child and Family Development *

HELEN KORNBLUM and BARBARA J. ANDERSON

It is now recognized that insulin-dependent *diabetes mellitus* (IDDM or Type I diabetes) influences the tasks of normal human development throughout the lifecycle (Hamburg & Inoff, 1983). There is increasing empirical study of the impact of this serious chronic illness and its complex treatment on diabetic children and their families (Anderson & Auslander, 1980). The influence of diabetes in the parent on child and family development, however, has been virtually unexamined. In this chapter we provide a brief overview of IDDM and its treatment. Second, we discuss background and rationale for our exploratory study of parents with diabetes. Disease-related factors that have an impact on the developmental tasks of these diabetic parents are presented. Finally, we identify five areas in which diabetes significantly affects families: decisions about having children, spouse roles, psychological development of young children, interactions with extended family, and resources outside the family.

*The authors express their gratitude to Dr. Julio Santiago, who was generous with his time in discussing this project and who helped us secure parents for interviews. We also appreciate Karen Flavin, R. N., and Norma Finkelstein, M.S.W., who discussed substantive issues with us and helped identify parents for interviews. A special acknowledgement is extended to the parents who took time to talk with us so thoughtfully about their personal experiences and their families.

INSULIN-DEPENDENT *DIABETES MELLITUS*

Diabetes is a chronic disease characterized by impaired metabolism of food and by high blood sugar levels. This results from either a complete or a relative deficiency of insulin, a hormone produced by the pancreas and needed to metabolize the food we eat. Diabetes is an inherited disorder, although the exact inheritance patterns are not fully understood. There are two distinctly different forms of diabetes, which are often confused. In this chapter we focus on adults with insulin-dependent or Type I diabetes. This form of the disease is often called juvenile-onset diabetes because most individuals are diagnosed during childhood. Persons with Type I diabetes produce none or very little of their own insulin and must depend on daily insulin injections for life. Young parents with diabetes will most likely have this form of the disease. In the other major form of diabetes (non–insulin-dependent, Type II, or adult-onset diabetes) the pancreas produces some insulin. Therefore, the disease can often be controlled by diet and exercise without daily insulin injections.

Diabetes mellitus affects 10 million Americans and their families. About 5% of the population have been diagnosed as having diabetes, and the incidence appears to be increasing by 6% each year (Third Annual Report of the National Diabetes Advisory Board, 1980). Currently, there is no cure for the disease. Present forms of medical therapy are not able to prevent the serious long-term complications of diabetes, which affect the blood vessels, heart, kidneys, eyes, and nerves. However, there is increasing evidence to suggest that if the person with diabetes maintains blood sugar levels near normal, these complications may be delayed or prevented.

In addition to progressive long-term health risks, diabetic individuals taking insulin face the daily threat of acute metabolic crises. The tools for controlling diabetes are imperfect and cannot duplicate the precision with which the pancreas regulates blood sugar levels. Therefore, persons with insulin-dependent diabetes walk a tightrope, balancing between high and low blood sugar levels. This balance is achieved through a complex therapeutic regimen, the cornerstones of which are one or more insulin injections daily, a calculated meal plan coordinated closely with injections, exercise, and monitoring blood sugar levels through urine or blood tests. This complex treatment regimen affects the most basic components of daily life: food, activity, and time (Benoliel, 1975), and often conflicts with family routines. Finally, because stress influences blood sugar control, and blood sugar levels, in turn, influence emotional equilibrium, the diabetic individual must cope with a complex feedback cycle between physical and psychological states.

COPING BY DIABETIC PARENTS:
AN EXPLORATORY STUDY

There is increasing evidence that family interactions are closely related to the psychological and physical functioning of insulin-dependent diabetic children. The pioneering studies in this area were carried out by Baker, Minuchin, and Rosman in Philadelphia (e.g., Baker & Barcai, 1970). These investigators used a systems perspective to study reciprocal influences between physiologic responses of the diabetic child and specific family interactions. They concluded that the family's organizational style and patterns of interaction can contribute to physiological changes in some diabetic children. Likewise, the diabetic child exerts a strong influence on the family. The model of the family that is gaining acceptance in research on diabetic children is an interactive system in which both the child and other family members continually modify each other's behavior and influence the course of treatment (Anderson & Auslander, 1980).

Research with diabetic adults, however, has not focused on the impact of a diabetic parent on the family environment. Previous studies with diabetic adults have been extremely one-dimensional, focusing on deviant psychological consequences of having diabetes. This focus on pathological emotional responses to the disease and its management have often been undertaken in an attempt to identify a "diabetic personality." In their review of this research, Dunn and Turtle (1981) point out substantial methodological problems in these studies and provide clear evidence that a consistent psychological response to this disease—or the diabetic personality—is a myth. Research in the past has been concerned with extreme adjustment problems rather than with how the diabetic adult copes with other developmental tasks, such as becoming a parent and raising children.

Because there has been so little discussion of the impact of the parent's diabetes on the family environment of young children, we carried out a pilot study of 12 families with young children in which either the mother or father had Type I diabetes. We interviewed diabetic parents who received their medical care at Washington University Medical Center in St. Louis concerning how diabetes affects the roles, rules, and relationships in their families. Five themes were consistently raised during these interviews: decisions about having children, spouse roles, children's development and the parent–child relationship, interactions with extended family, and resources outside the family. Before discussing these five areas, we identify two disease-related factors— the age at which the parent was diagnosed as having diabetes and individual differences in disease severity—which had a significant impact on the major coping areas for these parents.

As a caveat, we want to emphasize that we are reporting examples from our interviews to illustrate the variability in the experiences of these diabetic parents. Above all, we want to point out that these are not pathological homes nor unhappy, disturbed families. But these parents are ones who must cope realistically with a tremendously difficult challenge as they incorporate diabetes into their roles as parents. Their strength and resiliency, especially in light of the limited supportive or counseling resources available to them, are impressive.

Parental Age at Diagnosis

When did the parent develop diabetes? What was the family situation at the time of diagnosis? First, it is important to consider the parent's age at diagnosis and the related issue of disease duration as they affect the parent's physical health. Epidemiological evidence indicates that, in general, the longer a person has lived with diabetes, the greater the risk of physical problems. A 30-year-old diabetic woman who has had diabetes for 20 years likely faces more serious consequences to her own health from the physical stress of pregnancy than does a 30-year-old woman who has had diabetes for only four years. The issue of shortened life expectancy was grappled with by all of the parents we spoke with. For example, one young father, who has lived with diabetes for 19 years, spoke eloquently about his concerns that he might not be able to support his family in the years ahead and that he might die while his son was still a child.

There is a second, more psychological consideration with respect to the parent's age at diagnosis. Whether or not the diabetes was diagnosed before or after a marriage, or prior to or following the decision to have a child, affects the parents' reactions to the disease, to each other, and to their children. One young mother who was diagnosed shortly before becoming pregnant emphasized how important it was to her that people not think that the pregnancy triggered the diabetes, as does happen with a particular form of the disease called gestational diabetes. She wanted it to be understood that the diabetes came first, then the pregnancy. It was foremost in her mind that others know that her child was not responsible for her diabetes. In contrast, another mother developed diabetes after her two children were in elementary school. Because she was diagnosed after her children were born, she was never able to consider ahead of time what it might mean to be a parent with a serious chronic illness. The time in the life cycle at which the diagnosis occurs has important physical and psychological implications for the parent and therefore, has an impact on relationships in the family.

Differences in Severity and Treatment of Diabetes

The diabetic person's level of metabolic control, which is influenced by how severe the illness is and how well the disease is managed, exerts a constant influence on diabetic parents and their families. Earlier we pointed out that blood sugar levels affect emotions and, vice versa, that stress and emotional states affect the control of blood sugar. The diabetic parent's metabolic control also affects number of acute physical symptoms and medical emergencies, which often have a direct impact on the children and spouse.

Parents with diabetes often follow different medical treatment regimens. Such treatment variations depend on differences among physicians who care for diabetic patients, as well as on patient differences with respect to knowledge, motivation to maintain good metabolic control, and resources for managing this disease. Some parents may follow a regimen that requires one daily injection of insulin; others may take two or three daily injections while others may wear a portable, insulin pump programmed for continuous delivery of insulin. With respect to monitoring blood sugar levels, some parents rely on urine testing, while others test their blood by fingersticks and reading the glucose content with the aid of blood glucose monitoring equipment.

Furthermore, some diabetic individuals will immediately suffer severe symptoms of low blood sugar if they deviate from a planned meal schedule, while others have more flexibility in their timing of meals. One father reported to us that when he urgently needs to eat supper on time and his family is slow to come to the table, he screams at them because of irritability from low blood sugar. Another parent usually handles this problem of delayed meals by changing her planned dinner and having a quick snack. These differences in obtrusiveness of symptoms and flexibility of diabetes treatment requirements affect many aspects of the family's interactions and routines.

Decisions about Having Children

Diabetes influences the experiences of pregnancy, childbirth, and family planning in several ways. First, there are several medical realities that diabetic parents must face. Genetic counseling is important for diabetic adults who are considering having a child but sometimes may also be frustrating because the complex inheritance patterns of diabetes are still not well understood. In addition, contraception options may be limited for the woman with diabetes. For example, birth control pills or the IUD may put some diabetic women at increased medical risk. Also, impotence is one of the long-term physical complications that may affect diabetic men.

There are several psychological aspects of family planning and pregnancy that diabetic parents must confront. Parents we spoke with had three major concerns: (1) that the physiological stress of pregnancy would jeopardize the diabetic mother's long-term health and the health of the newborn; (2) that parents may not live long enough to see their children grow up or that they may be in poor health, unable to provide for their children (and, in fact, dependent on their children for support); and (3) that the child would develop diabetes. Some adults with diabetes decide not to have children because of these very serious considerations (Ahlfield & Soler, 1983). The parents in our study already had at least one child, but several spoke of limiting their family size or of choosing to adopt additional children. Others talked about the apprehension around their decision to have more children. As one young woman told us, "I want to get pregnant—but I'm scared."

Pregnancy often makes it extremely difficult to control the blood sugar levels of a diabetic woman, and well-controlled blood sugar levels are crucial for the health of the baby. Until the last decade, diabetic women faced increased risks of prolonged hospitalizations to control their blood sugar during pregnancy, of spontaneous miscarriages, of a Cesarean delivery due to the large size of the baby, or of a newborn with congenital anomalies or metabolic problems. However, recent treatment advances, such as the portable insulin infusion pump and blood sugar monitors for the home, have increased the woman's ability to keep blood sugars near normal throughout pregnancy. Thus, while diabetes still represents a high-risk pregnancy, the prognosis for having a healthy newborn is greatly increased if the woman follows a strict management plan during pregnancy. Therefore, this may be a particularly stressful pregnancy, in which the woman is expected to exert a great deal of control over its course but is also a victim of her metabolism and as yet imperfect therapeutic tools (Merkatz, Budd, & Merkatz, 1979).

The second psychological concern affecting childbearing decisions is that the parent may have health complications or a shortened lifespan, which will not allow the fulfillment of the parental role. One diabetic father stated that his major fear was of reduced life expectancy and that he felt he "may spoil my child, not knowing how long I'll be around." Another father with diabetes reported that he began to take better care of himself and follow his treatment plan more conscientiously when his baby was born because he "wants to live longer for my son." A diabetic woman with a toddler indicated she felt she really pushed the development of independence in her child out of fear that he might have to take care of himself sooner than expected. The birth of a child makes most parents more aware of their own mortality. For diabetic parents, the birth of a child acutely underscores the possible long-term serious health consequences of their disease.

A third concern affecting diabetic parents is the fear that their child will develop diabetes. It should be pointed out that none of the parents interviewed had a child who had developed diabetes. But many parents voiced deep apprehension of this happening. For example, although knowing that diet does not cause diabetes, several mothers reported that they closely watch what their children eat and restrict their intake of sweets. In contrast, one diabetic mother bakes frequently and says that she wants her children to "eat while they can," as if their days as nondiabetic children were numbered. One of the fathers we spoke with told us that he knows that the fear that his only child will develop diabetes affects his interactions with her, that he tends to spoil her or treat her as more special. Another father with one child reported that he wants another child, but his fears that the second child may have diabetes will likely cause him to limit his family. A man who developed diabetes after his children were born indicated he will worry until his children pass their early 20s, the age he was when he was diagnosed. Yet this father was also aware that, realistically, his children could develop the disease at any age. Only one parent, who was also the only person interviewed who was seriously disabled by diabetic retinopathy, denied that she worried about one of her children developing diabetes. It is clear that the guilt and fear of passing on a serious

inherited disorder to their children are perhaps the most difficult issues with which many of these parents must cope.

Impact on the Husband–Wife Relationship

Concerning the impact of diabetes on spouse roles and relationships,
two themes were repeatedly raised by parents: (1) The uncontrollable
moodiness and irritability that occur when the parent's blood sugar
level is low affect other family members, and (2) The diabetic parent's
constant additional responsibility for self-care frequently conflicts with
the needs of other family members. Many parents reported that the
irritability associated with low blood sugar episodes took its toll on
family interactions and was perhaps hardest on the spouse. Every parent mentioned that their spouse's understanding and support were extremely important. As one father put it, "Most spouses understand this
diabetes-related moodiness or else they get divorced, yet the spouse
may still feel it personally at the time."

A related aspect of diabetes influencing family relationships is the
additional responsibility for self-care that must be incorporated into
the diabetic adult's roles of spouse and parent. It may be difficult for
the diabetic parent, especially for a parent providing primary care for
young children, to carry out child-rearing responsibilities if he or she
is often sick or in need of hospitalization. In such cases, the spouse
must assume additional responsibility or other caregivers must be se-
cured. Also, responsibility for daily self-care may at times be transferred to the spouse. Some spouses are directly involved in the
treatment plan of the diabetic parent, helping with injections and blood
testing. Other spouses are more indirectly involved in the planning and
scheduling demands of their diabetic spouse. Parents often reported
family disputes surrounding food and scheduling, two critical aspects
of diabetes care and also two areas in which other family members may
have needs that conflict with those of the diabetic parent.

The financial demands of diabetes for medical fees, insulin and other
supplies, and certain foods placed a burden on some marital relationships. In several families, these financial concerns are compounded
when the diabetic parent loses time from work or experiences discrimination in the workplace. Ahlfeld and Soler (1983) reported that more
diabetic women than men reported that the disease caused financial
hardships. Hamburg and Inoff (1983) have suggested that economic
strains from diabetes are often underestimated and can make the tran-

sition into marriage an especially stressful one for some diabetic adults and their spouses.

Clearly spouses of diabetic parents play a key role in the medical treatment and the psychological adaptation of their spouses to this disease. Research that incorporates the perspectives of *both* the diabetic parent *and* the spouse is needed to fill the gap in our understanding of the critical role played by the marital dyad in family adjustment to a diabetic parent.

Impact on the Developing Child and Parent–Child Relationship

Another issue concerns the psychological responses of children with a diabetic parent. An assessment of the child is essential in addressing this question, and we have not yet carried out any child assessments in our preliminary work. However, responses from the parent interviews suggested several issues that may be important for the psychological development of young children. First, in response to our specific question, many parents believed that diabetes did not have any special impact on their children. Nor did they indicate that their children might have a special need for information, which would change at different ages. There was a general tendency to downplay the psychological impact on the child and to assume that children easily accept diabetes as being "just part of Mom."

All of the parents we interviewed reported they were very open about injections and insulin pumps, diet restrictions, and urine and blood glucose testing in the home. Yet certainly for very young children, issues of bodily injury and illness are salient, and it would be important to explain injections and blood tests in developmentally appropriate ways. One mother who was already experiencing retinopathy reported that her children "don't ask questions, they just know I have blood tests, use no sugar in my diet, and give myself shots. Nothing phases my kids as long as I'm here. Diabetic retinopathy is too big to explain to them." Clearly, many parents (and health care providers) assume that because children do not *ask* questions, they do not *have* questions or a need for information about diabetes.

A second and related aspect of children's psychological responses concerns possible fears: fear of abandonment triggered by acute symptoms or hospitalizations, fear of parental disability or death, fear that this disease will happen to them. One woman reported that her teenage daughter was very anxious that her mother would become blind. This mother, who was afraid of the corrective surgical procedure that had been recommended as treatment, was refusing to undergo eye surgery. Another mother said that her young daughter once expressed fear of the mother's dying. Writing about children's reactions to parental illness. McCollum (1981) has stated:

> Children of ill parents struggle with worrisome questions: What is wrong with mommy, daddy? Will she get worse? Could it happen to me too? Is it my fault? Young children construct their own theories to account for illness; they frequently believe that it is the consequence of their own "bad" words, thoughts, or deeds. Older children, though often more realistic, struggle with feelings of sadness, guilt, helplessness, fear, or resentment when a parent is ill. (p.187)

The responsibility issues we discussed earlier may also have a psychological impact on the child. Children may come to feel very responsible for their parent's well-being, especially those children who are actively involved in the parent's treatment regimen. This may induce resentment in children, which is quite realistic because these children are frequently asked to compromise their needs and to consider the parent's health needs first. Children also have to confront the fact that they may inherit this disease, and this is bound to stir up strong feelings. Children have to deal with the fact that their parent is "different." This would be a complicating factor, especially during periods such as early adolescence when children have difficulty "being different."

Diabetes in a parent may also be associated with positive consequences in children's development. With respect to chronic illness in general, Rutter (1966) has suggested "not all parental illnesses lead to deviant development in the children, nor, when there are harmful conquences, are all children equally affected" (p.106). Children of diabetic parents have the potential opportunity to learn lessons about sensitivity to others and about family interdependence firsthand. Until the needed research is carried out, we can only speculate as to the range of positive and negative contributions to the child's psychological development resulting from having a diabetic parent.

Interaction with Extended Family

Little attention has been paid in the literature to the impact of chronic illness on relationships throughout the extended family. Yet extended families—especially grandparents—were significant sources of both stress and support to the diabetic parents we interviewed. These parents reported that their own parents, at times, had difficulty "letting go" of responsibility for diabetes management, and the entry of new grandchildren had not seemed to alter this concern for the diabetic parent's health. Yet when grandparents and other relatives were nearby and available, they were often able to provide valuable concrete assistance, especially in the form of babysitting and transportation.

The impact of the extended family on the diabetic parent is complex. Our sample was too limited to examine how factors such as disease duration, family structure, cohesiveness, and health status of extended family members influence relationships with the diabetic parent and his or her family. Hill and Hansen (1962) have postulated that when stress in the nuclear family is not acute but ongoing, a strong and involved extended family helps to mediate stress and fosters the regenerative power of the nuclear family. It is clear in this exploratory study that extended family members potentially play a crucial role in the adjustment of the diabetic adult to marriage and parenthood.

Resources outside the Family

There were few resources in the health care system or consumer diabetes organizations available for diabetic parents and their family members. It is especially difficult for the parent to handle his or her own emotional upheaval after the diagnosis of a chronic illness when the parent is also heavily involved in the care of young children. Certainly, it would be important for the parent to have access to counseling or a peer support network at the time of diagnosis. Also, because it is unrealistic to expect an individual to accept easily a chronic illness such as diabetes, which presents new challenges at each stage of the life cycle, continuing access to counseling and educational services for diabetic parents is extremely important (Kornblum & Anderson, 1982). This issue is complex, however, for there was also a reluctance on the part of some diabetic parents to seek psychological help. Many parents already felt pressured to find the financial resources and time to cope with the medical aspects of this disease and were, therefore, hesitant to make a commitment to follow through with counseling or educational sessions.

Parents also may need specific assistance in helping their children understand this complex disease and in adapting their explanations to the child's age. With respect to other family members, every person living with a spouse spoke of the stress on the marriage relationship, as well as the importance of the cooperation and support of their spouse in managing their disease. It would be important to learn what the needs of the nondiabetic parents are, for their adaptation to diabetes exerts a powerful influence on the diabetic spouse and children. Nondiabetic spouses would have much to share with each other in a support group and could likely be used more effectively by the physician caring for the diabetic parent.

Finally, it is clear that there needs to be more psychological awareness on the part of medical professionals who take care of diabetic parents. Cooperation is needed between diabetic parents and physicians in setting up management plans that are realistic, given the other demands on parents' time and energy. In the care of children with diabetes, physicians, nurses, social workers, dietitians, and psychologists are beginning to work together to provide care for patients and their families. This interdisciplinary and family-oriented approach would also seem to be very effective with diabetic parents.

A PERSPECTIVE ON FUTURE RESEARCH

This exploratory study has several implications for future research in the neglected area of diabetic parents and their families. First, diabetic parents cannot be considered as a homogeneous group. Researchers must consider the parent's age and family situation at diagnosis, metabolic control level, and specific treatment plan. In addition, five broad issues were identified that presented significant coping challenges to these families. First, family planning and pregnancy concerns were faced by all diabetic parents. Second, these parents reported that diabetes-related mood fluctuations, daily treatment demands, and increased financial responsibilities affected the spouse relationship, and they also spoke about the central importance of their spouse's support to their own personal adaptation. Third, parents and health-care providers tended to downplay children's responses to diabetes and needs for information about this disease. Fourth, diabetes played a prominent role in the interactions between diabetic parents and members of the extended family. Finally, few consumer organizations or hospitals provided family-oriented programs for diabetic parents, and it is clear that attitudes toward meeting the psychological needs of diabetic parents and their families need to be more closely examined. These issues chart a direction for future research and service delivery that focuses not on deviant responses of individuals to chronic illness, but rather on the coping tasks to be mastered by all members of the family system when a parent has diabetes.

REFERENCES

Ahlfield, J., & Soler, N. The impact of diabetes in youth on marriage and having children. *Diabetes*, 1983, *32*, 38A.

Anderson, B. J., & Auslander, W. F. Research on diabetes management and the family: A critique. *Diabetes Care*, 1980, *3*, 696–702.

Baker, L., & Barcai, A. Psychosomatic aspects of diabetes. In O.W. Hill (Ed.), *Modern trends in psychosomatic illness* (Vol. 2). New York: Appleton–Century–Crofts, 1970.

Benoliel, J. Q. Childhood diabetes: The commonplace in living becomes uncommon. In A. L. Strauss, & B. G. Glaser (Eds.), *Chronic illness and the quality of life.* St. Louis: Mosby, 1975.

Dunn, S. M., & Turtle, J. R. The myth of the diabetic personality. *Diabetes Care*, 1981, *4*, 640–646.

Hamburg, B., & Inoff, G. Coping with predictable crises of diabetes. *Diabetes Care*, 1983, *6*, 409–416.

Hill, R., & Hansen, D. The family in disaster. In G. Baker, & D. Chapman (Eds.), *Man and society in disaster.* New York: Basic Books, 1962.

Kornblum, H., & Anderson, B. J. Acceptance reassessed. *Child Psychiatry and Human Development*, 1982, *12*, 171–178.

McCollum, A. T. *The chronically ill child.* New Haven: Yale University Press, 1981.

Merkatz, R. B., Budd, K., & Merkatz, I. R. Psychologic and social implications of scientific care for pregnant diabetic women. In I. R. Merkatz, & P. A. Adam (Eds.), *The diabetic pregnancy: A perinatal perspective.* New York: Grune & Stratton, 1979.

Rutter, M. *Children of sick parents.* London: Oxford University Press, 1966.

Third Annual Report of the National Diabetes Advisory Board. NIH Publication No. 8-2072, 1980.

Families with Deaf Parents:
A Functional Perspective*

ROBERT J. HOFFMEISTER

INTRODUCTION

There is no problem which does not become increasingly complex when actively investigated, growing in scope and depth,
endlessly opening up new vistas of work to be done. . . There
is never any problem, *ever*, which can be confined within a
single framework. (Italics added)
                                        (*Braudel*, 1980, p. 15)

To obtain a proper perspective on families in which the parents are
deaf (hereafter referred to as *deaf families*), an understanding of deaf
history and the formation of the Deaf Community is necessary. The
purpose of this chapter is to give an overview of deaf families and to
present a number of issues that are in need of elaboration.[1]

*This chapter is dedicated to my parents, Mary E. and Alfred Hoffmeister. Each had
a physical impairment of the auditory mechanism that could be quantified as a disability
as measured by audiometric tests across the speech range. However, neither my sister,
Mary Patricia Hoffmeister, nor I have thought of our parents as handicapped.

[1]In this chapter an attempt is made to draw distinctions among the concepts impairment, disability, and handicap from the perspective of a hearing child of deaf parents.
Here, "Deaf" refers to a member of the cultural group termed the Deaf Community,
whereas "deaf" refers to the hearing loss or to nonmembers of the cultural group who
have a hearing loss.

THE DEAF COMMUNITY

The Deaf Community was formed in reaction to the hearing community's attitudes, stereotypes, and prejudice with respect to deafness; biases that developed from the centuries-old problem of the Deaf: communication. This, coupled with a negative attitude towards sign language necessitated the establishment of a community to minimize frustration and enhance positive functioning. Higgings (1980) states that "since childhood, members of the Deaf Community have experienced repeated frustration in making themselves understood [and have experienced] embarrassing misunderstandings and the loneliness of being left out by family, neighborhood acquaintances and others" p. 42). The need for self-esteem is stronger than family ties and years of education.

Self-respect and status are obtained within the Deaf Community. The community, its communication, and its culture were transmitted by unique circumstances. American Sign Language as used by the majority of the Deaf in the U.S. is passed on from child to child rather than through the traditional mother–child transmission, except where Deaf parents have deaf children. The ideal circumstances for the natural development of a positive self-image, exposure to adequate models for language development, and adequate personality development have been documented in families where both parents and children are deaf (Mindel & Vernon, 1971; Moores, 1982; Schlesinger & Meadow, 1972).

It is true that there is an audiological explanation of a hearing disorder for which the common or popular name is "deafness." The medical model of deafness restricts the term to a physical impairment that may be corrected through certain procedures. (However, to date there is no known cure for the hearing disorder that inhibits the functioning of the inner ear.) Very few people are aware of how deafness affects the everyday lives of those who are deaf. In this population the term 'deafness' is not easily defined. Deafness is a relative concept. Deafness, or the inability to hear, is viewed from the norm of hearing. Deafness exists relative to the corresponding concept 'hearing'. A person is only deaf, in a negative sense, when in the presence of a hearing person. That is because it is expected that one needs to have one's hearing in order to function and be successful. The view of deafness in this paper is not one of a defined population aspiring to hearing normalcy but one where the deficit of hearing is neutralized and "normalcy" has been achieved. This view is analogous to that found in minority groups in the U.S. Membership within the Deaf minority depends not on the amount of hearing one has but on how one functions within the Deaf Community. Communication within the community, the key to gaining entrance, is the same communication that isolates the Deaf from the hearing community. However, the issue is not fluent communication, but a positive attitude towards the Deaf Community itself. The inability to hear does not automatically establish one as a Deaf Community member. Membership involves an attitude about communication, about the world (hearing and deaf), and about oneself. To be an insider, a member, one must share the values, dreams, aspirations, and experiences common to the Deaf Community. Membership is so heavily dependent on deaf attitudes that there is a specific sign designated for deaf people outside the Deaf Community that loosely translates as "thinks like hearing." Historical events have resulted in restricting access of the hearing to this community to a relatively small number. A hearing child of deaf parents is considered an "in group" member by birthright, yet there is a very strong feeling in the community about hearing individuals:

> Some hearing individuals are courtesy members of the Deaf Communities. They may be educators, counselors, interpreters, or friends of the Deaf. Often they have deafness in the family; deaf parents, siblings, children, or even spouses. Yet their membership is just that, a courtesy, which recognizes the fundamental fact that no matter how empathetic they are, no matter that there is deafness in their families, they are not deaf and can never "really" know what it means to be deaf. (Higgins, 1980, p. 46)

The perspective of the Deaf as a minority group is unique in that Deaf cultural values and mores are not passed on from one generation to another within the family structure. Rather than being passed down from grandparent to parent to child, cultural values and mores are transmitted via peer interaction among deaf children in school (Woodward, 1982). Psychological development—including personality formation, self-esteem, acceptance, emotional stability, and language—are not learned from parental models but from other children (Chess & Fernandez, 1981). To my knowledge no other culture is transmitted and formed at the peer group level. Even though hearing authorities and models continuously interact with deaf children during their formative years, peer-group interaction ultimately plays a more significant role in the development of survival skills in the social domain.

Sociologically, the hearing and the Deaf need each other to establish boundaries and identities within each group membership. In order to form an identity, community members must compare and contrast themselves to other groups (Higgins, 1980). This comparison provides a set of rules within which the Deaf define acceptable and nonacceptable behavior. Deaf individuals are thus provided with an arena and with boundaries within which to function.

Functioning is another relative term, dependent upon the expectations of a specific group. Successful functioning is a major factor in sustaining membership in the Deaf Community. The deaf individual, because of his or her unusual circumstances must participate in both the Deaf and hearing communities. It is at this point that normalcy becomes defined. A deaf person may be a successfully participating member of the Deaf Community, but encounter difficulties within the hearing community. To achieve a sense of balance, the deaf person may typically participate in the hearing community in settings that are defined and structured, such as work. As adults, contact between the deaf and hearing persons is minimized, which results in a lack of knowledge about each other. Typically, stereotypes are carried by the hearing community, further fueled by this lack of interaction. One stereotype is that the deaf are not capable of interacting or socializing, hence they are inferior. More confusion arises when the Deaf and the hearing are required to interact. In many cases an interpreter (a hearing person using a signed language) is used as a go-between. The use of an interpreter is sometimes misunderstood by hearing persons, who view the use of signs as representing an intellectual deficit rather than being simply a language barrier.

Deaf family members make up a significant proportion of the Deaf Community. As previously stated, membership within the community is primarily dependent on attitude, hearing status, and use of a signed language. Attitudes derive from shared experiences.

COMMUNICATION

My only communication difficulties arose when I began doing business with the outside world.
                                            Jacobs (1980, p. 12).

Communication barriers have existed between the general hearing population and the Deaf since the first deaf person was born. However, the full impact of this barrier was not felt until the decision by the Abbé de L'Epée, in the 1700s, to modify French Sign Language so that it conformed to the syntax of spoken French. Implicit in this decision was the assumption that the language of the Deaf Community was insufficient for educational purposes, in particular for learning the language of the hearing community.

This same belief greatly influenced education of the Deaf in the United States. Laurent Clerc, a deaf student of de L'Epée, was brought to this country by Thomas Hopkins Gallaudet, in order to help establish the American School for the Deaf in Hartford, Connecticut. Operating upon the assumption that had prevailed in France, a form of Signed English became the language of the classroom, even though a signed language was already in use by the Deaf (Lane, 1980). Great success was claimed for the use of Signed English (see Annual Reports, American Asylum for the Deaf, 1817-1840). However, the use of sign language was dealt a deadly blow by Alexander Graham Bell in his numerous arguments against its use. These attacks focused not so much upon the accomplishments of the Deaf, but rather upon the fact that sign language was a vehicle that created a natural bond among deaf people (Moores, 1982). Bell participated in a conference in Milan, Italy, in 1880, which was well attended by the educators of the deaf from all over the world. Bell tried to have a resolution adopted barring the use of signs by deaf children and adults in schools for the deaf but failed. The educational establishment in the U.S. has never fully recovered from the intent of this resolution, and the Deaf Community has suffered because of it.

The change in attitude from predominantly manual to oral communication created a situation where deaf persons were expected to function as hearing persons whether or not they were able to. False expectations were established for hearing parents. Speech and lipreading became the paramount purpose for providing education to the deaf. This change was made to train the deaf to function within the hearing world (Higgins, 1980).

The Deaf were suppressed (see Lane, 1980, for more detailed discussion). As the economy changed from a trades and agricultural base to an industrial base, communication with the hearing became more and more of a requirement. The influences of the latter half of the nineteenth century have placed an overwhelming emphasis on the importance of speech for deaf children; that is, "to become like hearing" (Higgins, 1980, p. 17). Removing the natural means of communication isolated the Deaf not only from the hearing but from other deaf persons as well.

The negative views towards sign language have become internalized by the Deaf. Those who have poor speech, minimal understanding of

English, and who are undereducated feel inadequate for participating in the hearing world.

EDUCATIONAL INFLUENCES

The sociocultural influences of the educational institutions for the Deaf and for the hearing cannot be ignored. Within 100 years of the founding of the first school for the deaf, deaf students could choose from a residential school for the deaf or a school specifically for deaf students formed by a group of cities or counties, which was called a day school for the deaf. Day schools began to flourish in the middle of the twentieth century and preceded the day classes and "integrated" programs for the "hearing-impaired" now in vogue.

Currently forty percent of all deaf children in the United States are enrolled in residential schools for the deaf. Because of the complex classifications of school programs, the remaining 60% attend classes within day schools or regular hearing schools. The average deaf adult at completion of high school has an academic achievement median of 4.5 grades (Trybus & Karchmer, 1977). This figure is an indictment of the educational practices used with the Deaf. The academic achievement score is mistakenly thought to be a measure of intellectual competence; instead, it should be viewed as the result of inadequate education and societal attitudes (Hoffmeister & Drury, 1982). In an attempt to right the wrongs of the past, the current movement within the educational establishments to promote Total Communication (using signs, finger spelling, speech, audition, speechreading, and writing as pedagogical tools) should have positive influences both on educational attainment and societal attitudes toward the Deaf.

The plethora of educational programs creates a situation where the background of deaf parents may be extremely varied. For example, it would not be uncommon for a deaf parent to have begun in a regular school or an oral program, then transfer to a residential school Total Communication program as a day student during adolescence (previously a typical situation in Massachusetts). Or because of the current efforts to comply with "mainstreaming," a deaf child could be switched from a center school program (residential or day school) to a self-contained classroom or integrated into a regular school classroom. These varied backgrounds make generalizing about deaf families difficult. Therefore, this section applies to deaf parents who are members of the

Deaf Community. There may be a number of deaf adults who have families that do not belong to the Deaf Community but very little is known about them.

SOCIOECONOMIC STATUS

Employment options for deaf adults at graduation range from low-paying unskilled labor to high-paying professional categories (Schein & Delk, 1972). It is not uncommon for deaf college graduates to be employed as linotype operators or as operators of other machines having to do with printing or the computer industry (key punch or computer operator as opposed to programmer); less than 10% of the deaf population have professional positions (Boatner, Stuckless & Moores, 1964). The socioeconomic status of deaf families is generally lower than the general population: The median income of deaf persons is approximately 15–20% below the median income for hearing persons. High-level executive positions or advancement to positions of foreman, supervisor, or administrator are resticted because of communication problems.

Attitudes and stereotypes held by employers have consistently kept the Deaf in lower-paying jobs. When employer attitudes towards the deaf were surveyed, over 30% said they would not even consider a deaf person for employment. (It is important to note that once a job is obtained, the pressure on the deaf person to do as well or better than the hearing person is enormous.) Ironically, employers who have hired deaf employees tend to hire more deaf workers once they find their job skills and capabilities exceed the employers' initial expectations (Moores, Fisher & Harlow, 1974). The deaf adult is faced with a lifelong quest of living down stereotypes within the hearing community.

Although the average deaf adult earns less than the average hearing adult, deaf families live in average to better-than-average neighborhoods. More than 70% of households headed by a white deaf male are located in middle- to upper-class neighborhoods (Schein & Delk, 1972). Housing appears to be a measure of status and importance within the Deaf Community. A deaf family's sense of worth is based on adequate provision for those they are responsible for. Maintaining status by living in acceptable neighborhoods and obtaining self-esteem from positive participation in the Deaf Community appears to compensate for negative educational and employment experiences.

Characteristics of Deaf Families

The family is a symbol of accomplishment for deaf adults within the Deaf Community. It is within the family that the barriers of the outside world do not exist. "In the process of establishing one's own family, the deaf individual is creating an environment where deafness is the norm rather than the exception" (Becker, 1980, p. 54). The family and the Deaf Community become the central focus for intimacy, base of support, and generativity (i.e., the continuation of the family) (Schlesinger & Meadow, 1972).

Ninety-five percent of deaf adults marry deaf partners. Mindel and Vernon (1972) see the marriage of two deaf adults as a healthy adaptation to deafness. The divorce rate among deaf marriages is equivalent to that of the hearing population. Stability within marriages appears to be as strong for the Deaf as it is for the hearing. Marriage between two deaf adults serves to neutralize the dissonance in a Deaf person's life since both partners share similar experiences, communication mode, social values, and everyday problems.

Most deaf parents have had no real training or model for parenthood. It is a tribute to their competence and resourcefulness that they are successful parents in a significant number of families. Success in family interaction is not dependent on lineage; the families of deaf parents and deaf offspring function smoothly in the early years of marriage. The following is a discussion of some of the factors that can be attributed to this success.

Deaf Families with Deaf Children

Because deaf parents have had both positive and negative experiences, they are somewhat ambivalent about whether they prefer their children to be deaf or hearing. With so much of their lives consumed by "hearing problems" it is unavoidable not to have fears of what the children will be like. Conflicting views on whether deaf parents wish to have deaf children are seen in statements by Jacobs (1980), who experienced initial disappointment because his children were hearing (though only for a brief moment) and Goodstein (1981), who signs:

> In general our deaf friends have often expressed a desire for deaf children for the sake of easy assimilation into the family, but when reality set in—when they had children—they would either rejoice to find out that their offspring could hear, or experience temporary disappointment if the child was deaf. (p. 14)

This ambivalence is further complicated by the fact that hearing children tend to be born into deaf families. Research on deaf adults from deaf families suggests that they tend to be more complacent, (Becker, 1980), better socialized, better adjusted, more flexible and adaptable to new situations (Schlesinger & Meadow, 1972), pass through life stages with more positive attitudes, are least impulsive and most mature (Harris, 1978), acquire language—both American Sign Language (Hoffmeister, 1977, 1978, 1979, 1982; Kantor, 1981; Supalla, 1982) and English (Moores, 1971, 1980, 1982)—more easily, achieve better in school (Mindel & Vernon, 1972; Moores, 1982; Vernon & Koh, 1970), and are psychologically and sociologically equivalent to the hearing population (Becker, 1980; Higgins, 1980).

Deaf parents who have deaf children typically have deafness within the extended family. Membership in deaf families "provides ascribed status in the community" (Becker, 1980, p. 58). The deaf parents provide a sense of continuity to the children and to the family. Schlesinger and Meadow (1972) suggest that deaf parents are more successful in coping and raising deaf than hearing children because of a possible displacement of prior feelings. Deaf parents may possibly react negatively to having a hearing child because of the overall negative feelings toward the hearing population. Recently *The Deaf American,* a national magazine for the Deaf, published a series of articles by deaf offspring of deaf parents. Throughout these articles one theme is constant: communication and acceptance—acceptance of the child as a child, not as a "deaf" child; acceptance as a participating family member. Hughes (1981) signs that "we [family] usually spend hours and hours talking together during and after supper. My parents believe strongly in encouraging us to share our thoughts and feelings with each other" (p. 9). Easy communication permits not only the transmission of information but also feelings, respect, and role models.

Deaf parents present a situation that their child may wish to emulate someday. Communication in the home is not a foreign, isolated instance of which only bits and pieces may be perceived. The deaf child in the deaf family perceives daily events as an integrated whole. Deaf parents easily engage their children in Deaf Community activities. In fact, as families develop, the activities of the deaf club within the community tend to become more family oriented.

At the local clubhouse for the Deaf, where deaf people flocked mainly for social purposes, there was always a hubbub of activities on Saturdays. Dad was president of the club at that time, as we tagged along with our folks and became involved in the usual affairs of the club for the Deaf. We were exposed to business meetings, and "overheard" chitchat, gossip, and jokes. (Goodstein, 1981, p. 11)

Deaf children of deaf parents have great advantages over deaf children of hearing parents in adjustment because they are able to view their parents within the Deaf Community as leaders, active participants, respected members, and high achievers. The Deaf Community presents the opportunity for the deaf parent to function positively and maintain self respect.

Deaf Families with Hearing Children

A major problem for deaf parents appears to derive from the lack of exposure to good parent models. As discussed above, the typical deaf parent is a product of a hearing family. If the deaf person remained at home, the hearing parental model may have been characterized by frustration, guilt, overprotection, and a long list of other traumatic affects experienced by hearing parents and their deaf children (Meadow, 1980; Mindel & Vernon, 1971; Moores, 1982; Rainer, Altshuler, & Kallman, 1963; Schlesinger & Meadow, 1972). Moores (1973, 1982) further suggests that since little research has been done on families with deaf children, the total impact is not really known. If the deaf parents were sent to the residential school, exposure to parenting models would be through houseparents, dorm counselors, and teachers. I would not be remiss in suggesting that parenting models within this setting would be less than ideal. Therefore, because of the lack of research, little is known about parenting in deaf families.

Research involving the communication between deaf parents and their children was nonexistent until a seminal study was conducted by Maestas y Moores (1980). Since 1960, other studies of communication with and among the Deaf have been directed at American Sign Language (Klima & Bellugi, 1980; Wilbur, 1979, for a comprehensive review). However, a number of others are interested in the effects of life experiences and how this would influence communication with the children in deaf families.

Maestas y Moores (1980) reported a study of the communicative style of three deaf mothers interacting with their children between the ages of birth and six months. Her main conclusions support the fact that deaf mothers are similar in communicative style to that of hearing mothers. Two major components of the mothers' register (style of communicating with the children) consist of affective and cognitive (simplifying—clarifying) statements to their child. Additionally, all linguistic codes available to the deaf mothers were used depending on the specific communicative function. That is, only manual communication, only voice, and a combination of these were used depending on the situation. This supports Schlesinger's (1978) suggestion that deaf mothers are bimodal and that speech is felt to have a place within the deaf family. This is further exemplified by Jaech's (1981) explanation of how his family communicated: "We were content to use signs and fingerspelling because it was all we needed. We used voice, depending on who was talking with whom" (p. 6). Deaf parents recognize that a hearing world exists and properly prepare their children to co-exist with it and to adapt to situations in it.

The acquisition of language in deaf families has focused on the development of American Sign Language (ASL) in deaf children of deaf parents (Hoffmeister, 1977, 1978, 1979, 1980; Newport & Ashbrook, 1977; for a review see Hoffmeister and Wilbur, 1981; Hoffmeister, 1982). The process of acquiring ASL by deaf children of deaf parents appears to follow the same processes as children acquiring a spoken language.

Very little work has been completed on the language of hearing children of deaf parents. Conflicting reports indicate that family variables such as background of the parents, intelligibility of the speech of the parents, exposure to hearing adults, and so forth, are not the important criteria (Schiff & Ventry, 1976). It is important to point out that the hearing children who had deaf parents with unintelligible speech developed appropriate English and speech skills and that amount of exposure to the hearing population did not appear to be related to language and speech problems. "It may very well be that the quality of interaction with a child is more important than mere exposure to 'normal' language" (italics added) (Schiff & Ventry, 1976, p. 356).

It is remarkable that deaf families function as well as they do. The odds appear overwhelming against success, yet the majority of deaf families appear to succeed in basic child rearing, providing family nurture, and remaining close throughout adulthood. Becker (1980) suggests that the Deaf Community contributes substantially to the support of proper parenting procedures by providing a forum to air problems, compare practices, and learn from the experiences of others.

Interaction with the Hearing World

The previous section dealt with families and communication. Communication as a process is all-pervasive in deafness and deaf families. It is always part of every situation that the Deaf and those related to the Deaf encounter.

The birth of a child and the first few years of the child's life bring the deaf family in direct contact with the hearing world. New decisions must be made regarding parental beliefs. If my child is hearing, do I use sign? What if I have unintelligible speech; how will I compensate? Will my hearing child be ashamed of me? The negative feelings towards manual communication cannot be dismissed. A review of the literature shows no mention by deaf adults of their interactions with the obstetrician, pediatrician, speech and hearing therapist, audiologist, and other medical personnel; yet contact with these professionals and the resulting positive and negative attitudes are found in the literature concerning hearing families with deaf children (Mindel & Vernon, 1971; Moores, 1982; Moores & Maestas y Moores, 1981; Murphy, 1979; Schlesinger & Meadow, 1972).

Professionals, whether they have direct contact with deafness or not, cannot be assumed to understand the implications of deafness on the individual. Higgins (1980) suggests that historically the deaf are viewed as incompetent human beings. They are seen as dependent on society; therefore, people within the helping professions wish to fulfill the role of protector, provider, and director. Complicating interaction with the hearing professionals are the views that all deaf persons function at the lower elementary school level because of the false impression of the reported average achievement score. Any form of sign language is traditionally foreign to most helping professionals. Hence, deaf adults, at the birth of their first child, are very careful to select medical professionals (both obstetrician and pediatrician) on the advice of other deaf adults. It is not unusual for many deaf people to maintain this relationship with a particular doctor for a lifetime.

Contact with hearing professionals outside the work setting may be very frustrating for many deaf adults. Deaf adults (like hearing adults) want professionals to know about problems associated with that professional's speciality and expect him or her to think about little things in interpersonal relationships that are important. For example, it is becoming more common for husbands to be present during childbirth. Some problems may occur between deaf parents and the doctor, such as the fact that wearing the mask during delivery prevents immediate communication between doctor and mother. In some cases, a doctor may assume the mother cannot understand the procedure because she cannot hear; therefore, he does not explain it. Little things that compensate for increasing fear and anxiety help deaf parents interact more favorably with hearing professionals; for example, providing an interpreter, speaking slowly, or taking the time to explain through writing.

After childbirth the problems of parenthood and the question of competency arise. Pediatricians may refer children of deaf parents to speech therapists. Speech and hearing professionals who do not have much contact with deaf adults may not recognize the strong emotional feelings that surface from the new parent's childhood. A double bind occurs; the deaf parents, probably unsure of how to care for their new child (as all parents are) meet the same professional who they may have blamed for causing great trauma in their own lives. Feelings of inadequacy may develop in the deaf parents, which is exactly the opposite goal of the professional involved. Medical personnel make frequent referrals to social work agencies just because the parents are deaf. Again, lack of knowledge concerning the Deaf as successful, contributing members of society creates problems when a professional must make a decision concerning a family. Because the child is not "developing speech adequately," a suggestion may be made to remove the child from the parents, increasing feelings of inadequacy in the parents. Lack of consistent reports regarding measures of speech development in hearing children of deaf families results in confusion as to what factors influence maximal development of vocal language in children. Current awareness of deafness and the acceptance of sign language are lessening the frequency of inappropriate actions on the part of professionals who come in contact with deaf families. This is an area of extreme sensitivity and should be further researched.

In addition to problems with professionals who are involved with the deaf family, marriage and childbirth stages present difficulties for many extended family members. The majority of deaf adults have middle-class, hearing parents, who have tended to be overprotective and overcontrolling throughout the deaf adult's life (Mindel & Vernon, 1971; Schlesinger & Meadow, 1972). Independence from the family is not an easy accomplishment for deaf children and young adults who were day students and lived at home. It is probably much easier for the students attending a residential school. For them, independence from the *family* is automatic, yet other dependencies may develop. Hearing parents may forbid the marriage to a deaf partner for fear of deaf grandchildren or worse, for fear of incapability on the part of the young deaf adult. Conflict may arise after the birth of a child regarding proper child-rearing practices. The problem of presenting a proper speech model may reappear. With all these potential conflicts to escape from, the Deaf Community serves as a strong support system for the individual deaf person.

Discussion concerning the removal of the child or overemphasis on hearing status by grandparents may create a larger division between hearing parents and their deaf adult offspring. Most of the time hearing parents have worked through the fear of lack of competence and the impact of deafness by the time their deaf child reaches adulthood. But as in any family, the new grandchild will cause memories of the past to resurface. These can be very uncomfortable memories for grandparents to reconcile.

The Role of Hearing Children of Deaf Parents

As the firstborn child in the deaf family grows, his or her responsibility as liaison to the hearing world grows. Other children may follow, but the oldest child typically becomes the interpreter for the family. The hearing children of deaf parents do not have the skills to cope with the role of liaison but must perform in the role. In a survey of hearing children of deaf parents, 95% (217 out of 229) respondents answered "yes" to the question, "Did you interpret for your parents?" Most interpreted situations were of three kinds: phone, medical, and shopping (Bunde, 1979). Another question focused on how the hearing children felt about interpreting for their parents; 19% expressed no feelings and 65% did not answer. Most deaf parents are very sensitive to this issue. They try not to rely on the hearing child until the child feels comfortable with the role. Initially, this is not a problem for the child. It becomes a problem after a few negative experiences are encountered.

Hearing children of deaf parents tend to be put in a position of making decisions because the general hearing public and professionals do not understand the separation between being an interpreter, being a son or daughter, and acting as an intermediary for the parents. Royster (1981) states,

> Sometimes I found myself resentful of always having to interpret and always knowing about the family's financial affairs and problems. Mama and Daddy sensed this resentment at times and didn't force me to interpret for T.V. programs or when my hearing friends came over to play". (p. 20)

Deaf parents are cautioned that although parents have needs, "care must be maintained to meet the legitimate dependent needs of the hearing child as well" (Schlesinger & Meadow, 1972, p. 187). Deaf parents must be careful not to put their interpreting child in a position that creates conflict; for example, in a medical or court situation, because the child may not be prepared to cope with the information being transferred (see Royster, 1981). Hearing children of deaf parents cannot be expected to function as a participant and to interpret at the same time.

Hearing children are required to interpret on the telephone. It is through the telephone that the hearing child becomes a decision maker for the deaf family. Hearing people who called and wished to speak to the deaf mother or father did not understand how to communicate through an interpreter. They usually wanted an answer more rapidly than was available through the interpreter. In some cases the hearing child of deaf parents would assume the responsibility for the answer for a variety of reasons. For example, the pressure to end a conversation quickly, for whatever reason, results in the child's avoiding interpreting and answering an inquiry.

Very little work has been done on hearing children of deaf parents. Recent texts focusing on deafness, the deaf person, deaf adulthood, and deaf culture do not even list hearing children of deaf parents in the index (Becker, 1980; Bendelry, 1980; Higgins, 1980; Moores, 1982).

> The findings regarding hearing children with deaf parents are of sufficient interest to merit further investigation. Since guidance clinics sometimes appear to be at a loss when dealing with deaf parents, this group of hearing children suffers as much from the lack of appropriate mental health services as do the deaf themselves. (Schlesinger and Meadow, 1972, p. 188)

TECHNOLOGICAL INFLUENCES

TTYs and TDDs

Jacobs (1980) appropriately points out that Bell, in inventing the telephone and the technological developments related to it, has left the deaf far behind in the communication arena. The importance of the telephone may be found in the following passage:

> At long last, it was my turn. I got up and announced that my most favorite gift of all was a telephone. Everyone in class just stared at me with a blank expression, as if to say, "So what?" To them a telephone was nothing, to me it was the greatest gift in the whole world! It was at that moment I realized how different my life was from theirs. The telephone, a simple communication device, symbolized the blatant contrast between the deaf world and the hearing world. (Royster, 1981, p. 19)

The telephone, "instead of benefitting deaf people . . . became a hindrance and a barrier" (Gannon, 1981). The inability to access the telephone has created negative feelings towards it by many deaf people.

A lifesaving device was invented by Weitbrecht in the early sixties. This device is called a teletypewriter (TTY). "Teletypewriters are machines with a typewriter keyboard. When one key is struck, it activates a similar key on the machines on the other end and a message is typed out. These machines are used to send news, stockmarket and weather reports, and telegrams. And it was possible to link these machines and other telecommunication devices to the telephone and use the telephone to send a message (Gannon, 1981). Prior to the invention of the coupler, which provided access to the phone, the deaf person who wanted to contact someone else would have to drive to that person's house and either leave a message or see the person (Becker, 1980). In addition to bringing the telephone into the Deaf Community, the TTY has helped to relieve the anxiety of many hearing family members of deaf parents who used to have to rely on neighbors and the mail.

A national organization, Teletypewriters for the Deaf, Inc., begun by a deaf engineer, Lathan Breunig, has helped to make the Telecommunication Device for the Deaf (TTD), a more generic form that includes the older TTYs and the newer machines produced by the current technological advances in communication devices, a household word among the Deaf. This organization's power has encouraged businesses and politics to become more actively involved in the affairs of the Deaf. Most deaf families own one; many businesses and hospitals have installed them. Many congressmen and senators have machines and contact persons. These machines have opened up the Deaf Community to better communications and larger involvement in the politics of their own destiny. The deaf person's use of the telephone is not on a par with that of the hearing person's, but these machines have certainly decreased frustration and saved the Deaf a great deal of time.

Decoders

Recently another device has been developed: the telecommunications television adaptor. This device is called a closed-captioning decoder. It will print the captions on the television only in those homes that have the decoder. Offering the captioning service is, however, up to the major networks. Two major broadcasting networks (ABC and NBC) cooperate with the National Captioning Institute in Los Angeles, while CBS has developed its own system. This captioning process will make television accessible to the Deaf, thereby opening up another convenience of life previously denied.

The major difficulty in the captioning service is in determining the level of readable English by the average deaf person. Research has been conducted on how to provide a significant amount of information to the widest possible population and yet not become paternalistic and reduce the message to telegraphese (for details see Wilbur, Montandon, & Goodhart, 1983).

THE AGED DEAF

The social organizations that have played a central role in the deaf person's life have even greater significance as the person ages. As with elderly populations in any community, the search for alternative activities to fill time previously allocated to work is of major concern to the elderly deaf population.

As the children begin to leave home, the parenting process plateaus. The major support for the elderly deaf person is the Deaf Community. Contacts have been maintained over time by regular gatherings at the local deaf club or other organizations for the Deaf. The fraternization around the bar for a few drinks and good conversation turns to weekly card playing (bridge, poker) and monthly socials for the elderly deaf. Friends developed in high school are still in contact, and children growing up within the community maintain the continuity. Close friends help the adjustment to old age (Becker, 1980), and the community helps maintain close friends. There is security in the knowledge that friends will respond in an emergency or in time of need. This mutual aid helps to cement the deaf adult ties to the community. Deaf senior citizens groups flourish. Some have their own housing projects, completely funded or operated by deaf adults, who value the senior citizens' role in maintaining the community's perspective between the younger and older generations.

Very little has been published on the process of and adjustment to aging by the Deaf. For an excellent anthropological look at the elderly Deaf, see Becker (1980). Higgins (1980), in his sociological perspectives, points out the inherent difficulties of examining the lifestyle and passage through time of the Deaf.

An examination of the inner workings of the aging process is just beginning to be developed. When the Deaf feel more secure about themselves, outside examiners may raise the issues; but introspection by deaf adults will provide the true details of the passage.

CONCLUSION

An overview of families with deaf parents has been presented. An attempt was made to present the issues encountered during the life-span of the deaf adult, not focusing on deficits created by the hearing loss but on the successful functioning of the person within the community. Moores (1982) is the first professional who successfully defines the problem of deafness. He separates and defines *impairment, disability,* and *handicap.* An impairment is the actual physical or structural deviation from the norm; a disability is the loss of an important function in spite of any aids or treatment; a handicap is the attitudes, feelings, and barriers that increase the effects of a disability, turn it into a problem of living, and put a person at a disadvantage.

It is my hope that hearing parents and professionals will see that it is true that deafness is an impairment and is disabling in terms of an inability to hear. However, it is a handicap only when all measures of life depend on it. When the disability is neutralized as in the Deaf Community, the measures of life are seen in a positive, not negative, light.

REFERENCES

Annual reports. American Asylum for the Deaf, 1817–1840.
Becker, *Growing old in silence.* Berkeley, California: University of California Press, 1980.
Bendelry, B. *Dancing without music: Deafness in America.* New York: Anchor Press, 1980.
Boatner, E., Stuckless, E., & Moores, D. *Occupational status of the young deaf adult in New England and the need and demand for a regional technical training center.* West Hartford, CT: American School for the Deaf, 1964.
Braudel, F. *On History.* Chicago: University of Chicago Press, 1980.
Bunde, L. Deaf parents–hearing children. *Signograph Series #1.* Washington, DC: Registry of Interpreters for the Deaf, 1979.
Chess, S., & Fernandez, P. *The handicapped child in school: Behavior and management.* New York: Bruner/Mazel, 1981.
Gannon, J. *Deaf Heritage: A narrative history of deaf America.* Silver Springs, MD: National Association of the Deaf, 1981.
Goodstein, A. Three generations of loving memories. *The Deaf American,* 1981, 34(3),
Harris, R. Mental health needs and practices in deaf children and adults: A deaf professional's perspective for the 1980's. In L. Stein, E. Mindel, T. Jabaley (Eds.), *Deafness & Mental Health.* New York: Grune and Stratton, 1978.
Higgins, P. *Outsiders in a hearing world.* Beverly Hills, California: Sage Publications, 1980.
Hoffmeister, R. *The acquisition of American Sign Language in deaf children of deaf parents.* Paper presented at the meeting of the New England Sign Language Research Group. Boston, MA, September 29, 1976.
Hoffmeister, R. *Word-order acquisition in American Sign Language.* Paper presented at the Third Annual Boston University Conference on Language Development, Boston, MA; September 29, 1978.
Hoffmeister, R. The development of possessive pronouns by deaf children of deaf parents. *Journal of Communication and Cognition,* 1979.
Hoffmeister, R. The influential POINT. *Proceedings of the National Symposium on Sign Language and Sign Language Teaching.* National Association of the Deaf, 1980.

Hoffmeister, R. The acquisition of language abilities by deaf children. In H. Hoemann & R. Wilbur (Eds.), *Communication in Two Societies* (Monographs in Social Aspects of Deafness). Washington, DC: Gallaudet College, 1982.

Hoffmeister, R. The acquisition of pronominal anaphora in deaf children. In B. Lust (Ed.), *Studies in the acquisition of anaphora: Defining the constraints.* Dordrecht, Holland: Reidel, in press.

Hoffmeister, R., & A. Drury. English training for primary and secondary level deaf children. In D. Sims, G. Walters, & R. Whitehead (Eds.), *Deafness and communication: Assessment and training.* Briarcliff Manor, NY: Stein and Day, 1982.

Hoffmeister, R. & Wilbur, R. *The acquisition of American Sign Language: A review.* In H. Lane & F. Grosjean (Eds.), *Current perspectives on sign language.* New Jersey: Lawrence Erlbaum Associates, 1980.

Hughes, P. Nothing is Impossible: the Hughes Family. *The Deaf American,* 1981, *34* (3), pp. 8–9.

Jacobs, L. *A deaf adult speaks out.* Washington, DC: Gallaudet College Press, 1980.

Jaech, T. The Jaech family: From Dad with love. *The Deaf American,* 1981, *34* (3), pp. 5–7.

Kantor, R. *Communicative interaction in American Sign Language between deaf mothers and their deaf children: A psycholinguistic analysis.* Unpublished doctoral dissertation, Boston University, 1981.

Klima, E., and Bellugi, U. *The Signs of Language.* Cambridge. Massachusetts: Harvard University Press, 1980.

Lane, H. Historical: A chronology of the oppression of sign language in France and the United States. In H. Lane & J. Grosjean, *Recent perspectives on sign language,* New Jersey: Lawrence Erlbaum, 1980.

Maestas y Moores, J. Early linguistic environment. *Sign Language Studies,* 1980, *26,* 1–13.

Meadow, K. *Deafness and Child Development.* Berkeley, CA: University of California Press, 1980.

Mindel, E., & Vernon, M. *They grow in silence.* Silver Spring, MD: National Association of the Deaf, 1971.

Moores, D. *Recent research on manual communication.* University of Minnesota Research, Development and Demonstration Center in Education of Handicapped Children, Minneapolis, MN, Research Report No. 7, 1971.

Moores, D. Families and deafness. In A. Norris (Ed.), *Deafness annual,* Silver Spring, MD: Professional Rehabilitation Workers with the Adult Deaf, 1973, 115–130.

Moores, D. Alternative communication needs. In R. Schiefelbusch (Ed.), *Nonspeech language and communication: Analysis and intervention.* Baltimore, MD: University Park Press, 1980.

Moores, D. *Educating the deaf: Psychology, principles, and practices.* Boston, MA: Houghton-Mifflin, 1982.

Moores, D., Fisher, S., & Harlow, M. *Post-secondary program for the deaf: Summary and overview* (Monograph VI). Minneapolis: University of Minnesota Research, Development, and Demonstration Center in Education of Handicapped Children, Minneapolis, MN, Research Report No. 80, 1974.

Moores, D. & Maestas y Moores, J. Special adaptations necessitated by hearing impairments. In J. Kaufman & D. Hallahan (Eds.), *Handbook of Special Education.* New York: Prentice Hall, 1981.

Murphy, A. (Ed.). *The families of hearing impaired children.* Washington, DC: Volta Review, Alexander Graham Bell Association for the Deaf, 1979, *81*(5)

Newport, E. & Ashbrook, The emergence of semantic relations in American Sign Language. *Papers and reports in child language development* (No. 13). Stanford: Dept. of Linguistics, Stanford University, 1977, 16–21.

Rainer, J., Altshuler, K., & Kallman, F. (Eds.). *Family and mental health problems in a deaf population.* New York: Columbia University Press, 1963.

Royster, M. The Roysters: Deaf parents: A personal perspective. *The Deaf American,* 1981, *34*(3), pp. 19–22

Schein, J., & Delk, M. *The deaf population in the United States.* Silver Spring, MD: National Association of the Deaf, 1972.

Schiff, N., & Ventry, I. Communication problems in hearing children of deaf parents. *Journal of Speech and Hearing Disorders,* 1976, *40,* 348–356.

Schlesinger, H. The Effects of Deafness on Childhood Development. In L. Liben (Ed.), *Deaf children: Developmental perspectives.* New York: Academic Press, 1978.

Schlesinger, H., and Meadow, K. *Sound and sign: Childhood deafness and mental health.* Berkeley, CA: University of California Press, 1972.

Supalla, T. Acquisition of morphology of American Sign Language verbs of motion. Unpublished doctoral dissertation, University of California, San Diego, 1982.

Trybus, R., & Karchmer, M. School achievement scores of hearing impaired children: National data of achievement status and growth patterns. *American Annals of the Deaf,* 1977, *122,* 62–69.

Vernon, M., & Koh, S. Effects of manual communication on deaf children's education achievement, linguistic competence, oral skills and psychological development. *American Annals of the Deaf,* 1970, *115*(5), 527–536.

Wilbur, R. *American Sign Language and sign systems: Research and applications.* Baltimore, MD: University Park Press, 1979.

Wilbur, R., Montandon, B., & Goodhart, W. Comprehension of nine syntactic structures by hearing impaired students. *Volta Review,* December, 1983, 328–345.

Children of Physically Disabled Parents: Some Thoughts, Facts, and Hypotheses

BOBBY G. GREER

INTRODUCTION

"Dad, there's a new Atari cartridge out and I think you could play it; it's *real* easy!" This is a statement of an adopted son to entice his cerebral palsied father into buying a new video game. Do sons of non-disabled fathers target their "sales pitches" to their fathers on the basis of their "old man's" lack of manual dexterity and with the implication that even he can play it? Probably so in some instances and probably not in others. But the more intriguing facet of this rhetorical question is, Does the fact that the son's superiority at game playing and other endeavors over his father's impair or improve his own development? In other words, do children of such physically disabled parents display adjustment patterns that deviate from those of children of nondisabled parents? Or, as some might contend, does this early development of competence relative to their parents' abilities actually enhance such children's mental health? As yet, no clear-cut evidence is available to answer such questions.

The present chapter will examine some of these issues. First, it will focus primarily on parents who were disabled prior to parenthood. Second, it will examine the concept of parenting in modern America and attempt to relate this to situations involving parents who have some form of physical handicap. Third, some critical issues involving the physically disabled parent will be discussed with material taken from primarily anecdotal sources. And, finally, a research paradigm for empirical studies into the general area will be proposed and described.

PARENTING IN MODERN AMERICA

The topic of the physically disabled parent must be examined in the context of "parenting" as viewed in contemporary society. The adequacy of the physically disabled individual as a parent must be viewed from the perspective of the adequacy of parents in general. Yankelovich, Skelly, and While (1977) found that 63% of parents surveyed felt they were doing an adequate job of parenting. This sample also felt that 74% of other parents known to them were doing an adequate job. LeMasters (1974), on the other hand, found in an informal survey that his sample of middle-class parents felt they were "successful" with 50% of their children. These findings do not completely tell the story, due to the fact that these were surveys of parents. Surveys of children might yield different results, and surveys of others (i.e., older persons, professionals in mental health, etc.) might show even greater differences. Empirical evidence of the adequacy of parenting in current-day society is difficult to find and even more difficult to evaluate as to its accuracy and validity (LeMasters, 1974).

Despite a lack of such empirical research, there is an abundance of literature on what a "good" parent should be. In bookstores one often finds an entire section called "parent books." Much of the contents of these books are distillation of what society has come to regard as acceptable practices in performing the parents' role. Such acceptable practices can be conceptualized as one form of Galbraith's conventional wisdom. The concept has been discussed elsewhere in regard to rehabilitation practices (Jenkins, Greer & Odle, 1978). LeMasters (1974) contends that conventional wisdom, a system of beliefs that are widely held, yet have little or no support in facts, is similar to folklore. LeMasters then lists some twenty such beliefs regarding parenthood. Only those most pertinent to the current topic will be discussed here.

Among the folklore beliefs listed and discussed by LeMasters are the following:

1. Children are sweet and cute.
2. Children will turn out well if they have good parents.
3. Modern behavioral science has been helpful to parents.
4. There are no bad children—only bad parents.

Children are sweet and cute.   This may apply to infants and small toddlers, especially *someone else's* infant or toddlers. This, however, rarely holds true for the young organism residing in your own home. In many instances, the case of the parent as a hostage could easily be made, particularly in middle-class, child-oriented homes. Rather than being sweet and cute, the child in this case becomes a somewhat hostile terrorist. This is, of course, something of an exaggeration that is made to counter this belief. For example, an adult who would spread thumb tacks on a floor to deflate the tires on someone's wheelchair would be looked upon as sick. Yet, when it was done by the son of a woman in a wheelchair seeking to restrict his mother's mobility, some people thought it was creative and cute! To the mother, Linda, it was neither.

Children will turn out well if they have good parents.   Both psychoanalysts and behaviorists, despite their disparate views on other aspects of human behavior, place great stress on the parent's early influence on the development of the child. These theories put much emphasis on the early life events of the child in shaping the child's personality. More recently, others have begun to question these precepts. Thomas, Chess, and Birch (1968) postulate that children are born with certain temperaments that cannot be the result of their environment, but rather appear to be innate. These authors speak of "easy" children and "difficult" children. The difficult child will present a challenge to any environment he or she enters. Bandura (1982) points out that chance encounters can alter a person's life path. The early environment, according to Bandura, works to develop preferences and such preferences work to produce certain environments, but unintended events can permanently alter an individual's life. Should parents of such an individual feel guilt or pride when such events take place? LeMasters points out that the parent is only one of a multitude of influences that shape the development of the child. He points to schools, the peer group, the media, and other sources that have as much impact on the development of the child as does the parent. Yet, there are those who will pick out some characteristic of the parent to somehow explain a child's behavior. Despite their research showing that children of parents with multiple sclerosis are well adjusted, Kennedy and Bush (1979) cite one case of the daughter of one of their subjects who was 16 years old, sexually promiscuous and abusing drugs. These authors infer that this child's role confusion regarding her bedridden mother somehow played a part in the child's deviant behavior. Out of the myriad of influences to which this child must have been exposed, it is difficult to pick one, for example, a chronic illness in the mother, to explicate her behavior.

Modern behavioral science has been helpful to parents. LeMasters (1974) and Cooper (1974) both indicate that the greatest contribution of modern behavioral science to parents is an enhancement of guilt and confusion. A substantial case can be made for the fact that behavioral science has contributed to the current diversity in approaches to child-rearing, almost all of which emphasizes the role of the parent. Some books currently found in book stores admonish the parents on their role in formulating a child's intellect, while others caution against pressuring the child, for example, *The Hurried Child* by Elkind. If we can assume that physically handicapped parents are as anxious as other parents to meet their parental responsibilities, we can also assume that they are as mystified as other parents when seeking literature on the subject. Given the extra expenditure of time some physically disabled persons must devote to their day-to-day routine (DeLoach and Greer, 1981), advice regarding strict schedules for children hinders rather than helps.

There are no bad children—just bad parents. LeMasters (1974) and others (Rappoport & Rappoport, 1977) label those who belong to this school of thought "child worshippers." They seem to adhere fanatically to the concepts of Locke and Rousseau regarding *tabula rasa* and the innate innocence of children. Some of the previously cited works (Cooper, 1974; LeMasters, 1974; and Thomas et al., 1968) also apply this concept. Granted that while there are parents who inflict untold damage on children (Kemp & Helfer, 1973; Wilson, Trammel, Greer, & Long, 1977), it is still the case that most parents have the best interests of their offspring as one of their highest priorities. Since society has often been portrayed as viewing physical disability as bad (Wright, 1960), it is understandable that parents with disabilities might perceive any misbehavior on the part of their children as a reflection of themselves. It is yet to be demonstrated empirically that such parents feel any guiltier than other parents, nor has it been demonstrated that they have more valid reasons for such feelings than other parents.

Children themselves often exacerbate parents' guilt feelings by not-so-diplomatically pointing out weaknesses or other characteristics in their parents to explain any misfortune that befalls them. If the parents had earned more money, they (the children) would have had more opportunities. If the parents had only had less money, they (the children) would not have had so much leisure time and would have had to work harder for their opportunities. In essence, they blame their problems on a "hook"—any characteristic of the parent that is, in their minds, unique from other parents—and attribute many of their own failures to these hooks in the parent. A physical disability can become such a hook to a child. What must be remembered by both child and parent is that in states of anger, resentment, or bitterness, human beings search for something to excuse their shortcomings. This process does not always involve blaming negative outcomes on a parent's disability. There is a television commercial involving a famous professional football player who attributes his successful sports career to "my daddy who was in a wheelchair." Negative or positive, one must question whether one factor, in this case a physical disability, is the overwhelming influence some would have us believe, when we consider the almost infinite number of factors affecting the development of an individual.

CRITICAL ISSUES FACING PHYSICALLY DISABLED PARENTS

"Many disabled adults, like many able-bodied adults, become parents. When a person has a severe mobility impairment, the disability can complicate the already challenging situation of being a parent" (Brown, 1981, p. 32). Not only does this statement hold true for the mobility impaired, it holds true for impairments of other physical abilities.

The available literature in the area of parenting and the physically handicapped centers on four basic issues. First, there is the issue of becoming a parent. Secondly, there is the issue of providing the necessary nurture needed in rearing a child. Thirdly, there is the issue of the child's achieving an early physical superiority over the parent. And, lastly, there is the issue of intimate familiarity of the child with the long-term effects of permanent physical disability.

Becoming a Parent

For some individuals, becoming a parent is a natural process of marriage or some romantic liaison. For others, it seems to be a desired, yet physiologically or psychologically unachievable, goal. For the couple where the wife is physically disabled, the ability to have children naturally may be medically improbable or may present certain life-threatening hazards to both the mother and the offspring (DeLoach & Greer, 1981). In such cases, the couple may consider the possibility of adoption. However, certain adoption agencies have strict policies regarding the physical, and well as mental, capabilities of adoptive parents (Buck & Hohmann, 1981). Sandness (1981) quotes one employee of such an agency as telling her and her nondisabled husband, "Be glad you have each other. Don't try to be parents, too" (p. 23). Parenthetically, Sandness and her husband found, five years later, a new agency that speialized in seeking American homes for Korean–American children. The Sandnesses have adopted thirteen children! The current author, who is physically disabled, has two children, both of whom are adopted. He and his wife experienced no unusual reluctance on the part of the state adoption agency. However, his wife is nondisabled, and it may be that a couple where the wife is physically disabled would experience more difficulty approaching adoption agencies due to the current-day view of parenting as being the central role of the mother. Other variables such as occupational status and severity of disability would also be major factors considered by such agencies.

Greer (1965) conducted a study of the adjustment of 59 adults with cerebral palsy. One aspect of this study was the division of this sample into five groups based on mental health. Of those subjects who were parents, over 90 percent fell into the top two groups. Currently, there is a decreasing desire to assume the parent role on the part of young married persons (DeLoach & Greer, 1981). Therefore, it can be proposed that the disabled persons who become parents are (1) much above average in mental health and (2) most enthusiastic and committed to assuming this role.

Providing Nurture

Once spouses become parents, the proper care and nurture of the child, or children, is of paramount importance in the minds of many authorities in the field of child development. Rearing of a child entails providing for the child's basic needs. These needs are those of nutrition, physical health, physical safety, intellectual stimulation, and emotional security. Since the providing of such needs involves certain physical, mental, and emotional abilities on the part of the parents (i.e., the physical skills to prepare formulas, meals, etc.), outsiders are frequently concerned about the physically disabled parent's ability to manage these tasks. What is not considered many times is the fact that there exist an almost infinite variety of methods of achieving a specified task. For example, if one envisions the task of diapering an infant as cleaning up the child's excrement and then pinning a clean diaper on the child, it is very difficult to imagine a person who has palsy performing this task. However, there are diapers with snaps, instead of pins, and, currently, disposable diapers with strips of tape. Caring for and meeting the needs of the child then become a matter of creatively developing alternative methods that circumvent the parents' physical limitations.

The presence of a physical disability may be a hindrance to society's perceiving that a parent may be fit to provide for the child's needs in spite of the most undesirable circumstances. A severely disabled father was divorced from his nondisabled wife. During the marriage they had one daughter. After the divorce, the father remained unsuccessful in seeking permanent custody of the child, despite the mother's aberrant lifestyle involving several boyfriends and strongly suspected sexual molestation of the little girl. However, it did not help the case when the father took the daughter to another city without the mother's or the court's permission. Charges and countercharges resulted in a most regrettable situation for the child. In this instance, it might be that the disabled father could have provided a healthier environment for the child, but his impulsive, rash behavior only worked to reinforce society's view of his lack of ability to act as a parent. It is an intriguing question as to whether this father could have provided his daughter with a more positive style of nurture than the mother, even with his rather serious physical limitations. Brown (1981) cites several examples of families where the disabled parent's disability was a source of pride for the child, it involved the father's being in closer day-to-day contact with the children, and some of the children even developed career interests in the medical field due to their familiarity with disabilities. The available research in this area does not indicate any particular difficulties on the part of the disabled parents to provide physically, intellectually, or emotionally for the children. There is, however, some evidence to demonstrate that in such circumstances there is undue stress placed upon the nondisabled spouses (Buck & Hohmann, 1981).

Physical Superiority of the Child

"An issue most disabled parents must cope with is how much personal assistance to require from the child" (Brown, 1981, p. 35). Requiring too much assistance from the child could, in extreme cases, place unneeded stress on the child and could result in growing resentment of the parent's physical dependence. It is even suspected that physical dependence and emotional dependence are often interrelated (DeLoach & Greer, 1981; Wright, 1960). A physically disabled father states the issue succinctly when he relates, "It's really easy to get Melissa to work for me. She will do things I can't do. She'll go get a tool, or I hold her up to get things I can't reach. But disabled parents have to be careful. We have to let our sons and daughters be children and do the things they want. They have their own little minds and their own priorities. We can't let them become robots for our sake" (Brown, 1981, p. 35). From a different perspective, however, some physical dependence on a child could enhance the child's own feelings of competence. Whereas some children of nondisabled parents are forbidden for various reasons from doing tasks within their capabilities, children of the physically disabled in many cases do not meet with such restraints. At issue frequently is not the physical dependence of the parents, but the entire matter of the efficient use of time. Disabled parents are often faced with doing a task themselves that would require considerably more time than were they to allow, or require, their nondisabled child to do it in a much shorter length of time. It must be pointed out that the efficient use of time, while a practical consideration, is a poor rationalization for excesses in the misuse of a child's assistance.

In doing tasks around the home, the author relies heavily on both his children for getting tools, tasks requiring fine eye–hand coordination, and getting to small, out-of-the-way places. However, the author's son, who is more dextrous at twelve years of age than his father, does not yet match his father in strength and experience. "Trade-offs" are then made with the father applying the needed "elbow grease" to loosen an extra-tight nut or to instruct his son in the alignment of the rear wheel of a bicycle; while the son will use a screwdriver to start a screw, or a hammer to nail something, without the unsightly surrounding hammer marks that would be there if the father were doing the nailing!

Adlerian concepts of inferiority have been offered as one of the tenets of adjustment to physical disability in the past (English, 1971). One of these Adlerian tenets is that the child, being surrounded by more physically dominant and competent adults, develops early feelings of inferiority. A child who, on the other hand, quickly learns that he or she is physically superior to the most significant adult in his or her life, that is, one or both parents, can be postulated to have a somewhat different outlook. It would be interesting to develop a measure of self-perceived competence and to ascertain if differences exist between children of physically disabled parents as compared to children of non-disabled parents.

One area in which the physical superiority of the child presents serious problems is that of discipline. Many nondisabled parents do not encounter this until their children are well into adolescence. But for the physically disabled parents, the disciplining of even a very young child can present problems. Sandness (1981) states, "If you can't follow through on discipline, . . . have someone around who can. . . . [And] avoid making threats you cannot carry out" (p. 24). For example, instead of making dire threats to demonstrate one's anger, one should make statements that are so exaggerated that their ridiculousness is obvious to both parent and child. This conveys the parent's grave concern without leading to a "no-win" confrontation. For example, with an older child a parent might say, "I'm so mad I could run over you with my wheelchair!" I have used the line, "I'm so mad at you I am shaking!" With tempers flaring on both sides, such statements frequently defuse the situation with humor. At other times the discipline may take the form of restricting privileges or other sanctions that do not involve physical punishment.

The parent with a physical disability soon learns there are absolute limits to the degree to which they can go in the disciplining of a child. In many families where only one of the parents is disabled, discipline has been found to be primarily the responsibility of the nondisabled parent (Buck & Hohmann, 1981). To let such a responsibility rest too heavily on one parent, however, is not entirely fair to that parent, nor would it appear to be healthy for the relationship of the disabled parent and his or her children. At the core of the issue is how one conceptualizes discipline. If one envisions discipline as some type of physical punishment, then certain physically disabled parents, such as quadriplegics, might encounter many barriers to disciplining their children and, thus, would leave this duty to the more able spouse. On the other hand, if discipline is conceived to be the general establishment of rules of conduct and the enforcement of those rules, then nonphysical types of discipline could be enforced by both parents. Also at issue here is the establishment of mutual respect on the part of parent and child.

The author's son is almost physically equal to his father, but the father retains the upper hand mainly out of respect, not physical superiority. Here, one must consider the disciplining of a child as one of the coping strategies that must be developed to reduce disability-related stress (DeLoach & Greer, 1981). Sandness's guidelines, presented earlier, represent a good starting point for the development of such strategies.

THE CHILD'S FAMILIARITY WITH THE EFFECTS
OF PHYSICAL DISABLEMENT

One recurrent theme in some of the writing regarding children of physically disabled parents is the reference to such children's tolerance for differences in others. "Scotti's a smart child. . . . I have Alliance meetings here. She's helped all kinds of disabled people, each with different needs. . . . She can tell a person's range of motion by noticing where they can reach" (Brown, 1981, p. 33). From such references, one might easily develop the hypothesis that children with physically disabled parents would tend to be more tolerant of physical difference in others. This hypothesis, however, should be generated with some caution. First, the age of the child must be considered. Younger children do not generalize from parents to other adults with disabilities. One of the most fascinating incidents to occur to the writer was on an overnight visit with a couple, both of whom had cerebral palsy. In the writer's subjective appraisal, both of these individuals had a more awkward gait than the writer. This couple had two attractive, physically normal children. The oldest child was about four years old at the time and she would stare at the writer every time he walked. Finally, he asked the child why she seemed so curious. The child replied, "Why do you walk so funny? I've never seen anyone walk so funny!" It may be, therefore, that to very young children, Mommy and Daddy are Mommy and Daddy, but separate and apart, physically and emotionally, from others. Another factor to be considered is the parents' involvement with other physically impaired individuals. In the instance cited above, Scotti's mother was very involved with an advocacy group that brought the child into contact with many adults with all types of disabilities. What about parents whose social interactions are mainly with non-disabled individuals?

There are even some suggestions that children who have seen their parents struggle to achieve a normal lifestyle in spite of a physical disability are less tolerant of persons who complain of physical problems

(Buck & Hohmann, 1981). However, the research of Buck and Hohmann and that of others (e.g., Olgas, 1974) found no evidence to demonstrate that children of physically disabled parents viewed physical disability negatively. The present writer has had several students majoring in special education whose parents were physically disabled. Could this not be an indication of positive identification on the part of such students with persons who are disabled. It may be that Buck and Hohmann's subject were intolerant of the complaints of persons who were not truly disabled!

The speculative literature on the effects of parental impairment on the children of such families is, by and large, negative. "Much has been written regarding the beneficial effects of the patient, though disabled, of being at home with loved ones. It can nevertheless accentuate the already crisis situation which arises from illness of a family member" (Olgas, p. 319). However, the empirical literature presents no clear-cut evidence for such negative effects from a disabling condition in a parent on the long-term adjustment of children.

A PROPOSED RESEARCH PARADIGM

If we are to move forward in the promotion of knowledge in the area of parenting and the physically disabled adult, we must move in a more comprehensive frame of reference. The work of Olgas (1974) and Buck and Hohmann (1981) are good beginnings, but they have strict limitations. The number of subjects used was somewhat small in both studies and represented circumscribed samples of particular types of disabilities. This is not a criticism of these studies, but rather an admonition that much more needs to be done to yield a comprehensive body of empirical evidence in this topic area.

Table 8.1 displays a proposed paradigm, listing the variables that must be included in future research. The writer does not intend that one research project could encompass and control for all the listed variables. This is proposed merely as a listing of some of the major variables that must be taken into account if a more complete body of research is to develop.

Table 8.1 presents a partial listing of the variables to be included in researching the area of parents with physical disabilities. The variables are divided into three major categories: *parent variables, family situational variables,* and *child variables.* The listing of specific variables within the three categories is incomplete in each case. They represent

Table 8.1

Variables to be Considered in Studies Investigating Parenting
and the Effects of Parents with Physical Disabilities

Parent variables	Family situational variables	Child variables
Independent	Intact	Independent
Disability	Divorced	Sex
Severity	One parent disabled	Age
Age at onset	Both parents disabled	Birth order
Parent	Presence of step-parent	Age at disablement of
Mother	Disabled	parent
Father	Nondisabled	Dependent
Educational level		Self-concept
Socioeconomic status		Adjustment level
Employment status		Sociometric status
Dependent		among peers
Adjustment level		Attitude toward parents
Attitude toward		Attitude toward others
child rearing		with disabilities

those included in prior research as well as those that would appear to be important to the present writer. Obviously, many additional variables could be added to this listing. Under two of the categories, parent variables and child variables, the subcategories of *independent* and *dependent* are included. Much of the research done thus far has investigated only the adjustment level of the children. It seems obvious that the adjustment of the parent must be taken into account as well, along with the parent's attitudes toward child-rearing. The tediousness of the systematic inclusions of all these dependent and independent variables in one or two studies is all too clear to the writer. Rather, it will take many different studies to yield a comprehensive body of knowledge in this area. Until such a comprehensive approach is undertaken, however, few conclusions can be drawn regarding children of families where one or both parents are disabled.

REFERENCES

Bandura, A. The psychology of chance encounters and life paths. *American Psychologist*, 1982, 37(7), 747–755.
Brown, D. All in the family. *Disabled USA*, 1981, 4(3), 30–35.

Buck, F. M., & Hohmann, G. Personality behavior, values and family relations of children of fathers with spinal cord injury. *Archives of Physical Medicine*, 1981, *62*, 432–428.

Cooper, S. Treatment of parents. In G. Caplan (Ed.), *American Handbook of Psychiatry, II*. New York: Basic Books, 1974.

DeLoach, C., & Greer, B. G. Adjustment to severe physical disability: A metamorphosis. New York: McGraw–Hill, 1981.

Elkind, D. *The hurried child*. Menlo Park, CA: Addison-Wesley, 1981.

English, W. The application of personality theory to explain psychological reaction to disability. *Rehabilitation Research and Practice Review*, 1981.

Greer, B. A study of the personal adjustment of adults with cerebral palsy. Unpublished doctoral dissertation, University of Texas, 1965.

Jenkins, W., Odle, S., & Greer, B. Conventional wisdom: Is it really wise. *Journal of Rehabilitation*, July/August/September, 1978, *20*(3), 42–43.

Kempe, H., & Helfer, R. *Helping the battered child and his family*. New York: Lippincott, 1972.

Kennedy, K. M., & Bush, D. F. Counseling the children of handicapped parents. *Personnel and Guidance Journal*, 1979, *58*(4), 267–270.

LeMasters, E. E. *Parents in modern America*. Homewood, IL: Dorsey Press, 1974.

Olgas, M. The relationship between parents' health status and body image of their children. *Nursing Research*, 1974, *23*(4), 319–323.

Rappoport, R. N., & Rappoport, R. *Fathers, mothers and other*. London: Rutledge and Paul, 1977.

Thomas, A., Chess, S., & Birch, H. G. *Temperament and behavior disorders in children*. New York: New York University Press, 1968.

Sandness, G. Adoption by parents with disabilities. *Rehabilitation Gazette*, 1981, *24*, 23–25.

Wilson, C., Trammel, S., Greer, B. G., & Long, G. *An exploratory study of the relationship between child abuse and drug abuse by the perpetrators*. Unpublished manuscript. Memphis, Tennessee, 1977.

Wright, B. *Physical disability: A psychological approach*. New York: Harper-Row, 1960.

Yankelovich, J., Skelley, S., & White, A. *Raising children in a changing society*. Minneapolis: General Mills, 1977.

Onset of Disability in a Parent: Impact on Child and Family

DOROTHEA D. GLASS

PROBLEMS ASSOCIATED WITH ONSET OF PARENTAL DISABILITY

The sudden onset of a major disability in a parent, with the attending physical and psychological changes and losses affecting every aspect of the person's and family's life, often results in an interruption of life styles, goals, and expectations of crisis proportions, causing disruption of the family homeostasis in which the usual problem-solving means are inadequate to restore balance. This disequilibrium causes stress on all family members, including the children, and results in a process of response that may include a period of shock, denial, mourning, depression, and despair, followed by a process of trial and error, adapting and accommodation, then renewal of routines and roles, recovery and reorganization, at a level determined by the hardships of the disability, interacting with the family's crisis-meeting resources (Bishop & Epstein, 1980; Kossaris, 1979; Litman, 1966; Livsey, 1972). There is great variability in response of different families and thus variation in the amount of disruption, the physical and emotional cost, the time and effort needed to reach homeostasis again, and in the level of functioning finally achieved. Thus the onset of disability, which often means prolonged hospitalization and separation of the parent from the family, has an impact on the life style of the children as well as the parents and interferes with the physical and emotional routines of daily living, plans, and expectations of all family members. The challenge to the family's value system, role patterns, and communication networks results in problems for the family members not solvable by customary

145

methods, and causes acute continuing stress in the present, as well as mobilizing anxieties and problems associated with past events and future plans (Anthony, 1970; Cogswell, 1976; El Ghatit & Hanson, 1976; Parad & Caplan, 1965; Trieschmann, 1980).

Practically, the disability of a parent may result in a dramatic decrease in family income if the disabled person is a wage earner; a draining of the family's financial resources, not only for medical care, but for care of the home and young children if the mother is disabled; the need to assume new roles by the able-bodied parent and children and perhaps even forced change in the home environment to minimize architectural barriers and/or cost. Many of these have ripple effects causing changes in all aspects of the family members' lives, both large and very small.

These multiple and significant changes cause feelings of loneliness, abandonment, anger, guilt, depression, despair, and sometimes panic in both parents and children. The adults are more likely to have the cognitive ability to deal with the crisis appropriately within the framework of their established value system and life pattern. The children, on the other hand, have often not developed the cognitive and coping skills to understand the causality and contingency relationships surrounding the onset of disability.

The Very Young Child

The very young child's thinking is primitive and magical. Even in the latency years, the movement from magical to rational thinking is slow and gradual. Questions for the children, therefore, are concrete: what? why? how? The abstract concepts surrounding the changes brought about by the disability cannot be readily handled by the children and often result in overwhelming bewilderment and insecurity, which worsen the impact of sudden parental disability on the young child. The disabled parent precipitously disappears for a prolonged interval of unknown duration into the strange and frightening world of the hospital and rehabilitation center. The remaining able-bodied parent is visibly upset and unsure, or sometimes panic-stricken, unable to cope. There is general confusion and interruption of the normal routines of the home, all very frightening to the very young child. The able-bodied parent is often away for many hours at the hospital or attending to reality problems and, therefore, the child is deprived of both emotional anchors.

The anxiety, anger, guilt, and other negative feelings about the disability felt by the family's older members are perceived by the child.

The medical situation for the disabled parent is often unsettled or un-clear, producing in the child increased anxiety and fear of death of the parent. If it is the primary caretaker who is disabled, there is usually serious disruption of the family and home routines, increased disorder in the home, often with discipline relaxed, disarrangement of living conditions, and perhaps unfamiliar relatives or strangers in the home caring for the child.

The Older Child

The older child who is able to think in rational and conceptual terms identifies with the parents and their troubles and feels the same lone-liness, helplessness, apprehension, anger, and perhaps guilt. The med-ical situation of the disabled parent is often unclear or mystified because of ignorance and lack of appropriate feedback from hospital personnel. The child may feel anger because of a breach of the implied contract of family living, disappointment concerning future plans and possible or imagined changes. This may be accompanied by guilt be-cause of the anger, since one is not supposed to be angry at a sick par-ent. In addition, the child may experience fantasies of causation, because of previous differences with the parent, expectation of pun-ishment for secret sin or remorse at not having been "good" to the parent in the past. Feelings of shame may result from the embarrass-ment of deviance from societal norms, opening of private family trou-bles to the view of outsiders so that the family becomes vulnerable and an object of pity to others, and from the negative attitudes toward disability held by much of society (Richardson, Goodman, Hastrof, & Dornbusch, 1961; Romano, 1984). Often the older child feels he or she has to behave like an adult, take over for the hospitalized parent, sup-press his or her feelings in front of the younger children and/or the visibly troubled and perhaps overwhelmed able-bodied parent. Some-times teenagers may respond in the direction of acting out, doing poorly in school, withdrawal and disinterest, sexual promiscuity, or use of drugs or alcohol (Kennedy & Bush, 1979; Olsen, 1970).

ADJUSTING TO THE DISABILITY

Evolution of the process of adjustment to the disability will depend on many factors related to the integration of the family, its value sys-tem and coping skills, the nature of the disability, and the resources available to the family from within and from the society in which the family functions. The nature and extent of the disability will determine the resources needed to cope with it. If the disability is limited and stable, resources to handle it are more easily available; and the future can be predicted and controlled. If the disability is progressive, complicated, with multiple system damage, then more resources are needed, the future is unpredictable; and this may result in continuous instability and anxiety for the family members. The presence of even severe disability does not preclude the maintenance of an intact, interdependent, loving family unit, able to participate in work and play at a satisfying level. Medical and technological advances have made it possible for people with very severe disabilities to be full participating members of their family and society (Romano, 1984).

The adjustment of the family to disability in a parent is a process, not a state. The responses observed in the first weeks and months after onset are not necessarily what are going to be the family's long-term means of coping with the disability, though they are often so-misinterpreted by health-care professionals. Actually, families are constantly responding to the process of achieving homeostatis (Romano, personal communication). The effectively functioning family solves problems; the ineffectively functioning family may not.

Better integrated and adaptable families are less vulnerable and can more easily take crisis in stride without marked changes in organization and structure. Factors conducive to good adjustment include affectional relations among family members, good marital adjustment, companionable parent–child relationships, family council type of control in making decisions, previous successful experience with other crises, and social participation (Hill, 1965; Koos, 1946).

Hill (1965) has summarized the statements of many investigators in a formula that diagrams the adaptability of a family in crisis: The hardships of the event, A, lie outside the family and are an attribute of the event itself. Events outside the family tend to solidify the family. B and C, the family's resources and the definition the family makes of the event, are within the family and depend upon the family's structure and values, which vary from family to family. The more meager the family's resources, B, the more vulnerable the family is and the more severely will the stressor event, A, be defined as crisis, C.

The outcome of the crisis, that is, the disability, thus depends on the adequacy of the family's resources. Koos (1946) has described the basic criteria for adequacy of a family organization as including: (1) consciousness of, and acceptance by, each member of his or her own roles, responsibilities, and rights, and of the complementary roles, in the family; (2) willingness of family members to accept the common good of the family over their own individual goals and desires, so that the family thinks of itself as a unit, with open discussion and communication concerning this; (3) provision of satisfactions within the family unit so that the home is the center for the children's activities; and (4) existence of a family sense of direction and movement, however small, toward a commonly agreed upon objective or objectives.

The problem-solving process for the family responding to the onset of a disability can be assisted by the development of a program of problem-solving tasks. First, the family members must come to terms with the possible threat to the life of the disabled parent implicit in the disability and the absence of the parent from the household, with the accompanying loneliness, changes in routines and roles, emotional deprivations, and disappointments. Another task for the children is to master the threat of loss of self, based on the absence of a parent on whom the child depends for survival and on identification with that parent, causing anxiety in the child about his or her own vulnerability. Possible guilt about having unconsciously caused the disability because of angry wishes or inattention must be handled, along with the anxiety that the disability may be punishment for wrongdoing or wrong-thinking. There may be a need of the child to try to replace the absent parent. Contact with the disabled parent away from the home must be reestablished, and finally, there must be reintegration of the changed parent into the family, with restoration of the integrity and effective functioning of the family as close to the predisability level as possible.

It is important that the separation of the parent from the home be as brief as possible and that every effort be made to bring the disabled parent back to the home quickly, starting perhaps with day-long or weekend home visits. Should the disabled parent be unable to return home permanently because of the nature of the disability, a new crisis situation arises with a new and more difficult set of adjustments to be made.

Facilitating the child's adjustment to the parent's disability depends on the age and conceptual ability of the child. Older children should be helped to verbalize their concerns, questions, and feelings so as to work them through. Opportunities for appropriate activities in understanding and dealing with the newly disabled parent work to counteract feelings of helplessness. Meeting with the hospital therapists who are treating the parent, to explore and learn adaptive techniques and equipment and observe the parent develop increasing competence, is useful for this. Doing things for the disabled parent will not pose the problem of reversal of the parenting role if it is seen in the larger context of a reciprocal relationship satisfying a temporary need. Spending time with the disabled parent in the rehabilitation setting so as to share the parent's experiences, thoughts, and feelings and work them through together can help to increase feelings of competence and comfort in dealing with the disability and its effects both inside and outside the home (Kossaris, 1979).

The young child needs to spend time in the rehabilitation center with the disabled parent, too. She or he can explore the hospital environment, handle the adaptive equipment, push the wheelchair, and assist the able-bodied parent so as to be involved in the disabled parent's rehabilitation program. The child's questions about changes in the disabled parent's functioning need to be answered directly and simply at the level of the child's understanding, not in elaborate detail; for example, "Why can't Mommy walk?" "She hurt her back badly." "How will she get home?" "In her wheelchair in the car." This helps to set the child's expectation that the disabled parent's competence in her or his role will be resumed in the future, that Mommy will still be Mommy. It is also important to share and deal with the child's feelings by direct verbal acknowledgement: "You miss having Daddy at home." The young child may be helped to handle her or his adaptive process through creative play, which allows review of painful events in the disabled parent. Dolls, puppets, drawing materials, and storytelling have all been used. Content of such play should parallel reality sufficiently so that the child can identify with it (Strax & Spergel, 1980).

The first visit home is important for the start of the reintegration of the changed parent into the family, and careful preparation should be made for it. This allows for some understanding of what the parent can and cannot do, some discovering of what changes may need to be made in the home, and rehearsal of some of the daily processes while the patient is still a part of the hospital program, so that needed adaptations can be planned and made thoughtfully and without pressure. It is important on this first visit that the family have plenty of time together without visitors. Preparation of this sort serves not only to demystify the disability and reassure the child and other family members that the family can function with the disability, but also provides the child with models for dealing with reactions to the parent's disability by people outside the family. Often relatives, teachers, neighbors, and peers make thoughtless, pitying, or teasing remarks. Becoming familiar with the disability, gaining mastery over her or his own feelings and coming to terms with the events of the disability, makes the child better able to cope. For instance, Romano describes an 8-year-old child who was teased at school by his schoolmates who said that his father would never come home, that he had been punished by God because he was bad. The child, who had been participating in a familiarizing program, was able to reply that he was helping his father with his wheelchair, that his father loved him and was soon coming home (Romano, 1976).

EFFECTS OF PARENTAL DISABILITY
ON CHILDREN

Many dire predictions and projections concerning the ghastly effects of major disability on family life are made, but actually very little objective research has been done (Buck & Hohmann, 1981). Much of what appears in the literature indicates that able-bodied health professionals project their own negative fantasies onto families where there is a disabled parent, as if it were fact (Romano, 1982). Many articles have described a multitude of deleterious effects on the children of a disabled parent in the areas of psychological adjustment, sex role development, health patterns, body image, contemporary interests, interpersonal relations, school achievement, acting out, drug abuse, social responsibility, and parent–child relationships. These articles have been used in the courts and by adoption agencies as a basis for denying the rights of parental responsibility to disabled people. Actually, there have been only a few objective studies (DeLaMata, Gingras, & Wittkower, 1960; Olgas, 1974), and many of these are of limited scope and methodology without use of controls.

Little is known empirically about the effects of parental disability on children, although it is of vital interest to physically disabled parents and the rehabilitation professions. Buck and Hohmann (1981), in a comparison study of adolescents and young adults raised by veteran fathers with spinal cord injuries and by nondisabled veteran fathers, found no differences in psychological adjustment. These subjects showed appropriate sex role orientation; the male children were able to identify with a father who did not always assume the traditional male, provider role; and all showed good health-care patterns and ap-

propriate sick role behavior with no increase in hospitalizations, illnesses, or surgeries. Despite limitations in mobility, disabled fathers
participated in as many recreational activities as did the nondisabled;
and the children of the disabled expressed more interest in athletics
and recreation. There were no adverse effects on social skills, number
and closeness of friends, or dating patterns because of the social stigma
of having a disabled parent or from having increased responsibilities
at the expense of leisure activities. Nor was there any evidence that
the children felt ashamed of their disabled fathers or received negative
feedback about their fathers from friends and dates who met them.
There was no evidence of any adverse effect on the parent–child relationship; and the fathers in both groups were similarly perceived by
their children to be warm, affectionate, and helpful. Disabled fathers
were reported to express verbal and physical affection to their children
more often. There was no difference in discipline practices, which were
perceived as appropriately limiting but not overly authoritative or punishing, nor in methods of punishing misbehavior by spanking, yelling,
or reasoning, although these fathers withdrew privileges more often.
Fathers with spinal cord injuries did not delegate decision making or
discipline to mothers more, nor was there loss of authority by the disabled fathers. The children responded more quickly and willingly to
their disabled fathers' requests and commands, and had more positive
attitudes about their fathers. They also felt more protective of both
their fathers and mothers.

Olgas (1974), in a study of children of parents with multiple sclerosis, showed that they did not differ significantly in body image development from children with able-bodied parents. Severity of
disability was not a useful predictor of satisfaction or effectiveness in
family roles. Some of the physically limited homemakers, bedridden
and severely disabled, had not needed to relinquish their function as
home manager and provider of mothering and had well-organized and
smoothly operating homes. Similarly, a severely disabled father could
function as supervisor, manager, and task assigner of the family, even
though he was not physically active or the major wage earner (Litman,
1966; Livsey, 1972).

A major disability in a parent will result in inevitable changes both
inside and outside of the family; and in the marginal family, the post-
morbid adjustment may be more precarious than at the predisabled
stage. Where there is better premorbid integration of the family, the
postdisability problems will be coped with more effectively. However,
existing research and experience suggest that in many families the disability is not the true cause of the problems, though it is often blamed

by the family that holds negative beliefs and prejudices about disability and thus blames all problems on the disability, even though many families without a disabled parent are facing the same problems of rebellious children, financial difficulties, intrafamily hostility, and social isolation.

Much of the available literature depends on highly selected and biased samples, anecdotal case descriptions, or opinion based on personal experience. In addition, the literature centers on neuromusculoskeletal disability. In searching the literature for preparing this chapter, no reports were found that addressed age of onset of other disabilities (e.g., blindness, deafness, etc.). There is a great need for well-developed and well-grounded research using sound, scientific methods with application of standardized measurement and adequate controls. Of great interest and value would be cooperative longitudinal studies of families with a disabled parent, using a systematic and uniform method of obtaining data; controlled empirical studies of effects of parental disability on children of different ages and stages; comparison of the responses and adjustment of children to an already-disabled parent with the responses of children to a parent who later acquires a disability; study of children of families with one disabled parent compared with children in families where both parents are disabled; and comparison of the characteristics of coping and noncoping families. Solid information is needed not only for the guidance of disabled parents and of those working with their rehabilitation, but also to combat the current discrimination so often faced in society, in the courts, and in the agencies by disabled parents and their children.

REFERENCES

Anthony, E. J. The impact of mental and physical illness on family life. *American Journal of Psychiatry*, 1970, *127*(2), 56–64.

Bishop, D. S., and Epstein, N. B. Family problems and disability. In D. S. Bishop (Ed.), *Behavioral problems and the disabled*. Baltimore: Williams & Wilkins, 1980.

Buck, F. M., and Hohmann, G. W. Personality and behavior of children of disabled and non-disabled fathers. *Archives of Physical Medicine and Rehabilitation*, 1981, *62*, 432–438.

Cogswell, B. E. Conceptual model of family as a group: Family response to disabled. In G. L. Albrecht, (Ed.) *Sociology of physical disability and rehabilitation*. University of Pittsburgh Press, 1976.

DeLaMata, R. C., Gringras, C., and Wittkower, E. D. Impact of sudden severe disablement of the father upon the family. *Canadian Medical Association*, 1960, *82*, 1015–1020.

El Ghatit, A. Z., Hanson, R. Marriage and divorce after spinal cord injury. *Archives of Physical Medicine and Rehabilitation*, 1976, *57*, 470–472.

Hill, R. Generic features of families under stress. In H. J. Parad (Ed.), *Crisis intervention*. New York: Family Service Association of America, 1965.

Kennedy, K. M., and Bush, D. F. Counseling the children of handicapped parents. *Personnel and Guidance Journal*, 1979, *58*(4), 267–270.

Koos, E. L. *Families in trouble*. New York: King's Crown Press, 1946.

Kossaris, P. Family therapy. *American Journal of Nursing*, 1979, *79*, 1730–1733.

Litman, T. J. The family & physical rehabilitation. *Journal of Chronic Disease*, 1966, *19*, 211–217.

Livsey, C. G. Physical illness and family dynamics. *Advances in Psychosomatic Medicine*, 1972, *8*, 237–251.

Olgas, M. The relationship between parents' health status and body image of their children. *Nursing Research*, 1974, *23*, 319–324.

Olsen, E. H. The impact of serious illness on the family system. *Postgraduate Medicine*, 1970, *47*(2) 169–174.

Parad, H. J., and Caplan, G. A framework for studying families in crisis. In H. J. Parad (Ed.), *Crisis Intervention*. New York: Family Service Association of America, 1965.

Richardson, S. A., Goodman, N., Hastrof, A. H., Dornbusch, S. M. Cultural uniformity in reactions to physical disabilities. *American Sociological Review*, 1961, *26*, 241–247.

Romano, M. Preparing children for parental disability. *Social Work in Health Care*, 1976, *1*(3), 309–315.

Romano, M. The impact of disability on family and society. In J. V. Basmajian (Ed.), *Foundations of medical rehabilitation*. Baltimore: Williams & Wilkins, 1984.

Strax, T., and Spergel, P. Problems of larger systems. In D. S. Bishop (Ed.), *Behavioral Problems and the Disabled*. Baltimore: Williams & Wilkins, 1980.

Trieschmann, R. B. (Ed.), *Spinal cord injuries: Psychological, social and vocational adjustment*. Elmsford, NY: Pergamon Press, 1980.

Methodological Issues in Studying Children of Disabled Parents

DEBORAH L. COATES, PETER M. VIETZE, and DAVID B. GRAY

Developmental researchers have traditionally been interested in the influence of socialization practices and parental influences on the behavior and development of children. Until recently, a unidirectional path of causality was assumed in considering the relationship between parental and child behavior. It was assumed that variation in child behavior was influenced by parental behavior. For example, numerous studies have explored the effects of parental discipline techniques on aggressiveness, dependency, and morality (Baumrind, 1967; Chamberlin, 1974; Hoffman, 1963; Nevius, 1972; Sears, Maccoby & Levin, 1957; Winder & Rau, 1962). Other studies have investigated the relationship between parental control and cognitive development, achievement, creativity, and social competence (Armentrout, 1971; Baumrind & Black, 1967; Gecas, 1971; Healey, 1974; Hess & Shipman, 1965; Sprehn, 1973). The results of these studies have been mixed regarding the nature of parental influence on child behavior. However, it has been assumed that aspects of parental behavior account for variance in the child's behavior. In much of this research the focus on parent attitudes and behavior is often based on retrospective accounts (e.g., Sears, Maccoby and Levin, 1957) or on prospective studies of mother–child interaction (e.g., Hess & Shipman, 1965; Lewis & Goldberg, 1969; Moss, 1967).

More recently it has been acknowledged that there are aspects of the child's behavior and characteristics that relate to how parents interact with their children (Bell, 1971; Lewis & Rosenblum, 1974). Research on the effects of the child on the caregiver have begun to emerge. This research focuses on children who were known to be at risk for devel-

CHILDREN OF HANDICAPPED PARENTS   **155**

oping handicaps or on children known to be handicapped. There is general agreement that parents and children exert mutual influence on one another's behavior and that this mutual influence is often expressed in the child's development and behavior.

This view has led to the development of some new but limited methods and techniques for studying children's development in the context of bidirectional and multidirectional transactions between the child and the environment. Nevertheless, this research relied on available methods rather than devising methods to fit the research questions posed. Throughout these recent developments, a major methodological approach has been virtually ignored in understanding how parents and children influence each other. Relatively little attention has been afforded to families in which one or both parents were disabled in order to examine how extreme variability in parental characteristics might affect the behavior and development of children. There are, of course, some noteworthy exceptions to this observation. Researchers interested in how particular parental disabilities affected child outcomes did undertake such investigations. One example of this is the large-scale effort by Sameroff, Zax, and their colleagues at the University of Rochester. The Rochester Longitudinal Study investigated the mechanisms by which schizophrenic mothers might transmit their disorders to their offspring (e.g., Sameroff, Barocas, & Seifer, in press; Sameroff & Zax, 1978).

Several important lessons in experimental design can be derived from a careful examination of the work by Sameroff and his colleagues. In order to answer the question of the maternal contribution to the disturbed behavior of their children, test subjects must be selected that will allow possible answers to the problem to be tested. Sameroff and colleagues included four groups of women: schizophrenic, neurotically depressed, personality disordered, and normals. This approach allows a comparison among groups to examine base rates of disturbed children within each experimental group as well as a matched control group of normals. In this *discriminant validity* study results were analyzed for similarities and differences across groups. The results show that the general condition of having a mother with a psychiatric history was more important than knowing the specific psychiatric diagnosis in predicting the child's development.

Secondly, these investigators categorized their subjects by several invariant or static variables such as race, sex, and socioeconomic status that may have causal links to disturbed behavior in children. By examining these variables, Sameroff and colleagues were able to determine the variable's effect on the outcome measure. This design allowed the researchers to detect the fact that the developmental problems exhibited by the children were related more to their socio-economic status than to the fact that their mother was diagnosed as schizophrenic.

The example given above serves to demonstrate how important it is to consider the range and nature of variables that must be considered in undertaking research on the effects of parental disability on child development and behavior. Research on families with disabled parents affords a unique opportunity to understand the bidirectional effect of the parent–child relationship on child developmental status. In this chapter, we will present two alternative research paradigms for designing research in this neglected area. Next, we will discuss the range of independent and dependent variables that should be considered in conducting studies that focus on understanding how parental disability affects the behavior and development of children. And finally, issues of research methodology will be considered. It should be noted that in discussing these issues, we have tried to be inclusive and to identify all the relevant issues that must be addressed. We do not mean to suggest that all of the variables we discuss must be included in any investigation. However, we recognize that informed decisions in research design are to be preferred over uninformed choices. The variables to be included will depend on the research questions being asked.

CONGENITAL VERSUS ADVENTITIOUS DISABILITY: TWO RESEARCH PARADIGMS

In this section the different classes of variables necessary in studying children of disabled parents will be introduced. Specific variables within each class will also be described. It is important to distinguish the independent variables from the dependent variables in order to introduce the classes of variables that might be considered in any study of how parental disability affects child development and behavior. Different levels of independent variables should be considered depending on the origin of the disabling condition of the parent. Thus, the first question that must be asked is whether the disability is one that is *congenital* in origin or whether it is *adventitious*. In fact, the relationship in time of the onset of the parent's disability to the arrival of the target child may be the important factor here. We will discuss this distinction as well.

A research paradigm for understanding the effect of congenital parental disability on child behavior and development is presented in Figure 10.1. A hypothetical paradigm is presented in which several sets

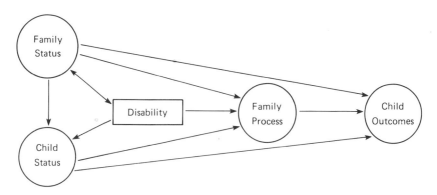

Figure 10.1   Cogenital disability paradigm.

of variables are indicated according to whether they are independent or dependent variables. In this paradigm, the *independent variables* are divided into *predisposing factors* and *process factors.* The predisposing factors include the characteristic of central concern, the *disability,* as well as two sets of status variables, *family status variables* and *child status variables.* The arrows drawn are indicative of hypothetical directions of effect.

The family status variables include demographic variables that might be important in characterizing the sample and in helping to account for variance that might otherwise be attributed to the disabling condition or conditions being studied. As Sameroff (1975), Sameroff and Chandler (1975), and Bronfenbrenner (1977) have pointed out, the context of development is an essential ingredient in understanding the course of development itself. The family status variables serve to index the social and environmental context in which behavior occurs. It is assumed for the research questions being addressed that these variables are relatively invariant factors, as compared with child status variables, which may illuminate or predict the particular processes and outcomes being studied.

The child status variables, on the other hand, are not as invariant as the family status variables. These may also be affected or mediated by the levels of the family status variables although they are not seen as affecting the disability variables themselves. Rather, some of them may have been affected by the disability of the affected parent prior to the research and will continue to change as a result of the transactions between the child and the other family members. In the case of some congenital disabilities, the child too may be disabled. This might also serve as a background factor to be considered in the research design.

Variables concerning the disability itself are of central concern. The variables to be considered in describing the disability, including whether it is congenital or adventitious, pose a major problem for research design. As indicated above, if the disability is congenital or if it occurred prior to the arrival of the target child, its status is relegated to that of a predisposing factor, and is not as sensitive to family process variables as child status variables. This is the major point of distinction between the two research paradigms. Thus, the occurrence of a disability prior to the appearance of children will affect the child outcome variables as well as the mediating family process variables. Figure 10.2 presents a hypothetical paradigm representing adventitious parental disability and indicates that, in the case of adventitious disability, family process variables may be both independent variables affecting some of the disability variables and outcome variables influenced by the disability variables. Thus, consideration of the onset of the disabling condition may be the single most important factor in studying the effect of parental disability on child development. Including both congenitally and adventitiously disabled parents in the same research design may make it difficult or impossible to interpret the results of an investigation.

Inclusion of family process variables in studies of how parental disability affects child development may make a seemingly simple research design woefully complex. These variables may serve as independent variables, mediating variables, or outcome variables depending on the research question and the decision to study adventitious or congenital disability. It may be possible to ignore family process factors altogether in preliminary investigations and save more complex questions of how or why for more advanced stages of investigation. Nevertheless, it is important to examine the role of such variables in influencing how parental disability affects child development.

The major dependent variables to be considered are the child out-

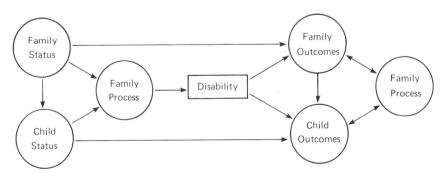

Figure 10.2 Adventitious disability paradigm.

come variables. This is true for both research paradigms proposed. Although several different domains of behavior will be considered, it is probably the case that any particular investigation will focus on a particular domain of development. It will also be of interest to consider changes in child behavior over time. Thus, Paradigm 1 (Figure 10.1) indicates only child outcome variables as dependent variables. Paradigm 2 (Figure 10.2), on the other hand allows for the possibility of considering how adventitious disability might be expressed in some family variables, family process variables, as well as child outcome variables. It is also evident that there might be continual interchange among the three sets of dependent variables as presented in Figure 10.2.

To summarize, we have outlined the two major alternative hypothetical paradigms that account for several sets of factors that might be considered, depending on whether the parental disability being studied is congenital or whether it is adventitious. It has been suggested that the distinction between these two types is one that must be made early in order to prevent errors in understanding that could arise from comparing the two types. This would result from the fact that important intervening factors of family process might operate in different ways in the two types of disability. It should also be pointed out that in addition to the ways in which each of the sets of variables might relate individually to the outcome variables, several of the independent variables might interact to produce outcomes apart from how each of them might predict the outcomes separately.

PREDISPOSING FACTORS

In this section, two sets of predisposing factors, family status and child status variables will be discussed. This will provide further detail regarding important methodological considerations in studying the effects of parental disability on child development.

Family Status

There are a number of background factors that are considered family status variables and can be taken into consideration in conducting any research in which the parent's influence on child outcomes is of interest. Perhaps the variable that has received the most attention is socioeconomic status (SES). This is a variable that needs little introduction. Its importance has been demonstrated in a wide range of topics from studies of cognitive behavior to research on mother–infant interaction. SES is usually derived from a number of characteristics that index the resources available to a family. It is generally a composite summary score of occupation of the adults in a household, income level, and highest educational level attained. Although various schemes for representing SES have been devised, it is also possible that the individual factors of occupational level and educational achievement might have some usefulness as independent variables apart from SES.

Another family background factor that might be considered is ethnicity, or cultural–social orientation. This variable may be an index variable for a family's acceptance of particular disabilities. For example, it has been reported that black families are more likely to accept mild mental retardation, without stigmatizing an individual affected in this way, than white families (Edgerton, 1979). There seems to be a greater tolerance for certain types of differences in the black community than in comparable white communities.

Religious orientation might also be influential in indexing an orientation toward disability in the family. This might be represented by a particular denomination or by the strength of religious conviction. Some families might rely on religious belief systems as sources of strength in coping with the difficulties engendered by having a disabled person in the family. Although not carrying as much causal weight as other factors, religion or religiosity might serve as an explanatory variable in understanding relationships between parental disability and child development outcomes.

If one considers that the family is a functional unit, one of whose purposes is to provide resources for maintenance, then family size and structure might be important factors to consider. The number of children and the spacing certainly affects how far the available resources will go, especially if one parent is disabled. The presence of extended family members in the home may also relieve the pressure that a disabled parent might have on the family. Finally, the marital status of parents may have an important influence on the relationship of parental disability to child development outcomes. Hetherington (1979) has suggested that children may have difficulty adjusting to the stress of having only one parent. If there is only one parent, and that parent is disabled, the psychological resources available to the family may be severely taxed. The combined effects of single parenthood and parental disability may further mediate the relationship of parent to child outcome variables.

It is conceivable that whether a family lives in a rural, suburban, or urban location may be important in understanding the relationship of parental disability and child development. Geography may be another indicator for opportunity for social support from other people. It may also be an index of community attitudes toward disability or availability of treatment programs. This is a variable that is often overlooked, but one that might impact heavily on the social environment.

Finally, it has recently been acknowledged in the literature on family relationships that families go through stages, just as individuals do, during the course of their development. It may be important to consider which phase in the family life cycle a particular family is in, in order to better understand the impact of parental disability on the child. A family that is in midcycle may be quite able to adapt to the added burden of one parent becoming disabled, while a family that is in an early phase may have more limited psychological and economic resources available for coping with parental disability.

It should be kept in mind that although each of these family status factors is discussed individually, some of them overlap with others. In fact, several of them may be used to index others. For example, the size of a family may correspond with, and thus be, an index of family life cycle phase. In a similar way, although SES might be a better predictor of the child outcome variables under study, the data to compute SES may not be available, although parental educational level is available. These two factors may be interchangeable but not for some groups (e.g., for blacks because of job discrimination and other social segregation). Taking all of these family status variables into account might make an unwieldy number of predictors or covariates and some scheme to reduce the number of these control variables might be undertaken. Preliminary cluster analyses or exploratory factor analyses might serve this purpose.

A number of strategies for utilizing the family status variables might be considered. It is possible to stratify the sample on one or more of these variables. On the other hand, it is conceivable that this might reduce the pool of available subjects to below a level that is reasonable. Thus, matching study groups subject by subject may not be a feasible strategy for subject selection. Another alternative is to try to locate a large representative pool of subjects and attempt to match groups according to the average representativeness on each independent variable separately. Still another way might be to use these variables as covariates. This may be a far more acceptable way to insure comparability among groups without studying exclusively unique study samples.

Child Status

In order to maintain optimal control and limit the amount of error variance attributable to extraneous factors, it would be well to consider a number of characteristics of the children being studied as independent variables. These include sex, age, developmental level, and birth order. In a review of family interaction in disturbed and normal families, Jacob (1975) indicated that over two thirds of the studies he surveyed had not analyzed results separately for males and females. It is clear that in the case of a disabled parent, there might be differential effects on boys and girls depending on outcome variables. Thus, it is probably important to insure that in order to fully understand the impact of parental disability on child development, both boys and girls be studied and sex differences be examined.

It is of even greater importance to evaluate the child's age in studying the effects of parental disability on child development. Research in other areas has suggested that children of different ages are affected differently by stressful environmental events. Hetherington (1979) has reported that divorce differentially affects children of different ages. Age is an important status variable, and children of different ages should be studied in order to understand more fully the role it plays in mediating the impact of parental disability on child behavior. For some outcome variables it might also be of some value to know the child's intellectual or developmental status within particular age groups. It has long been acknowledged that children with differing intellectual abilities perform differently on a variety of learning tasks. Thus, it seems important to have a representative sample of children's ability levels in a study population or to study only a homogeneous group with respect to intellectual ability. This is, of course, to insure that the outcomes can be attributed to different parental disability status or other disability factors and not to differences in intelligence or developmental level.

There has recently emerged a great deal of interest in the birth order of children. Zajonc (1976) has reported reliable differences between first and later-born children for a variety of cognitive skills. It is also evident that the impact of parental disability might vary according to a child's position in the family. At the very least, attempts should be made to control for birth order by either representing both first- and later-born children or selecting for a common birth order level. This variable will not usually, but could, be orthogonal with some of the family status variables such as family cycle phase and family size. The degree of child disability is a factor that must also be controlled. Although the central focus of a study may be on parental disability, it is conceivable that for some parental disabilities there will be a higher chance of the child's being disabled. Whether the child was born prematurely or was low in birthweight should also be taken into consideration. It might be best, in the interest of sample homogeneity, to exclude any children who have some sort of disability if such a decision would not eliminate difficult-to-obtain subjects from the available pool. Whatever the decision, child disability is an important predisposing factor that must be considered.

For the most part, the child status variables that have been indicated are independent of one another. Thus, taking these into consideration should not present confounding problems. These variables should be considered in forming groups so that there is comparability among the groups with regard to these independent variables. This would allow subsequent analyses of the covariance of these variables with major study variables.

PARENTAL DISABILITY VARIABLES

One of the central independent variables to be considered in research on the effects of parental disability pertains to the disability itself. One aspect of this set of variables has already been discussed and, as mentioned above, concerns the onset of the disability relative to the child's arrival. Although we have characterized this as being either congenital or adventitious, we acknowledged the fact that some adventitious disabilities occur prior to the child's arrival. For purposes of the present discussion, it will be assumed that such cases would have similar effects on the child as congenital disability. However, there are other aspects of disability onset that might be considered. It is conceivable that the suddenness of onset might also be a factor that accounts for outcome variation. There are certain disabling diseases that are progressive and make possible a period of adjustment and adaptation on the part of the family. These disabilities tend to be neurological in nature such as Parkinson's disease, Huntington's chorea, and "Lou Gehrig's disease." In some cases, these are terminal, such as the latter two, while in other cases, like the former, the disease can be controlled medically after onset. Disabilities that result from sudden causes, such as traumatic injuries, may have different effects on the family and children due to the lack of preparedness for the disorder. Thus, these two

aspects of onset—suddenness and relationship to the child's arrival—
are important variables to be considered in characterizing the disabled
groups being studied.

Perhaps the focal independent variable is the type of disability itself.
An important question is whether specific parental disabilities have
specific outcomes in the children and how the mere fact of having a
disabled parent affects the children. In order to explore these questions
it is necessary to include more than one group of disabled parents in
a single study and to study different disability groups across studies.
For some research questions, especially those of theoretical importance, the type of disability may be of central importance. For example,
it might be of great interest to study the language development of children with one or more deaf parents. In this case, the specificity of the
disability has some specific relevance for a particular child outcome
since it is assumed that the child's language environment influences
the development of language. In order to assure that it is the parent's
deafness or lack of vocal speech affecting the child's language, and not
the mere fact of having a disabled parent, it would be necessary to have
another type of parental disability as one sort of comparison group.
Suffice it to say that the type of disability groups to be studied will
depend on the research question being studied. The research question
may also dictate the nature of comparison groups to be employed in
the design. The issue of comparison groups will be discussed in a subsequent section on research methods.

Another factor of the disability groups to be studied is the severity
of the disability. Severity might be defined as the extent to which the
handicap limits the mobility and independent living skills of the involved parent. There are a number of ways in which this might be
taken into consideration. It may be possible to select parents who are
all disabled to the same severity level. For example, in considering
studies of physically disabled parents it might be possible to select parents who are either quadriplegics or parents who are paraplegics. However, it might be more interesting to examine the degree of paralysis
as a dimension and select parents at different points on the dimension
in order to study the relationship between severity of physical disability and outcome in the children's behavior. In similar ways it might
be possible to scale severity of any of the disabilities being studied in
order to evaluate the relationship between severity and outcome for
more than one disability orthogonally.

Another factor by which to characterize parental disability has been
identified as chronicity (Sameroff, Barocas and Seifer, in press). Chronicity of disability has been defined as the length of time the person

has been disabled. In the Rochester Longitudinal Study, chronicity of mental disorders was related to a variety of child outcome variables. It is important to account for variability in chronicity of disability in any study of parental disability and its effect on child development. It is not clear, however, what sort of predictions might be made for this variable. It most certainly would also interact with severity of disability. For some outcome variables it might be reasonable to predict that parents with the most chronic disorders have children with the most extremely negative outcomes. However, for some other outcome variables it might be expected that the longer the parent has been disabled, the less likely is that the child will be affected. This might be especially true for outcomes that have an emotional component or outcomes such as adjustment or adaptation for which time would attenuate the effect. No doubt, there are some disabilities for which chronicity and severity would be related, while for other disabilities the two might be orthogonal. Once more, the specific study question would determine the appropriateness of this dimension.

Another factor that might be considered is related to the time since the onset of the disability. However, this factor is more abstract than those discussed thus far. We will refer to this factor as *phase of the disability*. It is a psychological dimension and it is based on theories of family and patient response to the course of time following the onset of disability. Although there are several theories in the rehabilitation literature describing different stages in the adjustment to a disability, selecting any one of these theories and ordering disabled parents along the dimension might lead to interesting findings in child outcome. For example, Bray (1977) posits three phases following the occurrence of a disability: anxiety, acceptance, and assimilation. It is possible that the behavior of children with disabled parents in the anxiety phase might differ on a number of outcome variables from children whose parents were in the assimilation phase. Considering such a dimension would necessitate the researcher's ability to divide disabled parents according to the phases suggested by the particular theory. Nevertheless, this is not a difficult task to imagine and might be useful in the treatment or counseling of disabled parents and their children. It might also be important to account for the length of time and the quality of experience associated with each phase for a particular family.

Yet another important disability factor to be noted is the stage of treatment that the disabled parent is undergoing. This treatment factor is one that may not be equally relevant to all disability groups that might be studied. There may also be different outcomes for which treatment stage may be more relevant than it is for others. This variable might function merely as a covariate or stratification variable within disability types. The mechanism by which treatment status might operate may relate to the time taken for treatment and hence time that cannot be spent with the child. This variable might also be treated dichotomously as "being in treatment" or "not being in treatment."

Finally, as is obvious, it is important to consider which parent is disabled or whether both parents are disabled. It is likely that, since fathers and mothers seem to influence different aspects of their children's development (Lynn, 1974; 1979), which parent is disabled might determine how the child's behavior is affected. Some studies have demonstrated that fathers of infants engage in more rough-and-tumble play and, therefore, offer more kinesthetic stimulation than mothers. Children whose father's disability prevents this type of interaction might show poorer sensory–motor functioning as compared to children whose fathers were not disabled. On the other hand, a disabled father might be able to spend more time at home with his children and enhance the development of their verbal or other skills. Which parent is disabled might also account for sex differences in outcome for the children. Therefore, it is important to control for the gender of the disabled parent as well as that of the child.

In summary, then, we have suggested a number of important characteristics of the disability being studied that must be considered in the design of research on parental disability effects. These include (1) onset of the disability, whether before or after the child becomes part of the family and the suddenness of onset; (2) type of disability; (3) severity of the disability; (4) chronicity of the disability; (5) phase of adjustment to the disability; (6) stage of treatment; and (7) which parent is disabled or whether both are disabled. It is important to note that these factors must be taken into account in designing a study of parental disability effects on child development. In specific cases some of these may not be relevant dimensions. However, it would seem that for the most part these are important dimensions to control in carrying out such research.

FAMILY PROCESS VARIABLES

Theory building in psychology and sociology has historically used static or status characteristics of individuals as causal factors in predicting developmental or social status outcomes. These status variables are quite familiar and include sex, social class, race, residence, and occupation. More recently, it has been recognized that these variables may be simply "marker" variables or representations of particular underlying processes, contexts, or experiences, which vary systematically for members of a particular variable group. Parental disability status can be assumed to be a type of status variable that "marks" or represents an underlying process of consensual experience for families with disabled parents. Several methodological issues need to be considered if family process is to be treated as a mediator of the effects of parental disability on child and family outcomes.

Family process[1] theory and research, dating from the 1950s, usually refers to ongoing family interaction and communication patterns (Broderick & Pulliam-Krager, 1979). These interaction patterns can include literal and emotional messages, verbal and nonverbal interactions, and metacommunication, or awareness or knowledge about family interaction style. Family process has been conceptualized more specifically in theoretical and research contexts to include a variety of constructs such as problem-solving effectiveness, social process, marital adjustment, resource exchange or power, decision making, discipline, support, and affect (Scanzoni, 1979). There are basically three general classes of family process variables: (1) power–decision-making style, (2) communication and (3) problem solving effectiveness. Family researchers and theorists have defined these major classes of process variables in a variety of ways. This is evidenced by the wide array of operational variables described in numerous studies on family process (for futher discussion see Aldous, 1971; Jacob, 1975; Klein & Hill, 1979; Rausch, Grief, & Nugent, 1979; Scanzoni, 1979; Watzlawick, Beavin, & Johnson, 1967; Weick, 1971).

Power, communication, and problem-solving effectiveness are defined very briefly here for purposes of discussing methods relative to interaction in families with disabled parental members. Power and control are theoretically more relevant as predictors of socialization outcomes than other family behaviors.

The social network of the family represents another class of variables that is related to family process but is external to family interactions. Characteristics of social networks relevant to family processes

---

[1]The term *family process* is used interchangably with the term *family interaction.* The former has been used more commonly by family theorists, primarily sociologists, who have described models that explain family interaction styles. It represents a more comprehensive view of the nature of interrelationships that exist among family interaction and socialization outcomes. The entire process of family interaction and its effects are implied here by the use of this term.

might include kin-base, size, frequency of contact and degree of support provided. Social network variables have been demonstrated to influence family process although the nature of this influence has not been conclusively established (Aldous & Strauss, 1966; Blood & Wolfe, 1960; Bott, 1971). Social network factors are not discussed in detail here, but disability may predictably affect the family social network and indirectly influence family process.

In exploring the impact of parental disability on the child, family process variables can be conceptualized in three ways. They can be considered as predisposing or historical-context variables, as mediating causal variables, and as outcome variables (see Fig. 10-3).

The situation in which all three conceptualizations apply is offered by the adventitious paradigm. Family process variables can also be considered in the congenital paradigm as simply the representation of family process as a predictor or outcome for a particular type of family.

There are several variables that have been identified in family process research and theory that may be particularly sensitive to parental disability status. These variables, therefore, if explored in conjunction with research on disabled parents, may require special or unique methodological considerations. Variable sensitivity implies that certain family process variables may interrelate or be related to child outcome variables differently in families with a disabled parent than in other families. Variable sensitivity also implies that the disabling condition may allow for a certain previously examined family process variable to be isolated for futher examination. This assumption might be expected to hold for several other family types that might be identifiable because of some static condition or status. It seems, however, that the situation posed by the adventitious disability paradigm offers a unique methodological design for examining the influence of disability on

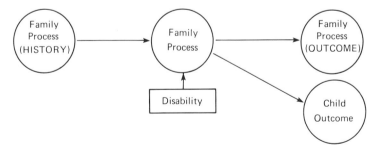

Figure 10.3 Family process variables as predisposing, mediating, and outcome variables.

family process. In this situation, as illustrated in Figure 10.3, the family represents its own family process comparison group.

Power or control and problem-solving effectiveness seem to raise the most critical methodological issues in research on disabled parents. Numerous studies have documented the existence of power structures in both conjugal and child-parent relations (e.g., Baumrind, 1966; Blood & Wolfe, 1967). Power and control techniques in the socialization process have been defined in numerous ways. Most commonly, power has been conceptualized to include spheres of influence and the process of resource exchange. It is not possible or necessary to discuss these definitions exhaustively, especially as this topic has been treated comprehensively elsewhere (see reviews by Rollins & Thomas, 1979; Scanzoni, 1979).

Rollins and Thomas (1979) suggest that parental power is a continuous quantitative variable as are other social power constructs. And, following the lead of Smith (1970), they concur that in parent–child relationships, power involves combining the use of rewards and coercion to obtain compliance with parental wishes. How parents use this combination of reward and coercion affects child behaviors. Specifically, type of discipline used and use of the complementary behaviors of support and affection can explain various child outcomes (Baumrind, 1966; Hoffman and Saltzstein, 1967). Parental power and control structures and discipline techniques may have predictable constraints placed on them for families with disabled parents. This may pose a methodological issue that needs to be considered in designing research with disabled parents as participants. The natural constraint placed on discipline style of disabled parents may also provide a unique situation in which to test theoretical models that explain the child effects of discipline style.

Parental disciplinary techniques have been categorized as verbal or physical and further categorized within each of these dimensions as love-oriented positive, love oriented negative, or power assertive (Steinmetz, 1979). A disabled parent, particularly one with a physical disability, may not have access to physical control, either positive or negative and may rely on verbal control exclusively. Methods may need to be designed in studies of disabled parents' discipline styles that account for more variability than those used in previous studies of verbal control. It has also been established that discipline style may also be differentially influential for male and female offspring as a function of parental sex. For example, several studies have found the greater the father's support, the greater the masculine sex role orientation for boys, and the greater the mother's support, the greater the feminine sex role orientation for girls (See Rollins & Thomas, 1979, pp. 338–348, for a further discussion). Thus, sex of the disabled parent may further complicate understanding the impact of disability on discipline and control patterns in the family.

Problem-solving effectiveness also presents unique methodological issues for research on family process and disabled parents. Disability condition may increase the emergence of family problems and may influence the nature of these problems. There may also be problems that occur in families with disabled parents that are unique to these families. Problems that occur in these families, that also occur in other families, may be recast in nonrecognizable forms. For example, disabled parents may be much more dependent on their offspring and thus reconstrue the nature of power relationships and the nature of dependency as a socialization outcome variable.

Several design and sampling considerations are necessary in order to address the issues raised by family process variables in research with disabled parents. While these process variables have not been discussed exhaustively, the considerations offered illustrate how family process variables might be incorporated into the study of parental disability status and its influence on child behavior.

OUTCOME VARIABLES

In discussing the outcome or dependent variables that might be studied in research into the effects of parental disability on child development, it seems important to divide these outcomes into two groups. Although the major focus of these studies should probably be on measures that can be taken with the child as the unit of analysis, we recognize that the family is an important theoretical and methodological unit of analysis also. It is evident that there are parental disability factors that will affect particular family variables and thus indirectly affect the child outcome variables. Therefore, a discussion of selected family outcome variables seems warranted prior to describing the range of child outcome variables to be considered in studies of parental disability.

Family Outcome Variables

The presence of a parent with a disability in a family may affect several characteristics of the family. Family process variables are affected for the adventitious disability paradigm. These have already been discussed above and are not presented again. As suggested earlier, family process variables may be considered as outcome variables as well. In addition, there are certain structural family variables that might be affected by the presence of a disabled parent.

One of the major effects of a parent's becoming disabled is that the roles assumed by each parent in the family may change. For example, in a family where the mother becomes disabled, many of the tasks she previously carried out might be taken over by other family members if she is no longer able to do them. She, in turn might assume some new tasks previously conducted by others or may be unable to assume any clearly defined roles. Such changes in responsibilities may affect child development. Whether the disabled parent can continue to work outside the home may determine how the role relationships in the family are structured. The role relationships might be the endpoint in a causal chain that began with the onset of the disabling condition. Nevertheless, changes in the family other than disability (e.g., divorce, incarceration of a family member, death of a family member, bankruptcy) often lead to realignment of roles. It might be important to investigate the extent of such changes in studies of parental disability.

Another structural change that is possible as a result of one parent becoming disabled is that the able-bodied parent leaves the family. This is an outcome that must be taken into account in understanding the effects on the children. Hetherington (1979) and others have been studying the effect of divorce on child behavior and development.

Finally, since families with a disabled member may incur new financial burdens not previously experienced, the disability might result in a loss of tangible resources. This too could effect the children in ways similar to downward social mobility. These structural factors of family life might easily be overlooked as explanatory variables in understanding the effects of parental disability on child behavior. It is important, therefore, to consider how family variables might be directly affected by the presence of a disabled member and how these variables in turn can be included in studies of child outcomes.

Child Outcome Variables

Child outcome variables, which are the effects to be studied, may include a broad range of behaviors. Many discussions of this type tend to focus on the deleterious effects of such influences as divorce or disability. This is the result of obsessive concerns with describing the normative experience in the social sciences. It would be a relatively easy task to provide a long list of *problem behaviors* which occur as the result of a child's having a disabled parent. It would be less common to see a research project focus on the *positive outcomes* of having a disabled parent. Therefore, in the present discussion, an effort will be made to include outcome variables that might be considered positive effects, as well as those that might be labeled as negative effects. It should be kept in mind that many of the variables that will be discussed may depend on the child status variables included in a study. Thus, the age of the child may have a profound effect on the type of outcome behaviors selected for study. Of course, the particular research question will have the greatest influence over the particular outcomes to be measured. In order to facilitate the generation of a list of relevant outcome variables, several children who have a disabled parent were interviewed by one of the authors. Although specific results of these interviews will not be given, the responses to several of the questions serve to clarify important outcome variables.

Perhaps the most salient set of outcome variables that might be used to characterize the effects of parental disability on children can be labeled *adjustment.* Under this heading it might be fruitful to consider such personality dimensions as independence, self-confidence, and self-esteem, among others. A child who has a disabled parent may be given new responsibilities to carry out. Although these are tasks that the child ordinarily might not do, this may serve as an opportunity for learning new skills. Acquisition of these responsibilities might serve to build self-confidence and in turn contribute to the child's self-esteem. The way the child reacts emotionally to the parent's disability may be an important determinant of how beneficial these changes are for the child. How various emotions are expressed may also be an important aspect of the child's adjustment to having a disabled parent. This of course will depend on the child's age and perhaps the family interaction context. Whether a child exhibits generally happy or positive emotions may be indicators of positive adjustment to the parent's disability. It is important to note that there may be little evidence of emotional effects of the parent's disability on the child. On the other hand, there may be evidence of negative emotional response, such as aggressive outbursts and sadness or even, in extreme cases, depression. Whether the researcher chooses to focus on these aspects of the child's behavior will be determined by the research question.

Another set of outcome variables that might be studied are social in nature. How the child relates to other people may be of interest. One of the children interviewed indicated that having a disabled parent may be a way of getting attention from peers. The child may be afforded a higher status in peer groups because of the responsibilities incurred while helping the disabled parent. Alternatively, because of some increased responsibilities, extra time may be spent that would otherwise be devoted to interactions with friends. Being engaged in special activities at home might provide a different bond with siblings than might otherwise be experienced. A different attitude toward people who are different might allow the child of a disabled parent to have a more heterogeneous social network than other children.

Which parent is affected by disability might have some effect on sex role of gender orientation. These outcomes might further be affected by the sex of the child. If the father is disabled, this might have a different effect on boys than on girls and these effects might depend on the child's age. Such differential results have been found in the research reported for children of divorce and in research on discipline mentioned earlier.

Certain disabilities in parents might affect children in specific ways. Without specific interventions to prevent language impairment, deaf parents might have children whose language is affected. It would be especially important to study the cognitive functioning of children who had a retarded parent or parents. Zetlin and associates (Zetlin, Weisner & Gallimore, Chap. 5, this volume) have presented some evidence on retarded parents, although they did not focus on the children's intellectual behavior. Thus, language and cognitive development are two sets of outcome variables that might be appropriate targets for study of a particular type of disability. The particular disability would probably affect which aspects of language and cognition would be of interest. These sorts of outcomes are specific, dependent measures that might be more closely tied to the type of parental disability than some of the other outcomes that might be studied.

Achievement and achievement motivation could also be of interest in families where a parent is disabled. Here again, which parent is affected might differentially affect girls and boys. There might be indirect effects on achievement and performance in school since children with a disabled parent might have more responsibilities at home than other children. This could detract from time spent on school work and in turn could affect achievement. Achievement motivation might also be enhanced by increased compensatory pressure to do well. Direct behavioral measures as well as attitudinal measures might be informative in this domain.

It would of course be of great importance to study problem behavior among children with a disabled parent. In a family environment that did not encourage open expression of feelings or understanding, acting out might be prevalent. It may not be important what specific form the acting out took. These might be determined by the family processes evident in the home. However, behavior disturbance might be of interest in understanding the effects of parental disability on the children. Once again, compensatory processes might be operating to reduce the incidence of acting out and result in lower rates of such problem behaviors as substance abuse, delinquency, and running away from home. The incidence of these might be harder to estimate in families with disabled parents since the study populations might not be large enough to get reliable estimates.

In short, there are a large variety of outcome behaviors that might be studied in children with disabled parents. They range from basic domains, such as language, cognition, and social behavior, to problem behaviors, like emotional disturbance, behavior disorders, and psychopathology. The choice of outcomes will be directed by the type of disability of interest as well as specific research questions.

RESEARCH METHODS

Up to this point the discussion has been focused primarily on design issues related to the research paradigms and control factors. In this section, several issues regarding other aspects of research methodology are addressed. These issues include choice of research instruments, sample selection, bias control, and data collection strategy.

The choice of instruments with regard to child outcomes may not be affected by the type of parental disability being studied. If it is assumed that the children are not disabled, then it is evident that there are no precautions, based on disability, that must be taken in instrument selection. The particular outcomes under study and the judgments of the researcher and other characteristics of the children participating will be the dictating factors in selecting appropriate instruments. However, to the extent that data will also be collected from the disabled parents, selection of instruments becomes a more salient issue. This is especially crucial if more than one disability group is studied. For some disabilities, self-administered instruments might be difficult to use. In these cases it would appear that there are two alternatives. One is to modify the instruments so that all parents will be able to provide comparable data. For standardized instruments, this may present problems related to the conditions under which the instruments were developed. Another alternative is to utilize observational methods that could be applied equally well to all groups. Detailed descriptions of the various issues in observational research are amply provided in Sackett's (1978) two-volume edition on the topic. Which of these alternatives is selected will depend on the particular disability groups being studied, the focus of the investigation, and the adaptability of the researchers.

If there is to be any conclusion regarding the attribution of outcomes to parental disability, some care should be taken to minimize bias in data collection. It might be easy to assure that those collecting data from the children have no information regarding the group membership of the children's parent. However, if it is necessary to carry out observations on the parents, it may be impossible to prevent the observers from knowing the disability of the parent. It is essential that the observers be uninformed regarding the purpose of the investigation. This may preclude intentional bias from influencing results. However, it seems almost impossible to eliminate unintentional bias that might result from the observer's knowledge of the parent's disability. If this is seen as a problem, then the choice of observational methods would be unwise. It may also be difficult to keep child interviewers uninformed about parental disability if information about the disability is desired. However, if no such information is collected then precautions should be taken to keep examiners and observers who have contact with the children from discovering the parent's disability status.

Another issue that must be considered is sample selection. It seems clear that since disability is an uncommon occurrence, truly random sampling may not be possible. In light of this, sampling strategies must be selected that do not favor one group over another. Selecting disabled adults from treatment clinics might introduce problems by oversampling individuals who have greater economic resources. Such a strategy might also favor disabilities for which treatments are readily available.

Decisions to include nondisabled parents and their children should be considered. Existence of such "normal" or variant comparison groups will allow inferences regarding the influence of parental disability on child behavior. Without such comparison groups, any conclusions will be subject to a host of alternative explanations. It would be easy to attribute any negative outcomes to the presence of parental disability. However, if there is no normal comparison group, these conclusions would be highly suspect. Similarly, inclusion of merely one type of disability may lead to gratuitous conclusions regarding the influence of parental disability on child behavior or development.

Subject selection must insure comparability of groups. Without accurate epidemiological data on incidence and prevalence of the various disabilities of interest, it will be very difficult to know the representativeness of a particular sample. This makes it extremely important to insure comparability among groups. Although matching often creates problems regarding generalizability of results, it might be fruitfully done in the case of disabled parents. It should be noted that since it will be necessary to select subjects on the basis of the parent's disability, problems may arise in the availability of children to be studied. Only painstaking efforts will lead to having children of comparable age, sex, and birth order among different groups. Since sample selection will be such a difficult problem, the researcher may choose to study all the children in the family. This may afford opportunities for comparing children of different ages on the outcome variables being studied. Furthermore, the fact that the sample finally selected will be a "precious commodity" may influence the researchers to conduct a longitudinal investigation in order to take maximum advantage of the sample.

The decision to conduct cross-sectional or longitudinal investigations will depend on a number of factors. First there are the usual criteria for making such a decision. These include cost, attrition, and time constraints. If developmental outcomes are of interest, then almost by necessity cross-sectional strategies are precluded. The possibility that developmental effects could be confounded with cohort effects are increased in studying the influence of parental disability on child outcomes. Therefore, it would be advisable to plan a longitudinal study or a cross-sequential study. This sort of design is a set of overlapping short-term longitudinal investigations for the purpose of estimating cohort effects while examining developmental changes in the behavior of interest.

It would seem that the greatest contribution to understanding the effects of parental disability would be gained by studying effects of parental disability longitudinally. This would allow more accurate estimates of developmental outcomes. As noted above, it might be best to capitalize on the opportunities presented by multichild families and study several children in families if this is possible while controlling for sex and birth order effects. These studies would necessitate very complex designs, but it would be possible to measure child, cohort, and intergroup effects all at once.

The methodological problems inherent in studying the effects of having a disabled parent on various aspects of a child's behavior and development are enormous. It would be easier to approach this problem with simplistic designs. However, if methodological rigor is not observed, the risks of producing uninterpretable results or invalid findings are great. Studying children of disabled parents provides natural experiments that can serve to further the understanding of how parents and children influence one another despite the difficult methodological problems.

REFERENCES

Aldous, J. A framework for the analysis of family problem solving. In J. Aldous, T. Condon, R. Hill, M. Straus, & I. Tallman (Eds.), *Family problem solving: A symposium on theoretical, methodological, and substantive concerns.* Hinsdale, IL: Dryden Press, 1971.

Aldous, J., & Straus, M. A. Social networks and conjugal roles: A test of Bott's hypothesis. *Social Forces,* 1966, *44,* 576–580.

Armentrout, J. A. Parental child-rearing attitudes and preadolescents' problem behaviors. *Journal of Consulting and Clinical Psychology,* 1971, *37,* 278–285.

Baumrind, D. Effects of authoritative control on child behavior. *Child Development,* 1966, *37,* 887–907.

Baumrind, D. Child care practices anteceding three patterns of preschool behavior. *Genetic Psychology Monographs,* 1967, *75,* 43–88.

Baumrind, D., & Black, A. E. Socialization practices associated with dimensions of competence in preschool boys and girls. *Child Development,* 1967, *38,* 291–328.

Bell, R. Q. Stimulus control of parent or caretaker behavior by offspring. *Developmental Psychology,* 1971, *4,* 63–72.

Blood, R. O., & Wolfe, D. M. *Husbands and wives: The dynamics of married living.* New York: Free Press, 1960.

Bott, E. *Family and social network.* (2nd Ed.) New York: Free Press, 1971.

Bray, G. P. Reactive patterns in families of the severely disabled. *Rehabilitation Counseling Bulletin,* March 1977, 236–239.

Broderick, C. B., & Pulliam–Krager, H. Family process and child outcomes. In W. R. Burr, R. Hill, F. I. Nye, & I. L. Reiss (Eds.), *Contemporary theories about the family.* New York: Free Press, 1979.

Bronfenbrenner, U. Toward an experimental ecology of human development. *American Psychologist,* 1977, *32,* 513–531.

Chamberlin, R. W. Authoritarian and accomodative child-rearing styles: Their relationships with the behavior patterns of two-year-old children and with other variables. *Journal of Pediatrics,* 1974, *84,* 287–293.

Edgerton, R. B. Another look at culture and mental retardation. In M. Begab (Ed.), *New perspectives on mental retardation.* Baltimore: University Park Press, 1979.

Gecas, V. Parental behavior and dimensions of adolescent self-evaluation. *Sociometry,* 1971, *34,* 466–482.

Healey, R. E. Parental behavior as related to children's academic achievement. Unpublished doctoral dissertation, Catholic University of America, Washington, DC, 1974.

Hess, R. D., & Shipman, V. C. Early experience and the socialization of cognitive modes in children. *Child Development,* 1965, *36,* 869–886.

Hetherington, E. M. Divorce: A child's perspective. *American Psychologist*, 1979, *34*, 851–858.

Hoffman, M. L. Parent discipline and the child's consideration for others. *Child Development*, 1963, *34*, 573–588.

Hoffman, M. L., & Saltzstein, H. D. Parental discipline and the child's moral development. *Journal of Personality and Social Psychology*, 1967, *5*, 45–57.

Jacob, T. Family interaction in disturbed and normal families: A methodological and substantive review. *Psychological Bulletin*, 1975, *82*, 33–65.

Klein, D. M., & Hill, R. Determinants of family problem-solving effectiveness. In W. R. Burr, R. Hill, F. I. Nye, & I. L. Reiss (Eds.), *Contemporary theories about the family.* New York: Free Press, 1979.

Lewis, M., & Goldberg, S. Perceptual–cognitive development in infancy: A generalized expectancy model as a function of mother–infant interaction. *Merrill–Palmer Quarterly*, 1969, *15*, 81–100.

Lewis, M., & Rosenblum, L. (Eds.), *The effect of the infant on its caregiver.* New York: Wiley, 1974.

Lynn, D. B. *The father: His role in child development.* Monterey, CA: Brooks/Cole, 1974.

Lynn, D. B. *Daughters and parents: Past, present and future.* Monterey, CA: Brooks/Cole, 1979.

Moss, H. A. Sex, age and state as determinants of mother–infant interaction. *Merrill–Palmer Quarterly*, 1967, *13*, 19–36.

Nevius, J. R. The relationship of child-rearing practices to the acquisition of moral judgments in 10-year old boys. Unpublished doctoral dissertation, University of Southern California, Los Angeles, 1972.

Raush, H. L., Greif, A. C., & Nugent, J. Communication in couples and families. In W. R. Burr, R. Hill, F. I. Nye, & I. L. Reiss, (Eds.), *Contemporary theories about the family.* New York: Free Press, 1979.

Rollins, B. C., & Thomas, D. L. Parental support, power and control techniques in the socialization of children. In W. R. Burr, R. Hill, F. I. Nye, & I. L. Reiss, (Eds.), *Contemporary theories about the family.* New York: Free Press, 1979.

Sackett, G. P. (Ed.), *Observing behavior.* Baltimore: University Park Press, 1978.

Sameroff, A. J. Early influences on development: Fact or fancy? *Merrill–Palmer Quarterly*, 1975, *21*, 267–294.

Sameroff, A. J., Barocas, R., & Seifer, R. The early development of children born to mentally ill women. In N. F. Watt, E. J. Anthony, L. C. Wynne, & J. Rolf (Eds.), *Children at risk for schizophrenia: A longitudinal perspective.* New York: Cambridge University Press, in press.

Sameroff, A. J., & Chandler, M. J. Reproductive risk and the continuum of caretaking casualty. In F. D. Horowitz, E. M. Hetherington, S. Scarr-Salapatek, & G. Siegel, (Eds.), *Review of child development research* (Vol. 4). Chicago: University of Chicago Press, 1975.

Sameroff, A. J., & Zax, M. In search of schizophrenia: Young offspring of schizophrenic women. In L. C. Wynne, R. L. Cromwell, & S. Mathysse (Eds.), *The nature of schizophrenia: New approaches to research and treatment.* New York: Wiley, 1978.

Scanzoni, J. Social processes and power in families. In W. R. Burr, R. Hill, F. I. Nye, & I. L. Reiss (Eds.), *Contemporary theories about the family.* New York: Free Press, 1979.

Sears, R. R., Maccoby, E. E., & Levin, H. *Patterns of child rearing.* Evanston: Row, Peterson, 1957.

Smith, T. E. Foundations of parental influence upon adolescents: An application of social power theory. *American Sociological Review*, 1970, *35*, 860–873.

Sprehn, G. C. Correlates of parent behavior and locus of control in nine to twelve-year-old males. Unpublished doctoral dissertation, Emory University, Atlanta, 1973.

Steinmetz, S. Disciplinary techniques and the realtionship to aggressiveness, dependency and conscience. In W. R. Burr, R. Hill, F. I. Nye, & I. L. Reiss (Eds.), *Contemporary theories about the family*. New York: Free Press, 1979.

Watzlawick, P., Beavin, J. H., & Jackson, D. D. *Pragmatics of human communication: A study of interaction patterns, pathologies and paradoxes*. New York: Norton, 1967.

Weick, K. E. Group processes, family processes and problem solving. In J. Aldous, T. Condon, R. Hill, M. Straus, & I. Tallman (Eds.), *Family problem solving: A symposium on theoretical, methodological and substantive concerns*. Hinsdale, IL: Dryden Press, 1971.

Winder, C. L., & Rau, L. Parental attitudes associated with social deviance in preadolescent boys. *Journal of Abnormal and Social Psychology*, 1962, *64*, 418–424.

Zajonc, R. B. Family configuration and intelligence: Variations in scholastic aptitude scores parallel trends in family size and the spacing of children. *Science*, 1976, *192*, 227–236.

11

The Handicapped Parent in the Community: A Synthesis and Commentary

J. R. NEWBROUGH

The purpose of this book is to explore the effects of a handicapped parent on a child. The handicapped parent is of particular concern, since for some disabilities, there is an additional risk that the child's development and care will be affected in ways that are not typical of children with nonhandicapped parents. In some cases, this leads to an increased likelihood that the child will become a public responsibility.

The family has come to be a matter of considerable national interest since the major policies in the society seem to take it for granted and to continue to treat families as if they were a renewable resource; yet, marriages have been dissolving at a high rate, and there are indications that the many problems in the public schools are strongly associated with families that are antisocial or marginal. The family has been recognized as a basic socializing structure for children and in recent years, a basic mediating structure for all members. There have been discussions of "empowering" families (Berger & Neuhaus, 1977) and "strengthening" families (Hobbs, Dokecki, Hoover-Dempsey, Moroney, Shayne, & Weeks, 1984) that seem to call for social policy that would improve family functioning.

There is a basic set of tasks that a family must perform for its members. Fotheringham (1980) lists the following minimal conditions for retarded persons to be parents. They are paraphrased here as applicable to all families:

1. Sufficient financial resources to make available food, clothing, housing, and recreation.

2. Sufficient supervision and assistance to make certain that the children experience a minimally acceptable degree of order and care in their lives.
3. Minimally acceptable levels of intellectual–educational–learning experiences and opportunities for the children in their home and in the community.
4. Advice and support to the parents who may be new to the tasks of parenthood.

All families confront these matters and many devise ways to manage them. These are also useful dimensions for considering families with a handicapped parent, where the handicap may make it more difficult for the person to perform the functions of being a parent.

THE HANDICAPPED PARENT

A central issue in this book is the extent to which parents who are handicapped are different from the general run of parents. Their ways of parenting may be different; they may look different and act differently. If the handicap is a motor one, then the coming and going may take different patterns, but the experience of words, of understandings, and of feelings may be similar to those other families. If there is a major sensory (hearing, seeing) or communicative disorder, then the psychological experience for the parent is different. What he or she have to transmit as experience may be different. And what the child learns about his or her own self in the world may be limited or dysfunctional.

From a cultural point of view, it is often considered that deviant or marginal people have a double socialization task—learning their own settings and learning how to be adequate in the modal settings as well. These are bicultural skills. Some children seem to learn by themselves how to be bicultural. Others seem to require the direction and support of someone they trust to show them how to fit in.

NEEDS AND NEED MEETING

Children's needs are experienced, expressed, and met in the course of their daily rounds. As with all members of the species, security, food and water, and shelter are basic ones, usually part of the home in relationship to their mother (or to both parents). Handicapped parents may have particularized problems in providing for these needs; one would wish to inquire into this. Assuming that these needs are met, then the desirable childrearing outcomes are (1) social and cognitive skills that allow the children to enter and participate in the usual range of human settings, without which the child would be handicapped; and (2) the ability to identify as a regular member of the community and to move into settings to participate and to lead, as appropriate. Having a marginal identity would be a substantial handicap. These are outcomes that concern the community for if they are not realized, chances are increased that the children would, at some time, be dependent upon public sustenance.

INTERVENTION

As discussed by Gilhool and Gran (Chap. 2, this volume), intervention should be considered from the perspectives of *right to intervene* and *goals for intervention.* One essentially wishes not to intervene in private matters where there is no undue hardship on any party. But where there is a substantial burden placed upon the primary caretaker, there is a real possibility that personal resources will not be sufficient and that his or her welfare, as well as that of the others in the family, will be endangered. In this instance, the community has an interest in the welfare of the family and often makes available some services for dealing with the burden. Often, the services are not adequate and the primary caretaker or the family as a whole feels abandoned by the community—left to try to cope on their own resources.

Goals for intervention would be similar to those for the handicapped person: to enable the family to function adequately. In the instance of a handicapped parent, access to opportunities may be limited; for example, the mother may not be able to be a Brownie leader or the father active in the Little League. Transportation necessary to get to activities may not be possible. Resources outside the family would have to be used to make the difference.

Intervention should probably be considered within the context of the social contract that each person has, implicitly, with their community (usually divided between local, state, and national government). There are *civil rights* that concern private ordering of self and family; these are rights that are staunchly defended. There are *welfare rights* that seem often to be in conflict with civil rights. These are the rights to have needs met sufficiently so that one can pursue one's life within the context of civil liberties. It is on the basis of welfare rights that families feel that they can demand services for their special situation and the basis on which public interventions are pursued.

RESEARCH CONSIDERATIONS

In approaching the matter of effects of handicapped parents on their children, one has to decide what outcomes (or dependent variables) are of particular interest and what variables, processes, or mechanisms seem tied to those outcomes. The child can be globally described as having the task of growing up with good health and the skills to become integrated into the society as a contributing member. A disabled parent could be thought to be unable to provide the kind of upbringing that stimulates the learning and development necessary for the child to become that contributing member. The tasks of the child of a disabled parent are the same as for any child; and where the parent does not have the ability or resources, it would be socially appropriate to consider making up for them in certain ways. Research needs to be directed toward learning whether certain categories of parental handicap have characteristic outcomes and what might be the most appropriate interventions.

COMMENTARY ON THE CHAPTERS

Chapter 2 by Gilhool and Gran offers consideration of whether handicapped persons have the right to marry and bear children. My first reaction was, Of course they do! But they go on to raise the question of whether the child will get proper care. In most cases, there is insufficient knowledge in the field to predict whether there are certain arrangements of the family, in a categorical sense, that will have untoward outcomes. With regard to abuse and neglect, the law has defined some conditions that impinge upon the child, but that has to be determined in the case of the particular child and is not established prior to due consideration and judgment.

Two social contracts have to be considered here—the *rights of the handicapped person* to marry and bear children and the *rights of the children* to be reared in a situation where there is sufficient support and nurture to prepare them to pursue happiness and to be a part of society. There are certain conditions under which handicapped people could not provide adequate care and certain conditions in which the child should not be reared. It is possible, through research, to identify these conditions. This should be done in order to decrease the risk of poor outcome for the child.

When I consider what it means to put this knowledge into practice,

I stop short of going the complete distance. It is one thing to use such knowledge for counseling handicapped persons or helping them get additional services. It is another to set up conditions, such as for having children, that would affect all persons in a particular category, such as a family. I can imagine a policy that separated the right to have children from the right to marry. These are separable decisions and each could be a licensable step. Thus, persons could be allowed to meet the basic human needs for companionship and love through marriage. The choice of having children and what their number should be might be somewhat controllable. Such a policy would require new social legislation that would redefine the right of privacy in the family.

Gilhool and Gran note that the civil rights of handicapped persons were clarified in the 1973 Vocational Rehabilitation Act, the 1975 Developmental Disabilities Assistance and Bill of Rights Act, and the 1976 Education for All Handicapped Children Act. In these, handicapped persons are defined as being allowed to aspire to as normal a life as possible. Yet, the court cases cited (in California, Arkansas, and Idaho) were decided on the basis of "the best interests of the child."

Rawls (1971) proposes the basis for a more equitable test than deciding in favor of only one interest. When there is a conflict of interest, the best interests of the child and the parent (or parents) should be advanced simultaneously. One could imagine that disabled parents might have the chance to show that they could (with appropriate assistance) meet the needs of the child and their own as well. In this case, the best interests of the child and the family might be able to be asserted simultaneously.

A basic issue in the concept of *private ordering* is that individuals are free to define what constitutes a good quality of life. Although this is implicit, the concept of *standard of living* also implies a categorical definition of life quality. It has come to mean middle-class standards of housing, education, income, styles of consumption, and participation in the community to those who study families. The poor and the disadvantaged are expected to aspire to this standard and to be motivated to work toward that goal. Other patterns of high-quality life have been asserted and pursued; for example, the communes of the 1960s. Localities have been threatened by these patterns and have often run the people out—probably violating their right of private ordering. One might expect that similar reactions will occur in reaction to handicapped persons, particularly the retarded, wishing to become parents. To what extent can their own standards for the good life be acceptable?

Thurman, in Chapter 3, urges us to consider the family as an ecological system in which there is more or less congruence, harmony, and tolerance. These attributes become salient when there is a handicap, since some family functions cannot be performed and there is either an insufficiency or an imbalance in the system. Said another way, it may be difficult, if not impossible, to balance the family and to enable it to function adequately. Balance implies oscillation around certain midpoints, which can be seen as levels of functioning. Balance in household functioning suggests a minimal level of participation by all members that is defined as acceptable. One parent may or may not do all the housework; either pattern will work so long as the housework gets done and everyone can tolerate the way in which it is carried out. This illustrates the systems principle of equipotentiality—the assertion that there are many paths to the desired goals.

In addition to the consideration of levels and balances, there are limits that have to be considered. These limits are the lower or upper level of functioning of a component between which the processes can be sustained and beyond which the function breaks down. Failure of the primary caretaker to fix meals or to do the laundry can be adjusted for if there is another adult or older child in the picture. If it is a single person who is disabled and has one or more preschool children, the system may have gone beyond its limits to function, depending on the nature of the disability. Resources have to be imported to enable the ecology (the system) to function; that is what has been specifically asserted in Public Law 94–142.

Thurman's variables seem to describe perceptions of family members about the adequacy of family functioning; specifically, *competency* refers to a judgment about how adequate someone is, *deviancy* refers to a judgment about how acceptable someone is, and *tolerance* refers to a judgment about how much a particular person will accept. Whether these are mutable functions that will respond to intervention will have to be discovered in future research.

I am persuaded that Thurman's model, while presenting us with complexity, does not at the same time take us beyond the technology for measurement offered by the computer and mathematical software programs. Self-reports and observations both have an acceptable usefulness. The basic questions are (1) What are the correct variables? (2) When and where does one measure them? and (3) Where are the connections that link the variables together?

Chapter 4, by Sameroff, Seifer, and Zax, presents us with the case of mentally ill patients and their effects upon the children. In a search for early determinants of later negative outcomes, Sameroff and colleagues have found little that continues in later life. They borrow Waddington's self-righting tendencies (from embryology) and apply them to child outcomes. The self-righting influences, a kind of balancing, are expected to come from the caretaking environment that can compensate for the various differences found among children. They suggest that the following variables might describe the important self-righting mechanisms used by the parents: (1) The level at which the parent can place the child in a developmental context, (2) the parent's developmental model, (3) sociocultural norms, (4) personality of the parent, and (5) interactional resources of the parent. All are intertwined and have to be understood in their interconnectedness.

What is needed for Sameroff's conceptualization is a small systems model that would specify direct linkages, indirect influences, and the spread of effect of any happening in the system. The system includes child, family, kin, friends, and locality. If these are levels of abstraction, then each level has its own variables and patterns of functioning. Time would be an organizing concept. Effects, happenings, and events could all be arranged along the timeline and provide a way to conceptualize the interactive effects of the elements. The kymograph, for temperature and barometer readings of weather, and the electroencephalograph are examples of continuous recording of such variation on a moving record.

Forrester (1967) has used this basic approach in the development of a dynamic model of a factory. He later tried applications of this to a city (Forrester, 1969) and to the world (Forrester, 1971; Meadows, Meadows, Randers, & Behrens, 1972). The idea was to use the computer in place of the moving record and to specify the relationships found among all variables mathematically. The model, when specified, then allows for collection of data on one variable or a few variables. Fed into the computer, it will show how the other variables should look when displayed with the previously specified mathematical relationships. The computer model provides a way to predict what would be expected to be found. To use this model as a research instrument, one needs to collect data on the same variables as in the model and to check the accuracy of the mathematics. Forrester's approach could be a very fruitful approach to the study of the dynamics of the family.

Zetlin, Weisner, and Gallimore, in Chapter 5, report field research on 4 families selected from 13 families that had at least one retarded parent. These 4 families illustrated a range of parental competence, where the mother was the more responsible parent and where there were both competent and noncompetent levels of childcare being provided. In the two cases of clear noncompetence, the grandparents and relatives stepped in and provided the necessary support. In all cases, family was available for support and help. The help typically involved

(1) survival resources, such as finances, and adequate food, (2) childcare tasks, and (3) integration among family roles. Much of the help seemed to fall in the domain of planning and management skills.

This chapter raised for me the question of whether the potential caretakers (parent of the retarded person, etc.) should have a voice in decisions about having children. Since more than one child often becomes too much of a burden (Zetlin et al., Chap. 5, this volume; Fotheringham, 1980), I would want the extended family to be included in the decision making along with the couple.

Zetlin et al. note that longitudinal research is necessary to study how the different stages in child development will require differing amounts and kinds of support from the family. If the extended family falls way at any time, it is very likely that the adequacy of care will fall below minimal acceptable levels and the child(ren) may have to be removed from the family. There has been little evidence of adequate community help through formal agencies. Thus, without the family, the chances of failure of the retarded parents is exceedingly high.

Glass, in her consideration of a disability occurring after the family is formed, in Chapter 9, indicates that the disability precipitates a crisis reaction around the major readjustment that has to be carried out. She focuses on the family as the coping unit without explicit consideration of the family and friendship support networks. Hers is a sensitive consideration of what is involved in the reintegration and readaptation of the family unit, with particular consideration to the age/life–stage placement of the child.

Adaptation can be successful with children who are not apparently handicapped by a parent who has a severe handicap. This conclusion is mostly observational and anecdotal. There needs to be some good longitudinal research into family coping and adaptation.

Kornblum and Anderson, in Chapter 6, could find no literature on the diabetic as parent; it was only on the diabetic child within a family context. Their interviews with 12 families led them to identify five themes to be considered important for the family with diabetic parents. The themes include whether the child grows up with a parent who has diabetes, whether the treatment and maintenance affects the family directly, whether the parent is hard to get along with, and whether the parent has frail health and has to be taken care of. All these refer to changes and adjustments that the child has to make. In addition, they noted that there are few resources in the health-care system or in consumer diabetes organizations for dealing with the psychological strains, tension, and needs to adjust to new situations.

Hoffmeister, in Chapter 7, describes the child of deaf parents as growing up as a bicultural person, having learned to be a member of the Deaf Community as well as the dominant community. The Deaf Community seems to be the most well developed social group of all for handicapped persons. It seems to have all the characteristics of a minority group. There are strong social groupings and social activities that provide for group identity and cultural development. Given the strong social supports that the deaf family usually has in the Deaf Community and the tradition of family self-reliance in contrast to the hearing community, Hoffmeister reported that the deaf children of deaf parents are much better socialized and adjusted than their hearing counterparts.

The effects of the handicapped on their children are not at the basic levels, but at the socializing and educational levels. The family tends to be sign-language oriented. The child learns that language and serves as a go-between and interpreter. This places the child in a very responsible role early in life, often placing him or her in a parental role in relation to the parents. Hoffmeister reports that a number of children (himself included) resented that role shift very much.

Greer writes Chapter 8 from the perspective of being a handicapped parent. His children and others that he has known seem to have adapted to their parents' handicaps with ease. The basic needs of all parties seem to have been met; the children may have more responsibility in helping the parents than children of nonhandicapped parents (as Hoffmeister reported for the deaf family).

The adjustment process and its long-term effects are generally not known since no research has been done on that adjustment. As with normal children, adjustment is a complex process that one category does not predict well—except in a negative sense. If the disability gets in the way of the parent performing the critical functions, the effect as a deficit for the child's experience may become apparent when there is no way to compensate for it.

Coates, Vietze, and Gray, Chapter 10, went to the literature to identify methodological issues in studying children of disabled parents. They first distinguished between congenital and adventitious origins of the disability. This allowed them to consider separately (1) those parents who begin family life with a disability and (2) those who experience a disability after the family is formed. In the former instance, it is considered to be a *predisposing factor*, while in the latter case, it affects and is affected by *family process variables*. The authors believe that these variables will account for the largest amount of variance in child outcomes. Why this is so, is not clear but is presumably based on the notion that a family that has to change and reestablish new patterns will affect the child more than a family in which the child learns to live with a disabled parent from the outset.

They consider child outcomes to be of three sorts: psychological adjustment, social–behavioral interaction, and goal attainment. They make a strong point of looking to see whether there have been salutary outcomes, not just negative effects.

This chapter is very helpful because it identifies issues in design and methods that take into account the complexities of the impact that a handicapped parent can have on a child. The handicap is a single factor in a complex system that produces a person who is insufficient in some life functions but not in most others.

PERSPECTIVE

This volume makes the very clear point that parents who are disabled are more similar to other parents than they are different. There are aspects of the process of parenting that they cannot participate in; but with help and support, many can be adequate parents. Even with mentally retarded parents, where one might expect global inabilities, Zetlin et al. document the fact that some retarded people are quite adequate (see also Budd & Greenspan, 1984; Greenspan & Budd, 1983; Fotheringham, 1980).

The demonstration that handicapped people can be functionally adequate makes clearer the fact that families are not socially independent elements. Families, handicapped and normal, require resources, networks, and supports to function well. The family, neighborhood, and larger community have usually provided this. The good community is often judged to have been the place where one feels helped and feels allowed to help others.

The question always arises with the handicapped parent of whose responsibility it is to provide the resources necessary for life. The basic assumption in the United States is that the family has the responsibility to provide the finances and to bear the burden of the caretaking. The theory of state responsibility for deficits in the family has begun to be redefined through the passage of Public Law 94–142 (Education for All Handicapped Children Act). The local community, through the schools, has to be responsible for basic education of the handicapped child before the age of majority. Once an adult, however, the handicapped person becomes the total responsibility of the family. Only in those cases of a complete lack of family (or other resources) does the state enter in.

The effect of this is to cast each family adrift with its own resources—many of them insufficient to the task of caring for a dependent member (Gorham, Des Jardins, Page, Pettis, & Schreiber, 1975). Where not insufficient, a parent usually has to make a life career out of caring for that person. There is no choice. The strain of the caretaking often produces unhealthy psychological adjustment patterns and often disrupts the marital relationship (Wikler, 1981). Such a lack of social investment in family support leads to a deficit in human capital development and to an increased amount of mental ill health in the local community.

Part of the solution to this problem probably lies in the redefinition of social services. Professionalized social services are based on a belief in expertise and superiority in the service providers and operates with specific categories and rules so that management and record-keeping can be simplified. Human needs are divided among the agencies; few agencies try to deal with the family as a system. As a consequence, social agencies tend to be more difficult to use than they are helpful. They usually adopt an adversarial role with the family, making cooperative enterprise difficult.

Services that consult with a family about how to live their lives in new ways, such as a diabetes clinic, seem to be much more functional. They aim to strengthen the family, not to substitute for it. The Direction Center (Brewer & Kakalik, 1979; Halpern, 1983) is a social form, rather like the California Regional Center for the developmentally disabled, that seems to have major potential for strengthening the abilities of individual families to cope. Technical support has long been available for families who are in agriculture through the extension and home demonstration programs. This is a model that could be expanded to the family with a handicapped member. And someday, perhaps, society will come to see that all families are not socially independent and need consultative and supportive services at various stages in their lives.

RESEARCH

The computer can be seen to be as much of a breakthrough for the study of behavioral dynamics as the movie was in its ability to handle time-relevant information. Dynamics of variables and their interrelationships require many measures and a lot of easily accessible storage space for the information. Technology, as described above in relationship to Forrester's work, is not sufficiently developed to begin to study types of family systems across long stretches of time in order to show how they function and how they react to, or process, change. It should be possible to develop dynamic models for different types of handicap. These models could provide an opportunity to simulate research with families and to see how various changes (such as use of, or loss of, supports) would impact on the family functioning. This will allow research to gather and take into account the various kinds of moderating variables.

The second focus for research should be oriented to discovering the nonfamily arrangements that can provide a high level of care and a good quality of life for people who are not fully adequate for filling their parental roles. Perhaps the small-community approach, such as that used in Camphill (Richards, 1980) and l'Arche (Clarke, 1974), are the most effective—where the structure is like a village or an extended family with a broader sharing of responsibilities. These forms are much to be preferred to the large institution or the group home or the foster home. Yet the nonretarded members often burn out emotionally, just as many parents do. Some alternatives to bureaucratization should be found for sustaining the basic living environment, but at the same time, systematized socialization procedures can to be quite effective (Budd & Greenspan, 1984, 1983). There is a need in America today to live simultaneously in two worlds at once, the small village and the large urbanized city (Johnson, 1977). Working with problems posed in these chapters can hasten the time when society is more balanced in its recognition of minority interests and in its provision of resources for dealing with the handicapped as "people of the village."

REFERENCES

Berger, P. L., & Neuhaus, R. J. *To empower people: The role of mediating structures in public policy.* Washington, DC: American Enterprise Institute for Public Policy Research, 1977.

Brewer, G., & Kakalik, J. *Handicapped children: Strategies for improving services.* New York: McGraw-Hill, 1979.

Budd, K. S., & Greenspan, S. Mentally retarded mothers. In E. A. Blechman (Ed.), *Behavior modification with women.* New York: Guilford Press, 1984.

Budd, K. S., & Greenspan, S. *Parameters of successful and unsuccessful interventions with mentally retarded parents.* Unpublished manuscript, 1983.

Clarke, B. *Enough room for joy: Jean Vanier's l'Arche.* New York: Paulist Press, 1974.

Forrester, J. W. *Industrial dynamics.* Cambridge, MA: MIT Press, 1967.

Forrester, J. W. *Urban dynamics.* Cambridge, MA: MIT Press, 1969.

Forrester, J. W. *World dynamics.* Cambridge, MA: Wright-Allen Press, 1971.

Fotheringham, J. B. *Mentally retarded persons as parents.* Unpublished manuscript, 1980.

Gorham, K. A., Des Jardins, C., Page, R., Pettis, E., & Schreiber, B. Effect on parents. In N. Hobbs (Ed.), *Issues in the classification of children* (Vol. 2). San Francisco: Jossey-Bass, 1975.

Greenspan, S., & Budd, K. S. *Research on mentally retarded parents.* Paper presented at an NICHD-sponsored conference on Research on Families with Retarded Persons, Rougemont, NC, September 1983.

Halpern, R. Direction service: Linking handicapped individuals and their families with needed services. *Journal of Community Psychology,* 1983, *11,* 187–198.

Hobbs, N., Dokecki, P. R., Hoover-Dempsey, K. V., Moroney, R. M., Shayne, M. W., & Weeks, K. B. *Strengthening families: New strategies for child care and parent education.* San Francisco: Jossey-Bass, 1984.

Johnson, E. S. How to live in two worlds without confusing them or ourselves. *Journal of Community Psychology,* 1977, *5,* 189–196.

Meadows, D. H., Meadows, D. L., Randers, J., & Behrens, W. W., III. *The limits to growth.* New York: Universe Books, 1972.

Rawls, J. *A theory of justice.* Cambridge, MA: The Belknap Press of Harvard University Press, 1971.

Richards, M. C. *Toward wholeness: Rudolf Steiner education in America.* Middletown, CT: Wesleyan University Press, 1980.

Wikler, L. Chronic stress of families of mentally retarded children. *Family Relations,* 1981, *30,* 281–288.

Author Index

Numbers in italics refer to the pages on which the complete references are cited.

Subject Index

Discipline practice of disabled parent, 152, 170–171

E

Ecological congruence in handicapped family, 35–43
Ecological congruence model, 38–40
competency continuum in, 38
deviancy continuum, 38
dimensions of, 38–39
tolerance for difference in, 38
Ecological system
development of, 37
effect of individual's characteristics on, 40
Ecology, definition of, 37
Education for the deaf, 116–117
Emotional handicap of parent, effect on early child development, 47–68
Employment, and deaf adults, 117
Environment
interaction of individual with, 36–37
role of, and schizophrenia, 51–53
Equality of treatment in federally funded programs, 14–15
ESPRIT program, 26
Ethnicity
and retarded parent, 94
and tolerance of disability, 161
Etiological models of schizophrenia, *see* schizophrenia
Eugenics, demise of, 12–14

F

Familiarizing program for child with disabled parent, 150–151
Family ecology
effect of handicap on, 40
factors in degree of congruence, 42
Family
in crisis, adaptability of, 148–149
involvement of grandparent in, 88
Family member, relationship to retarded parent, 83–86
Family outcome variables, and parental disability, 171–172
Family planning, and parent with diabetes, 102

Family relation, and schizophrenia, 52–53
Family size
and effect of disability of parent on child, 161
influencing competence of parent, 86
Family status variable, and development of child with disabled parent, 158
Family variables, and child development, 1
Family with handicapped parent, overview, 1–8
Fear of child
with diabetic parent, 105
with disabled parent, 146–147
Federally funded programs, equality of treatment in, 14–15
Financial aspects
of diabetes, 104
of disability, 146

G

Grandparent
involvement in family life, 88
responsibility, 87
in Polynesia, 83, 87
and retarded parent, 87

H

Handicap of parent, *see* Parent
Handicapped family
coping patterns in, 6
ecological congruence in, 35–43
policy regarding, 3–4
Hatz v. Hatz, 21
Heredity of schizophrenia, *see* Schizophrenia, transmission of
High-risk model, for schizophrenia, 55–56
High-risk pregnancy, and diabetes, 103
Human-environment relationships, 37

I

IDDM, *see* Insulin-dependent diabetes mellitus
Illness versus disability, 4
Inadequacy of parent, *see* Competence of parent
Independent Living Amendments, 15
Insecurity of child, with disabled parent, 146